T0083494

Off the Beaten Track

Off
the
Beaten
Track

The Story of
My Unconventional Life

SAEEDA BANO

Translated by Shahana Raza

zubaan

PENGUIN BOOKS

An imprint of Penguin Random House

ZUBAAN

128B Shahpur Jat, 1st Floor, New Delhi 110004, India

Zubaan is an independent feminist publisher based in New Delhi, set up as an imprint of India's first feminist publishing house, Kali for Women. Zubaan publishes in the areas of the humanities, social sciences, as well as in fiction, general non-fiction, and books for children and young adults under its Young Zubaan imprint.

in collaboration with

PENGUIN BOOKS

USA | Canada | UK | Ireland | Australia
New Zealand | India | South Africa | China

Penguin Books is part of the Penguin Random House group of companies whose addresses can be found at global.penguinrandomhouse.com

Penguin Random House India Pvt. Ltd
7th Floor, Infinity Tower C, DLF Cyber City,
Gurgaon 122 002, Haryana, India

First published by Zubaan Publishers Pvt. Ltd and Penguin Random House India 2020

ISBN 9789385932991

Printed at Replika Press Pvt. Ltd, India

www.zubaanbooks.com

www.penguin.co.in

Contents

Why I Translated This Book

SHAHANA RAZA

I believe *Dagar Se Hat Kar* is my grandmother Saeeda Bano's amaanat, her legacy to me, which I received through some cosmic-karmic good fortune, for safe-keeping.

From the earliest that I can recall, Bibi (everyone called Saeeda Bano Bibi) was different from other grandmothers. She drove a car, lived by herself in a posh South Delhi colony, corrected my English pronunciation with authority ('It's "K"-wality not Kwality with a "qu"') recited Urdu poetry verbatim and pleated her saree the other way round with the pallu draped over her right shoulder. Bibi was also brutally frank. She could say what she felt, pretty much to your face, without any hesitation whatsoever. This quality rubbed a few people the wrong way. She and I also had our differences, but I always marvelled at the remarkable flair with which she could make up with the ones she loved. Despite being aware that publishing *Dagar* was a slightly contentious issue in the family – that by mentioning certain personal incidents she was making the proverbial cut, too close to the bone – she nevertheless went ahead.

Around the time the book was published, Bibi suffered a paralytic attack that left her bedbound. One day when I went to meet her she asked me if I would read *Dagar* and translate it. 'But Bibi you have written it in Urdu, you know I can't read Urdu.' She grew silent. This was in the summer of 1997. Shortly afterwards, just as I was leaving for America to make a life for myself, eight neatly marked audiocassettes were handed to me. Bibi got her friend Nazneen

(Baby Baji) to read and record the entire book for me onto analog audiotapes. The tapes travelled with me first to New York, then Tampa and finally to Dubai where I settled in the year 2000 and started a family. Unfortunately, I was so absorbed with the rhythm of my own life I couldn't translate *Dagar* in Bibi's lifetime. She passed away in 2001.

Years later when my children were slightly older, I began listening to the tapes. As I heard Baby Baji's rich voice read out one page after the other easily, I felt stumped. Though I am from Lucknow and understand Urdu, the rich vocabulary Bibi used so effortlessly throughout *Dagar*, those exquisite sounding words, the wonderful analogies, appropriately chosen Urdu Farsi sher-o-shayri simply slithered and fell to the sides of my limited understanding, *Ahbaab ka dayra mehdood... Zindagi mein mua'ashrat ke bandhanon ne ek hum ahangii payda kar dee thee... Ai roshani tabah tu barman bilashudi.* Nevertheless, I had to figure it out; I was already way behind.

As I got acquainted with the intricacies of Bibi's unique life, I felt more people need to hear her story to understand that what we take for granted, is what she fought for: the right to make a choice for herself – as a woman, back in the days when they were kept behind purdah – a choice she didn't have, but one she fearlessly carved out. In the 1930s no one would have condoned or accepted incompatibility as a reason to walk out of a marriage, especially when two children were involved. Bibi exercised choice when she packed her bags and left the comfort of Lucknow society to tackle the hardships of living and working in Delhi as a single woman. In a strange way I feel this is why she wrote *Dagar*, to explain what she went through and how hopeless she felt at times. As Simone de Beauvoir explains in *Memoirs of a Dutiful Daughter*, 'The writer is a traitor to his despair as soon as he writes a book.'

Throughout the amazing journey of translating *Dagar*, whenever I needed help, the right person miraculously appeared. I am grateful to my father Saeed Raza for reminding me that I should consider translating the book even though Bibi had passed away. That it was, after all, not too late. I'd like to thank Baby Baji for taking the trouble to read and record the entire Urdu book onto audio cassettes for Bibi. That started the process going. I Google searched 'Urdu

tutors Dubai' and found Syeda Shan who not only read the entire
book out slowly enough for me to transcribe it, but also happened to
have this massive Urdu *lughat* dictionary that had meanings of every
imaginable intimidating word.

A very special thank you goes out for my aunt Zakia Zaheer
without whose help I would never have had the confidence to even
consider publishing this book. With her expert abilities, Zakia
Chachi patiently helped me unravel the meaning of words beyond
the scope of my narrow vocabulary and dig deeper through layers
of language to sculpt in English the emotions Bibi has expressed so
beautifully in Urdu. A well-known Urdu litterateur, translator and
writer, Zakia Zaheer has translated William Dalrymple's *The Last
Mughal* aside from co-authoring *Gold Dust of Begum Sultans*.

I am extremely grateful to Chitra Singh, friend first then sister-
in-law, who has been with me throughout this entire process, every
little step of the way, who took the time to listen to all my anxious
rantings at any given time of day (and night) and helped me calm my
ever restless mind. Only because I knew I could whet my writing off
of you Chitra, did I find the courage to move ahead. Once I started
translating I became acquainted with Mr Naved Masood through an
article he wrote about Nuruddin Ahmed sahab in which *Dagar* was
mentioned. His arrival was extremely timely, he threw light on people
and incidents mentioned in the book while telling me to march
on and complete this translation. Quite by accident I contacted
historian Siobhan Lambert-Hurley whose article on 'Intimacy and
Sexuality in Muslim Women's Autobiographical Writings in South
Asia' featured excerpts from Bibi's book. Dr Lambert-Hurley was
kind enough to respond to as many emails as I sent out and gave
me crucial background information on the Begums of Bhopal. As a
novice translator while pondering over little details such as whether I
should change street names to what they are called now… do I need
to verify the author's recollected memory in an autobiography… and
how much of the Urdu does one leave in, I met Kalidas Swaminathan
(Kalida to those of us who have had the pleasure of working with
him) who promptly introduced me to noted historian and translator,
Saleem Kidwai. Saleem bhai helped me clear these doubts as well as
sort out several more, all part and parcel of the art of translating a

book. I am also grateful to Neeta Gupta for encouraging me to take the leap of faith and publish *Dagar*.

A huge thanks to my family, my husband Prabodh and my children Aliya and Arjun for bearing with me and the almost constant 'shhhh, be quiet… I'm writing…' that I subjected them to. Knowing you guys were around in some not-so-quiet corner of the house was emotionally gratifying for me. When my sister Ayesha Raza Mishra heard I was working on Bibi's book, she immediately started sending images of monuments, people and artefacts mentioned in the book. I cannot thank her and my aunt Salima Raza enough for also taking the trouble to dig out Bibi's old albums and share invaluable pictures with me.

Thank you, Roopa Raveendran Menon for giving me time, again and again, to call and pick your brain while I was figuring out how to navigate the publishing industry. And of course to my friends Rathi, Ruchi, Jyotsna, Rajmohan, Debangshu, Shantanu, Sandeep, Neeta Thakur, Mamta, Sanjeev, Nishant, Urvashi, Jaina and Raees who shared contacts (and contracts) with me, listened to me talk endlessly about the book and always took the time to ask how the translation was coming along, whether in person, through messages or even long distance calls that were sometimes not free!

By being there for me each of you has helped Bibi realise her dream.

Preface

———— ❧ ————

Why did I think of writing the story of my life? Well, the entire credit goes to my friend Sheila Dhar, whom I met during the most eventful time in the history of our country, back in September 1947. When she saw the unusual situation I was grappling with during those tumultuous days of Partition, it made a deep impact on Sheila's impressionable mind. She was quite young at the time; I came across to her as an unconventional woman – one who had chosen to take the road less travelled.

As time went by the circumstances I was dealing with became more exceptional. Sheila was witness to all this. She was older now, mature enough to understand what was happening in my life. Perhaps that is why she encouraged me to start writing.

Many moons ago, we had a family physician in Lucknow called Dr Lahiri. He was a sincere and affectionate Bengali gentleman, whose consultation fee was only five rupees. When he walked in on a house-call, he would make it a point to acknowledge everyone in the family, from the adults to us youngsters. He would ask us how we were doing, if we had any aches or ailments and if time permitted, he would even joke with us, trying to impress us with his knowledge of graphology and palmistry. One look at someone's handwriting and Dr Lahiri could tell you that person's nature! One day he started reading my palm and after studying it seriously for a few minutes, he said, 'you will write a book and become very famous.' I began to laugh. Not only was there no possibility of becoming famous, there was also no chance of ever becoming a writer.

Little did I know that one day my circumstances would change so dramatically that by 1947 I would become famous as the first Indian woman to read news for All India Radio's (AIR) Urdu service. And bless Sheila Dhar, she got me to write this book. I could never have imagined that Dr Lahiri's prediction would come true.

I worked for years as a news broadcaster and producer and got into the habit of writing something or the other regularly. Despite this, I didn't have the confidence in myself to actually author a book. I still don't, but well, now I have written it! What I found as uphill a task as penning this entire memoir was finding a suitable ending for it. I have a small group of close friends and just a few are well-versed in Urdu. Who do I speak to about this book? Who do I ask if this rusty old story of my life is even worth a read?

Rumours had begun doing the rounds that I was writing my autobiography. One day the celebrated Urdu fiction writer, Qurratulain Hyder (Aini Apa to many) sent word that she was keen to read the draft of my book. The message was conveyed to me by Sughra Mehdi, Professor of Urdu at Jamia Millia Islamia University. I was absolutely delighted that an acclaimed author of Aini Apa's ilk was interested in my book. A book I was finding difficult to end. I handed it over to Sughra to show to her. After a while, Aini Apa sent the draft back with a single remark, 'it is readable'. I couldn't comprehend whether she was praising my work or diplomatically skirting the issue of having to critique it.

The positive outcome of this episode, however, was that Sughra became interested in the book. For two years, she diligently helped me edit and organise it, in whatever way she could, by reading, re-reading and correcting its loose and scattered structure. More importantly, she has been instrumental in lifting my flagging spirits whenever I felt low. That's how I have been able to finally finish this book, in the way I think fit. Sughra Mehdi's presence in my life is nothing short of divine intervention. God knows how many more problems she will have to help me solve, before this book is finally published. To say that I am thankful to her, sounds superficial. I don't have words to express what I really feel.

1

At the Turn of the Nineteenth Century

———— ❧ ————

In today's fast-paced world the thrill one felt commuting in a car is all but gone; people have taken to the skies. They travel in helicopters and airplanes and it comes as no surprise that even young children can make it from one distant place to another by themselves. They're not afraid of travelling alone, nor are they anxious at the thought of making the trip without an adult. Science has made such astounding progress that man has reached the moon. Astronomers now converse with the milky way and the youth of today have hobbies we could not have fathomed, from scaling the peaks of rugged mountains and surfing fearlessly on crashing waves to rafting through the hearts of restless rivers. The world has changed so rapidly it is difficult to even try and imagine what life might have been like a hundred years ago.

Back in our times, when the gramophone, with its large conspicuous brass horn, first came to India, it created a massive uproar. People were simply flabbergasted at hearing music float magically out of a slow rotating black plate. My mother was probably fifteen or sixteen years of age at that time. She used to tell us that in her days, the cost of living was so cheap that a maid's salary was only eight annas a month – that's just *fifty paise*! This was probably around 1880–1885. What's even more amazing is that the servants managed to lead a pretty decent life within this meagre amount.

Another interesting fact back then was that men and women lived and socialised in two entirely different worlds, despite being in the same house. Men had the privilege of living in the mardana or main house, while women (since they observed purdah and could not be seen by men other than close male relatives) were cocooned in an area specifically cordoned off for them, called the zanan-khana or zanana. The man of the house lived in the mardana along with other male members of the family and boys who had reached puberty. Valets and houseboys took care of their everyday needs. Even in those days there was a considerable wage gap between the salary of the sexes; male servants were paid a rupee a month, while a maid, as mentioned earlier, earned just half this amount.

Within the zanana all household chores, simple or complicated, were handled by maids. During the hot summer months, it was customary for the entire family to sleep in the aangan or inner courtyard. Every evening these housemaids lugged all the mattresses and bedclothes, heavy and light, into the aangan to make beds for each member of the family. In the morning, they would fold, carry and put everything back in its proper place. Aside from this tedious task, the responsibility of running the entire house also rested on their able shoulders. There was a certain harmony in the way relationships worked between couples in that society. Since men and women met up and interacted with each other for only a few hours during the day, it greatly reduced the possibility of friction between them.

The chaos, which is a natural consequence of the immense progress science has made today, was completely missing back then. People led simple lives. They journeyed from one place to another on slow-moving bullock carts or were carried to their destination on wheel-less palanquins such as a doli or a palki. A lightweight wooden structure, the palki was fitted with two or four strong horizontal timber rods. There was an inbuilt opening on either side for the passenger to enter and sit. A cloth was draped over the opening for privacy. Then eight sturdy kahars or palanquin bearers would hoist the rectangular palki on to their firm shoulders and carry the traveller to their desired destination on foot. The most alert, vocally able and strong-armed kahars were chosen to lead the way as their job included warning those at the rear of any approaching danger or the condition of the road.

'Watch your step... I see an open drain,' the head kahar would shout out.

'Keep alert... potholes ahead.' The men at the back of the

palanquin would grow vigilant. 'Steady now… we are approaching a bridge.'

Another means of transport was the myana or doli. Smaller than a palki, it could accommodate only one or two lightweight people. The doli was mostly used to transport a young bride to her groom's house after the wedding. To ensure the safety of the commuter, a couple of strong guards and trusted servants were sent along with the doli. Since the entire distance had to be covered on foot, every four miles or so these men took a short break, before resuming their synchronized march again.

In 1901, my mother was around 27 years old. We managed to calculate this after she told us she was married at fourteen and had her first child, my sister Aliya Khatoon, some 13 years later. There is this really interesting story about Amma's wedding day. My father lost his mother during his birth. A couple of years later, my Dada (paternal grandfather) married again. Initially, his wife shouldered the responsibility of looking after my father rather well, but as the years went by, she began treating him in the proverbial stepmotherly fashion. When my father was a bit older, Dada decided to send him to Lucknow to study. My father was an extremely keen student. When he finished Matriculation (Grade 10) his entire family thought he had achieved the highest academic degree possible and that it was now time to get him married.

Since my father was the only child of his parents (and strangely enough so was my mother) my Dada celebrated the wedding with great fanfare and left no stone unturned during the preparations. As was customary in those days, after the nikah (wedding ceremony), the bride was sent off in a doli from her parents' home in Rudauli village, zilla Barabanki, to her in-laws house in Isauli, all the way in Sultanpur district.[1] After this long arduous half-day journey, when Amma finally reached her destination, she was greeted with complete darkness.

To show her displeasure as a stepmother, my grandmother refused to light even a single charagh (oil-lamp) to welcome the child-

---

[1] Roughly a distance of 57 kilometres which takes close to an hour and a half to cover by car. In a palanquin it would probably have taken 11 hours.

bride into her new home. The house was pitch dark. I'm sure my grandfather must have been livid, lamps must have been lit hurriedly and the tired bride asked to alight and come inside. Railway tracks had not been laid in that area at the time. Large caravans of people walked to their destination on foot. Those that were wealthy and had the means, travelled like I mentioned, in a palki with their wives. This is how my poor mother reached her in-law's house and had to deal with such an unpleasant situation at the tender age of 14. What must she have gone through?

Back in those days, the way of living was such that the moment a girl reached adolescence, her family would start reminding her that she had to leave her parents' home one day to go live with her husband in another house. She was conditioned to believe that she needed to make herself adept at sewing, doing intricate embroidery, cooking, cleaning and looking after her younger siblings in order to be prepared for this grand occasion. By the time a girl reached 12-13 years of age, her friends started teasing her, filling her impressionable mind with all kinds of romantic notions of what her husband would be like, the gorgeous clothes and exquisite jewellery she would wear at her wedding, gently stoking the child's nascent desire to be a beautiful bride. This was then further kindled into a robust flame with colourful stories of the legendary cruelty she would face from her would-be mother-in-law and sisters-in-law.

Educating a girl, teaching her to read and write was absolutely unheard of. In fact it was considered downright improper – especially writing. God forbid a girl fell for a cousin or someone else and started sending him love letters! In a patriarchal world, ruled by men, there were several fundamental advantages in keeping a woman illiterate. The rules men had made for themselves within this same society were glaringly different. They had the freedom to do as they chose and they did whatever suited their own conveniences and preferences. Whether they had countless servants to cater to all of their needs or not, they were constantly socialising and could entertain themselves in more ways than one. They had the privilege of pursuing serious hobbies, such as attending poetry symposiums, literary events and taking part in debates. They could indulge their creative urge in a wide range of activities from painting to art and calligraphy or they could simply pass their free time playing various board games – taash (cards), shatranj (chess), pachisi (ludo) and ganjfa.[2] If they gambled or consumed alcohol, society simply turned a blind eye. Even if they spent the entire night watching mujra[3] or went as far as to indulge in amrad-parasti (homosexual activity with underage boys), it was all forgiven and forgotten.

Women, on the other hand, were prisoners in their own homes. Constantly surrounded by scores of female relatives, they invariably passed time knitting and doing needlework. They were kept actively engaged in learning intricate stitching patterns, along with the various sewing techniques of Lucknow's traditional chikankari embroidery which included crafting elaborate zardozi patterns on cloth with gold thread and mastering the difficult art of the murri stitch. Experts at cooking muhglai food, they were forever in the kitchen, busy preparing one mouth-watering dish after another. These would then be sent off to the mardana for approval. As men savoured these flavourful delicacies they showered their womenfolk with praise.

'Wah… so and so's wife sure makes fantastic gilanee khushka,'[4] someone would comment as he lifted the lid of the aromatic rice dish placed before him.

'But have you tried her moti pulao… It is so delicious, you will be left licking your fingers.'

'Yes… but her ande ka halwa (egg pudding)… uff… it's outstanding! And don't get me started on the kachchi biryani[5] she made the other day.'

The yardstick by which women were being judged in this society was based on such hollow values that women found them suffocating. And they could not even complain or hint that they were 'imprisoned in the zanana while our menfolk are out there having a good time.'

Truth be told, it was a severe case of might is right. Their wings clipped, women were totally dependent on men and had no means

---

[2] A game played with 96 round cards between three people.
[3] A dance performed by courtesans and prostitutes.
[4] A rice preparation from the Gilan province of Iran made with aromatic spices.
[5] Layers of meat, rice and potatoes infused with aromatic spices.

whatsoever of looking after themselves. Any protest was futile. They had learned to compromise with these unfair double standards that were in evidence all around them. At times they were happy, at times they lamented the misery of their fate.

This was one aspect of our society. The other was that the zanan-khana had a sophisticated culture of its own which had to be adhered to at all times. When men entered the zanana, they would accept salutations from the servants (no matter how insignificant their position within the household) lovingly lift little girls onto their laps, pat their sons affectionately on their heads, bestow blessings on their daughters-in-law, respectfully greet their mothers and other older female members of the household with a courteous salaam and then sit down comfortably to chat with them. They would ask how each member of the zanana was doing. If any serious matter was brought to their notice, they would try and resolve it with utmost responsibility. As they walked in cheerfully, laughing and talking, the monotonous atmosphere of the zanana would bloom and radiate with life.

This same sense of propriety was taught by the adult male members of the family to their sons and nephews – that the tehzeeb (culture) of the zanana must be upheld. That politeness, decorum and the ability to know how to communicate respectfully with people according to their age and social status, must be maintained at all times, no matter what.

By making rules and customs such as this, men had given women an exalted status within the four walls of the house. Any wish or suggestion expressed by their mothers, wives and elderly female relatives was given sincere attention. Almost as a kind of atonement, that by giving women this importance they could somehow overlook the social injustices that were being meted out to the fairer sex repeatedly. Though it seemed as though most men did not even notice that there was a problem with the way women were being treated. The strict patriarchal norms followed in Muslim homes were also enforced and practised in Hindu families. In fact their way of life was much the same as what I have just described – their women also observed purdah and ruled both home and hearth with an iron fist, commanding tremendous respect and veneration, but within the four walls of the house.

I have gone to great lengths to describe the socio-cultural milieu of society at that time, as my mother was a product of this environment. Since she did not receive a warm welcome at her in-law's house, the very next day my father got her back to Rudauli and said to her, 'I am going to Lucknow to study further. I want you to live with your parents. I will keep coming and visiting you during my holidays.' This must have caused quite a stir within their community. People must have gossiped, but my mother never went back to her sasural again. I have no idea how my father managed to keep things cordial with his family, all I know is, Amma stayed in Rudauli till my father finished his Bachelor of Arts degree in 1885 from Christian College, Lucknow.

For an Indian to achieve this decorated an academic degree was quite unheard of in the late 1800s. Since the British were ruling India at this time, most of the principals and teachers in educational institutions were from England. They showered my father, Mir Majid Husain, with respect. One of them promptly recommended him for a job in the princely state of Bhopal. He was to teach the much coveted English language to the then ruler, Nawab Sultan Jahan Begum's son's, Nawabzada Nasrullah Khan and his younger brother Nawabzada Obaidullah Khan. An expert in English and a teacher to the royal princes: it was a highly prestigious position. In that day and age teachers were given tremendous respect. I have heard that both princes remained standing when they were in my father's presence, and only sat down once he had seated himself. This was around the year 1885.

As part of his living arrangements my father was given a house along with a horse-drawn carriage. When he settled in, he went back to Rudauli and brought Amma to Bhopal. Moving from a little-known hamlet like Rudauli to an urban municipality such as Bhopal, was similar to bringing a villager from the interiors of rural India and leaving him bang in the buzzing centre of Manhattan city.

2

Nawab Sultan Jahan Begum's Bhopal

───── ⌘ ─────

Unique to the royalty of those days, the princely state of Bhopal was ruled by women for almost four successive generations.[6] Veiled and regal, when Nawab Sultan Jahan Begum sat on her imperial throne, members of her cabinet – from ministers to wealthy dignitaries – came and presented their courteous salaams one by one, to Sarkar Aliya.[7] Despite being powerful in their own way, these men stood in her presence till such time as she majestically nodded for them to be seated. The unexpected result of having a woman as monarch was that by default the status of the fairer sex within this society improved. The suffocation women felt in the North Indian state of Awadh, where deep-rooted conservative values were being followed blindly, was completely missing in Bhopal.

As the sovereign of Bhopal, Nawab Sultan Jahan Begum was eager to prove she could match any man in intelligence and capability. She was worried about the wellbeing of her female subjects and wanted to eradicate ignorance from their lives by making provisions for them to receive a proper education. She was also keen to liberate

───────

[6] In 1819, after the assassination of her husband, Qudsia Begum became the first woman ruler of Bhopal. She was succeeded by her only daughter, Sikandar Begum, who in turn left the throne to Shah Jahan Begum in 1868. After her, in 1901 Kaikhusrau Jahan Begum or Sultan Jahan Begum became the Nawab of Bhopal. She maintained strict purdah and wore a burqa with a face-veil right till the final years of her life.

[7] One of Nawab Sultan Jahan Begum's honorific titles which can be translated as Her Highness.

women from a life of social confinement. One day Nawab Sultan
Jahan Begum called my father and said, 'Mir Majid Husain send
your wife to present her salaam to me. Where have you hidden her...
behind purdah?' Back then, my mother used to wear typical Awadhi
clothes.[8] A cumbersome 12 yard farshi pyjama,[9] a choli or short-
sleeved bodice and a two-and-a-half yard long dupatta. Gathering
her trailing heavy clothes about her, Amma presented herself to the
Begum of Bhopal.

'Sit down Bibi.' Sarkar Aliya generally addressed women as Bibi
or Lady. She would then proceed to enquire about their wellbeing
in such an amiable manner that for the short span of time she spoke
with them, the ladies forgot that in reality, a gaping chasm of rank
lay between them. This was another indication of Nawab Sultan
Jahan Begum's astuteness, her diplomatic strategy as a ruler, to treat
people in a way that made them feel at ease, despite being in the
intimidating presence of royalty.

This is what happened with Amma. She instantly felt comfortable
in the palace. During her initial visits, Sarkar did not make a single
remark about the restrictive clothes she saw Amma wearing. She
did however say, 'Asharfunisa come and see me every Friday.' Now
no matter how, Amma would hurriedly finish off her chores every
Friday and rush off to Ahmedabad Palace. Sarkar would ask her
what life was like in a small village like Rudauli, the customs they
followed there and how men and women stayed together in that
social milieu. During one such visit, Sarkar said to Amma, 'Bibi you
seem to be a prisoner to this voluminous dress you are wearing. Why
don't you wear what we do in Bhopal? You will definitely feel more
comfortable.' Then she turned to one of her secretaries and ordered
her to get a Bhopali joda from her own wardrobe for Amma.

'Take Asharfunisa Bea inside and get her dressed,' she commanded.

In Bhopal the word Bea is used for Begum. Amma wore the
clothes that had been gifted to her so magnanimously, went to the

---

[8] Clothes worn by people living in Awadh, which is now the state of Uttar
Pradesh.

[9] A two-legged gathered skirt, held at the waist with drawstrings, which was so
long it swept the floor or farsh behind the person who was wearing it.

Begum and offered her gratitude in the form of a courteous salaam. Then she asked permission to leave. We heard that when Amma got back she was quite miffed at this great adversity that had befallen her. But from that day on whenever she went to Ahmedabad Palace, she made it a point to wear the same Bhopali clothes. Ultimately one day Sarkar Aliya said to my mother, 'Bibi get some more sets stitched for yourself. Every time you come here you wear the one I gave you. Try and get in the habit of wearing Bhopali clothes.'

Amma had to get some churidar-pyjamas stitched for herself. Over time, she got used to wearing Bhopali clothes and realised that indeed they were far less restrictive than the 12-yard farshi gharara she had been trailing about behind her till then. Gradually she switched to wearing Bhopali jodas. But she never took to draping the lengthy five yard Bhopali dupatta. That to her, was as cumbersome as Awadh's farshi pyjama.

My childhood was similar to that of any child from a middle class family. The only difference was that I was born and raised in a city like Bhopal, where women had been in the seat of power for several generations, where the gender equation was evidently tilted in favour of the fairer-sex. The socio-cultural environment in Bhopal was not as restrictive and oppressive as it was in other towns and cities of North India. Situated north of the Vindhya mountains, in the state of Madhya Pradesh, Bhopal is a picturesque city that appears almost hewn out of the undulating rocks and vast plateaus that surround it. Also known as the 'City of Lakes' for its various natural as well as artificial lagoons, Bhopal has thick green jungles inhabited by countless wild animals such as tigers, cheetahs, deer, antelopes, hyenas and jackals. Accentuated by its inspiring natural beauty and heart-warming scenery, there was a heady sense of freedom palpable throughout the city. Aside from this there were also several impressive man-made structures in Bhopal that shed light on how people lived in that day and age. One such building was the sprawling Sadar Manzil Palace, which was so large, at least 20-25 families could live inside quite comfortably, without even being aware of each other's presence.

The palaces of Sarkar Aliya's sons were built atop two of the prominent hills of Bhopal. Heir apparent Nawab Nasrullah Khan's beautiful mansion Idgah Kothi or Qiran-us-Sadain Mahal was situated on Idgah Hill while younger brother Nawab Obaidullah Khan's airy manor, Shamla Kothi was on Shamla Hill. The view of the Upper Lake and its surrounding areas was absolutely breathtaking from here. The other noteworthy buildings famous for their unique architecture were the Shikar Gaah or hunting castle of Ahmedabad Mahal and the palatial Noor-Us-Sabah palace, which is now a heritage hotel of the same name.

Located within Ali Manzil was a ladies club, next to which was a massive children's park where metal swing-sets hung invitingly between trees, luring children to come and play. There were rows of slides within the park, an open field marked with a running track and a separate area to keep girl guides busy. Another playground had been cordoned off especially for older girls to play hide and seek. This was so vast and spread out that it was almost impossible to find anyone! The ladies club had been made specifically to give women the opportunity to step out of their homes without a male escort. Sarkar Aliya also issued a royal decree making it mandatory for the wives and female relatives of her courtiers to visit the club in large groups every Friday. This, despite the fact that purdah was strictly observed at that time and women only ever left home to either attend a wedding or a funeral, otherwise they were perpetually trapped behind the four walls of their home. Sarkar Aliya, Sultan Jahan Begum, was constantly in search of ways to improve the lives of women and by making it compulsory for them to attend the club, she ensured that they had the opportunity to roam about freely, at least once a week. Then gradually the women of Bhopal grew confident in venturing out of the zanan-khana by themselves and realised that even they could enjoy such simple pleasures in life.

When I grew older, I noticed women in that society were constantly going on picnics. Almost on a regular basis we would hear that we were going on a gote (pronounced goat) which is what picnics were called in Bhopal. Elaborate preparations had to be made prior to departure, the first of which was scouting for a suitable place. Generally this would either be a spacious garden, a village or a shikargah (a hunting lodge) located on the outskirts of the city.

Laden with an array of appetizing delicacies, the ladies would head out with us children, along with a couple of maids and one or two male servants who acted as guards. We maintained kaana purdah, from male servants and the driver of the sej gaadi (bullock-cart), which meant we had to keep our faces partially covered while interacting with them or they could simply turn and look the other way if they saw our shadow approaching.

Then off we'd go for our delightful picnic on a sej gaadi. In order to make the slow dawdling journey a bit more comfortable, the hard wooden slabs of the bullock-cart would be covered with thin mattresses, spread over a layer of soft supple straw. The cart's appearance was nothing much to talk about – basically it was just a carriage pulled by two oxen.

Well-planned and functional, most houses in Bhopal had huge luxurious rooms, massive verandas, a kitchen, servant quarters and several bathrooms. They were architecturally designed to incorporate both spacious habitable living-quarters as well as convenient areas for leisure activities. Each individual unit was attached to the adjacent house through a common boundary wall. Despite this they were completely autonomous, giving each family optimum privacy. Various design elements had been cleverly used to prevent the interior of the house from being exposed to the public eye. The façade was always window-less and all doors and windows opened onto the inner courtyard. This made it quite impossible for the women living inside to get even a glimpse of the outside world.

Typically, the kitchen was located at the opposite end of the house from the entrance, after the open quadrangular courtyard. Food was slow cooked over wood-fires. Since purdah was strictly observed and the bawarchi (cook) was mostly a man, a purdeh ki deewar or thick cloth curtain used to be drawn across the kitchen door. The bawarchi was able to access the kitchen and exit it through a passage adjacent to it, without having to walk through the house. This gave the womenfolk freedom to move about as freely as they wanted within their own homes without having to come face to face with an unknown male. When food was ready, it would be carried by maidservants from this almost detached kitchen to the dining area inside the house. Meals were generally eaten together in the daalaan or veranda on a takhat, a wide wooden bench which was covered with thin carpets, called dastarkhwaans. They served the purpose of a tablecloth. In my house, punctuality and cleanliness were of utmost importance. We were not allowed to discard even a tiny cardamom peel here and there carelessly. Dustbins had been strategically placed in every corner for this purpose.

The interior of the zanana was well-planned, keeping the requirement of women in mind. The lobby was divided into two sitting areas. There was a wide wooden takhat on one side, where Amma sat, reclining comfortably on a gautakiya or bolster. Next to her was a large silver paan-daan[10] along with a small bowl in which she would keep the round hard betel-nuts she cracked open and kept cutting into smaller pieces. A sewing machine could also be seen on the same takhat. This was Amma's informal drawing room. When friends came to meet her they usually sat here, ate paan and gossiped together casually.

'Ae ooyee Bibi, did you hear what happened the other day?' One of the ladies would start narrating an incident which would more often than not, end on a high dramatic point, '... Have you ever even *heard* of such a preposterous thing?'

The other friends would gasp in-sync, 'What? God forbid!'

'Oh, I'm telling you... Kalyug is here, doomsday, Kalyug.'

And so on and so forth. They would chatter on with each other through the day. My mother seldom spoke, but she was a good listener.

At the other end of the same lobby, there was a sofa with a few chairs arranged around it strategically. When missionary women visited our homes they were made to sit there. These women's main agenda was to spread Christianity as far and wide across India as possible. They took their job rather seriously but went about their business in a subtle fashion, trying not to reveal that the sole motive behind their social call was to proselytize. Well-mannered and extremely polite, they showed genuine concern if they heard someone in the house was unwell and would even share their wide

---

[10] A decorated metal box used for keeping betel leaves and other ingredients to make paan.

knowledge of western medicine with us. If anyone was hurt or had a deep gash, they would immediately start cleaning and treating the wound. Their simple intention was to try and win as many hearts as possible and they were quite successful at this as they managed to get accepted into our homes.

In our days women wore simple modest clothes. Along with the kurta pyjama, a five yard muslin dupatta would be draped across the torso. The dupatta was plain white and had to be handed over to a rang-rez or dyer to be coloured in bright vibrant hues each week.

The dyer was an integral part of our lives in Bhopal. An extremely skilled artisan, aside from colouring our dupattas, he was also adept at embossing ornate patterns and interesting motifs on them. Show him a diagram of a delicate flower or an interesting geometric design and he would expertly print the exact thing on to our dupattas.

Just like the washerman who comes to the house on a designated day of the week to collect dirty clothes, the rang-rez came home once a week, carrying his heavy bundle of clothes. We would rush and gather around him and start handing out our dupattas to him, turn by turn, for re-printing or re-dyeing. Since colours bled back then, our dupattas inevitably turned white again after they went for a wash. So on Friday, we would hand them back to the rang-rez again to breathe new life into them.

Like the rang-rez, the bangle-sellers were also regular visitors to our homes each week. Slipping their motley coloured glassware on to the wrists of our womenfolk, they enticed shy brides, giggling little girls, elderly ladies and even our maids to buy their delicate tinkling bangles.

The ladies of the household, as well as their efficient maidservants, were skilled at tailoring. They could stitch their own clothes as well as tailor attractive outfits for all the young girls of the family. Our house was called Anees Manzil. Who gave it this name or why, I have no idea and till we lived there, I must admit, I was not curious enough to find out. Anees Manzil was located within a residential area of Bhopal called Ameer Ganj which, when translated literally, means 'wealthy neighbourhood'. Now why in God's name would they call it that? Architecturally, all the houses here had more or less the same appearance – single-storeyed with roofs made of khaprail or terracotta tiles. This design itself rendered it impossible for the women to come and stand in their balconies. Bang in the centre of these rows of identical houses was Anees Manzil, the only one without a tiled roof. Taking full advantage of this lapse in design we kids would create a huge ruckus every time we went up there to play, which was quite regularly.

We had no TV, video, or cinema to entertain us. But we shared a close relationship with the children of our servants. I remember, when I played with my friends they joined in and played along with us. Our free time was spent playing tricks and pranks on various people within the neighbourhood, sometimes even on our elders. If we got to know that an old servant (male or female) or some aged lady had a certain dislike for something or a pet peeve, we would purposely pester and tease them about it. There was this old servant called Kaloo miyan who got furious if anyone mentioned something as harmless as the word jalebi (a fried sweet soaked in sugar syrup) in his presence. We often crept up softly behind him and shouted out loud, 'ja-le-bi… ja-le-bi'.

Kaloo miyan would be livid! He would drop whatever he was doing and start screaming angrily, 'There is no way I can finish my work now, these kids have said "that" word. Oh God… I am already feeling sick… Oh, I feel so unwell… My head is beginning to spin… my arms, ohh… my legs look… look, they are swelling up! See? Oh my God I think I am going to die…. Look, look… there I can see djinns… they are calling out to me.'

The old man created such a racket! We had stiches in our stomach from laughing at his antics. The adults also enjoyed this drama, but they had to play at appeasing Kaloo miyan. Someone would rush to fan him as he lay writhing and fainting about on the floor, another would run, hiding her giggles, to get him a glass of water.

'Here Kaloo miyan have some cold water, I'm sure you will feel better soon.'

The entire house was entertained and good old Kaloo miyan got some needed respite from work for an hour or so.

Everybody in the neighbourhood knew each other well and people were quite familiar with each other's idiosyncrasies. If we heard the sound of commotion from a nearby house, we knew immediately that another hapless victim had fallen prey to a prank. As children we were quite innocent and led simple lives. Our means of enjoyment were limited to gadding about with each other, playing games or attending school. Though there were times when we mustered enough courage to play a practical joke on our elders.

One of our girlfriends had an older brother whom we also called Bhaijaan. Sometimes Bhaijaan came to play with us; whichever team he was on, always won. We always pleaded with him to join our side and if he agreed we would be thrilled to bits. Bhaijaan was extremely particular about saying his namaz five times a day. Behind the lobby of his house there was a large room which served the purpose of a modern day living room. The floor was covered from wall-to-wall with mattresses fitted over with white bedsheets and bolsters were arranged here and there for people to recline on while sitting. One usually saw the Begum sahab of the house sitting here leisurely, reclining regally on a bolster, paan-daan ugal-daan (spittoon) lying within easy reach, surrounded by female relatives, friends or visitors, busy doing some household chore or just sitting and making paan. In another corner of the room young girls could be seen playing a game of pachisi or doing something or the other to stay busy. When it was time for namaz, Bhaijaan would spread his janamaz (prayer mat) in this room and start praying. Out of respect the ladies and young girls would either leave the room or lower the volume of their chatter.

One day we girls thought up a trick. Bhaijaan started his namaz, then as is the protocol during prayer, we saw him bend halfway from his waist to do ruku and then he went into sajda.[11] When his forehead touched the janamaz, his hips, naturally, moved about eight to nine inches above ground. We moved in stealthily and slid a used ugal-daan in this gap. When Bhaijaan finished his sajda and sat up, he found himself seated on top of a dirty spittoon!

La-haul-villa quuvat! God save us and give us strength to ward off evil! That was the end of his namaz. We were hysterical with laughter and couldn't stop giggling. Of course we were caught,

---

[11] A prayer position in which the forehead, nose, both hands, knees and all toes touch the ground together.

punished and let off with a serious warning that we must never dare do such a thing again. We hardly got another chance, Bhaijaan became ultra-vigilant!

In our days, the norm was that at least two or three maidservants worked in every household. The salary of an efficient maid (one who was alert, active and smart) was two rupees a month. (In my mother's days it was just fifty paisa!) If the cook was brilliant, he could earn a high salary of five rupees per month and if he could prepare continental dishes, he could notch that figure three fold, to fifteen rupees. This was considered a top wage for a chef in my days. Within this same amount of money one could also hire professional housemaids (au pairs), who were highly trained and equally hard working.

I often wonder where these capable women have gone today. They had mastered the art of knowing how to get along with every member of the household. If they felt intimidated by the eldest Bea they worked out a friendly informal rapport with the youngest. They were affectionate and loving with children and felt responsible towards them. Some were of course lazy and inefficient as well, but most had this peculiar knack of tolerating and accepting all sorts of complicated situations that would usually arise in households, making it possible for everyone to live together amicably.

There was this maid at Bhaijaan's who was in the habit of sleeping every afternoon. After completing her chores, she would make her way to a secluded corner of the living room, cover herself with a thin sheet and fall fast asleep. She usually took her siesta between three and five in the evening and slept so soundly that at 5pm, we would have to call out her name repeatedly, even to get her to stir. Bee Rehmat was a very heavy sleeper.

One afternoon, she waddled into the room in her usual manner, stretched out on the mattress, covered herself with a thin sheet and quickly fell into a deep contented sleep. When we were absolutely sure she was oblivious to the world, we took a needle and thick thread and hastily stitched the edges of her covering sheet onto the white bedsheet spread on top of the mattress.

It was a hot summer afternoon, the large living room was being effectively cooled with the help of a slow whirring fan and khus ki tatti.[12] Not a soul was stirring. No one had so much as a clue about what we had done. Now you can only imagine what happened at 5pm when people started calling Bee Rehmat's name and she tried to get up. It was a hilarious sight! That day we were severely reprimanded.

I have mentioned earlier that women had been ruling the state of Bhopal for several generations and that they were called Nawabs. Ministers, secretaries, administrators, judges, police officers and District Heads of State, were all men but they performed their official duty under the authority of a woman. Role reversals such as this have taken place rarely in the history of the world. Whenever they have, the socio-cultural environment becomes glaringly different.

When a man assumes power he is at liberty to encourage the good deeds he sees around him and ignore the wrongdoings. But in this ancient world of ours it is rarely, if ever, that a woman gets the chance to hold the reins of power in her hands. Which is why Nawab Sultan Jahan Begum's entire concern, during her tenure as monarch, was to make Bhopal a progressive nation. She wanted to introduce and implement dynamic strategies to make the lives of her subjects content and comfortable. She was also extremely focussed and keen to get women out of the dark confines of ignorance. By 1903–1904, she launched several schools for girls and compelled orthodox families to enrol their daughters so they could receive a proper education. Who could dare disregard her orders? Though of course there was some opposition from those who were fundamentally against the idea of female education.

My father was extremely broadminded. He had already made arrangements for my elder sister to be tutored at home. When Sarkar Aliya launched the Sultania Girls' School they only had classes till Grade VI. My sister passed out of this grade, which was called Middle School, by around 1912. To felicitate her on this accomplishment Nawab Sultan Jahan Begum organised a special darbar court and rewarded her with gold bangles and a doshala or reversible shawl.[13] It

---

[12] Vetiver roots woven into a coir mat. When soaked with water, they are used for cooling.

[13] The Mughal Emperor Akbar is credited with having started the fashion of wearing two shawls, sewn back to back called do-shalas.

was customary for the government of Bhopal to honour its deserving citizens with safas or turbans and doshalas. In fact the traditional garment for men working in the Bhopali administrative services was a safa and a sherwani.[14]

It is worth mentioning another relevant fact here that demonstrates the level of importance women had in this society. When an official invite was sent for my mother, it would be addressed directly to her. The card carried her name, Asharfunisa, rather than the more traditional Mrs Mir Majid Husain. At social gatherings, women were introduced by their own names, not as so-and-so's wife or so-and-so's daughter. This was the start of making women aware that they had an individuality of their own.

In our house we had a harmonious environment with a visible lack of emotional upheavals. I never saw my parents fight or so much as argue with one another. Peaceful and balanced, the ambience of Anees Manzil was joyful. Yes from time to time, disagreements and fights did take place but these were mostly amongst the servants. If the problem was serious, Miyan (we called our father Miyan) would intervene otherwise Amma resolved the matter on her own.

Then one day I was admitted to school. When I started attending classes I found I was constantly being compared with my elder sister.

'Did you know Saeeda is Aliya Khatoon's sister?' This was the teacher.

'Really... but they are so dissimilar? She is not interested in studies, just keeps playing games all the time,' this from another teacher.

Truth be told, that is really all I wanted to do. I loved being on the sports field; attending classes was just about bearable. The teachers began complaining to my sister about me. She would glare at me angrily and warn me to start mending my ways. But my personality was a complex blend of peculiar traits. I was extremely obstinate, mischievous, immensely playful, anxious and God knows what else. This lethal combination had in turn made me quite fearless towards both my older brother and my sister and I never felt sorry for myself

---

[14] A knee-length coat, buttoned to the neck, worn by men, traditionally belonging to the Indian aristocracy.

when they scolded or reprimanded me. The years went by and one fine day I also graduated from Middle School. But this time there was no grand darbar, nor was I felicitated by the Begum of Bhopal.

In 1919 my sister Aliya (who was 12 years older than me) was married to a young man from Lucknow by the name of Syed Ali Zaheer. My recollection of this wedding is rather vague but based on the fact that she would be residing in that city permanently from now on, I was admitted to the Karamat Husain Muslim Girls High School as a boarder. Miyan was very keen I get a good education and study till as far as it was possible for a girl back then. I was simply content at the thought of seeing a new world.

But suddenly it felt as though I had been uprooted from the special inimitable environment I was accustomed to and flung into an unfamiliar society. This world was also unique, but in a peculiar way: the teachers, for example, seemed more progressive in their thinking, they were highly educated and well-travelled.

Established in Lucknow in 1922 by Justice Karamat Husain, the sole purpose of Muslim Girls Karamat Husain School was to provide Muslim girls with a proper education. By the time I joined in 1925 it had been more than successful in its mission. About 50 girls from different parts of India had been admitted into the boarding. Another 250-300 students, were studying as day-scholars. Lorries had been arranged to transport them to school each day.

The school was run efficiently, the staff was extremely competent, principals and professors were elected according to their abilities. There was no differentiation between Hindus and Muslims. The campus was massive with an enormous, spread-out compound that housed a tennis court, a badminton court and a basketball court. It was not long before I became an expert at these games. But academically I was an average student. From the start, I sensed I was different from my classmates; yes I was from another state, but aside from this, my personality was in complete contrast to that of my peers. I believe the bold, daring, mischievous qualities so obvious in me were a result of my Bhopali upbringing. The staff related better to the girls from Lucknow, who were far more gentle. For them I was simply an outsider, someone who had come from a far-off city to get educated in Lucknow. And since I wasn't interested in studies and was forever wanting to be on the sports field, my equation with the teaching faculty started getting strained. Those that were experienced and wise handled me with understanding, love and a bit of compassion. But the strict teachers were constantly miffed.

'Go stand in the corner!'

'Get out of my class.'

As insults and reprimands grew frequent, I adopted a stubborn stance.

Somehow I managed to complete Grade VII after failing in Farsi and Mathematics. Teachers of both these disciplines disliked me immensely and were constantly complaining to the principal about me. Even she had started getting annoyed with me. I had become a source of anguish for the matrons in boarding as well since I was constantly up to some mischief.

The one trick we looked forward to playing was lifting a petit girl on our shoulders and making her jump through the window into the warden's room! Once in, we would order her to open the rather well-stocked larder, empty it of whatever was lying in there – biscuits, packets of savoury snacks, cooked food items such as potato sabzi and delicious pasanda[15] meat, a variety of assorted breads, poori, paratha, and more – and hand it back to us quickly. We'd hurriedly stack these delectable goodies into a coarse sack, get the girl to climb out the way she got in and then oh, what a delightful feast we would have!

Later we would be summoned and interrogated. 'Who stole from the matron's room?' We'd stand there, heads bowed, trying to look as innocent as possible. Then we would be scolded, punished, taken to the principal's office and one would get to hear, 'Saeeda is a big nuisance.' Basically I used to be in the bad books of both the principal and the matrons quite regularly. Then by some divine intervention our Principal changed. An English lady by the name of Mrs Rollo was appointed as head of the school. I maintained my rebellious attitude with her as well. She came to our class for a lesson, greeted us with a cheerful 'good morning' and before leaving gave

---

[15] A north Indian dish of sliced meat cooked in a sauce made with tomatoes, yogurt, cream, and spices.

us some homework. The next day she came into the class and said, 'Girls keep your homework notebooks on my table.'

We did as we were told. I had not bothered to do the assignment, but I went and placed my notebook on the table. After class Mrs Rollo took the books with her and left. On the third day she had corrected our work. 'Girls, come and take your books,' she said, getting busy with the lesson. I was anticipating a scolding for not doing the work. But here was Mrs Rollo deeply engrossed in explaining some finer nuances of the English language to us.

Before class ended, she gave us homework, smiled and left. Once again I didn't do the assignment but went and kept the blank notebook on her table. The following day she came to class and in a cheerful manner said, 'come get your books'.

Class ended, she gave us another assignment and as she was leaving, turned to me and asked, 'Saeeda which game do you enjoy playing most?' I was silent. I couldn't find it in me to answer her. 'What kind of teacher is this,' I thought to myself. 'She isn't angry with me, hasn't scolded or even humiliated me.' That evening on the badminton court she praised my moves. I was thoroughly ashamed of myself. The next day, my notebook was not blank. I had completed my work and Mrs Rollo gave me 'Good' for it. Suddenly I turned a new leaf; I started completing my homework on time and was getting 'Good' 'Very Good' for it!

Aside from this I excelled on the sports field. No one could beat me in tennis; I won several prizes and awards at Inter-School and Inter-College competitions. Mrs Rollo enjoyed both tennis and badminton and I gradually starting doing well in both these games. But the biggest change in me was that I started concentrating on my studies. The credit for this goes entirely to Mrs Rollo. Her wisdom and innate ability to understand the mindset of a young rebellious girl saved me from becoming a worthless child. The remaining three years in school passed without any untoward incident.

In 1927 Nawab Nasrullah Khan, heir apparent to the throne of Bhopal, fell seriously ill. God knows what kind of life-threatening disease it was, but he never recovered. Strangely just a few months earlier, his younger brother, Nawab Obaidullah Khan had also passed away. What an unprecedented turn of events! But nonetheless they did happen, as history is witness. The effect of their twin deaths had an inexplicable impact on my father, both princes were after all his pupils and respected him immensely. Everyone in Bhopal knew that Miyan had a very special relationship with Nawab Nasrullah Khan and Nawab Obaidullah Khan.

Their sudden death placed Sarkar Aliya in a predicament; she had to decide who would now be heir apparent to the throne of Bhopal. According to Islam, if the parents are alive and the successor to the throne passes away, his brother is automatically chosen as the next heir-apparent. But according to the British Law of Succession, the son of the deceased must rightfully take his father's place. The question now was, should Nasrullah Khan's youngest brother Hamidullah Khan be appointed heir to Bhopal or his son, Habibullah Khan. Caught between a rock and a hard place, fate had deliberately placed the onus of an extremely grim decision on Sarkar Aliya's shoulders.

Though everyone knew that Hamidullah Khan was Sarkar's favourite child, no one could have imagined, even in their wildest dreams, that both her older children would suddenly die, one after the other and that Hamidullah Khan may get the chance of being Nawab of Bhopal. During extraordinary times like this, it is quite common within princely states that the riaya or subjects, try and ascertain what the mood of their ruler is. Bhopal was no exception. Its well placed nobility, land-holders and members of the advisory committee, knew very well which way the wind was blowing. No one so much as dared step, even by mistake, in the direction of Nawab Nasrullah Khan's palace, Idgah kothi.

Our house was comfortably nestled at the foot of Idgah Hill. It was part of Miyan's routine, to visit Qiran-us-Sadain palace and meet the heir-apparent either every Friday or whenever he found free time during the week. In keeping with his practice, despite the fact that Nawab Nasrullah Khan was no longer alive, Miyan would go to the palace to enquire after the health of his widow Qaisar Dulhan.

Sarkar Aliya, Sultan Jahan Begum had in the meantime, filed a law suit challenging the British Law of Succession. According to her, after her demise the state of Bhopal should be governed by her youngest son, Prince Hamidullah Khan as that was Shariah. She also decreed that late Nasrullah Khan's son, Habibullah Khan had been officially removed from the line of succession. Sarkar fought her legal battle right up to the Privy Council and at the end of approximately two long years, won the case.

Suddenly my father began to feel uncertain about his future. He went to meet Sultan Jahan Begum and decided to tell her truthfully, what was on his mind. 'I have had strong ties with the residents of Qiran-us-Sadain palace and Habib Manzil for a long time because of my association with the families of my pupils. Even though they are no longer alive, I have been meeting with Nasrullah Khan's sons, Masters Habib and Rafiq regularly and I do enquire, within the boundaries of social protocol, after the well-being of his widow as well, just as I used to when he was alive.'

Begum Bhopal knew my father well. After 45 years of shouldering various responsibilities in her court, his loyalty was tried and tested. She heard him out patiently and seemed absolutely unperturbed or even disappointed by what he had just said. And so it came to be that, once again, one would see Mir Majid Husain climbing Idgah Hill either on foot or travelling up its gentle slopes on his tumtum.[16] At the time there were only two houses in that direction, Qiran-us-Sadain Mahal and Kothi Habib Manzil. The path leading up was unpopulated, if anyone took that route, they could easily be spotted from a distance. I am sure people must have gossiped about my father's weekly visits; they may even have tried to poison Sultan Jahan Begum's mind against him, but Sarkar had the knack of knowing the core character of a person. She did not allow doubts about my father's loyalty to cloud her opinion of him.

After winning the case against the British government, in order to further consolidate Nawab Hamidullah Khan's position legally, Sultan Jahan Begum made a surprise announcement – that she would be abdicating the throne of Bhopal. A grand ceremony was held in 1928[17] to celebrate Nawab Hamidullah Khan's coronation. According to his designation, as an employee of the State, my father

---

[16] One-horse carriage, usually two-wheeled with two transverse seats set back to back.

[17] Some accounts put this date as 1926. I have, however, chosen to leave this date as it is in order to be faithful to the author's recollected memory.

remained in court and participated in all the royal functions. After the pomp and show was over, Miyan went up to Sultan Jahan Begum and respectfully handed her his resignation.

'Oh! what is this Mir Majid Husain!…. Why?' Sarkar Aliya asked.

My father replied, 'Sarkar you know my work and my personality very well. You are also aware that along with being your faithful servant I am seen as a well-wisher of late Nasrullah Khan's sons. For Nawab Hamidullah Khan, I am a total stranger. There is a strong possibility that several misunderstandings could crop up between him and me in the near future because of my deep loyalty to the family of the deceased Nawab. If I can be released from my duties with dignity and peace I feel it will be better for me in the long run.' Sarkar Aliya realised that there was a great deal of truth in my father's words. She accepted his resignation. By this time Miyan had decided he would leave Bhopal and go settle in Lucknow for good.

3

Leaving My Childhood Home

———— ❦ ————

Even in my worst dreams and wildest thoughts, I had not imagined that one day I would leave my beloved Bhopal forever and live somewhere else. That I would be obliged to move out of Anees Manzil, the home I grew up in. The anxiety of separation was so intense that when my friend Masood Bano came to see me, we would simply look at each other and without exchanging a single word, tears would start streaming down our faces. The anguish, the pain, the sadness of leaving Bhopal, my true motherland, stayed with me for a long time and the truth is, even today I feel a tremendous attachment towards this city. I miss the unique carefree world I grew up in, the delightful evenings I spent there at the premier Ladies Club and the gorgeous faces one saw amongst the crowd of women, each more ravishing than the other.

Several hundred years back, a 'soorma pathan', a brave soldier from Afghanistan by the name of Dost Mohammad Khan conquered and founded the city of Bhopal. Following his lead, numerous families of pathans came and settled in this area. Several years after Dost Mohammad Khan, the reins of his beloved kingdom fell in the efficient hands of women for four straight generations and Bhopal became famous for its Nawab Begums.

When Sultan Jahan Begum entered the Ladies Club, women from various social backgrounds, young or old, would vie with one another to appear before her to say adab, in the mere hope of being acknowledged by the grand Begum of Bhopal. As young girls, we stood at a distance and watched this fascinating scene unfold. We were amazed at the number of good-looking women we saw in the crowd. Ladies of the royal family were exceptionally beautiful, their stunning looks enhanced with the exquisite pearl and diamond jewellery they wore. They had a certain grace about them, a natural air of dignity which comes to those blessed with both money and power. But on the whole they were completely uneducated.

The most commendable aspect of Sultan Jahan Begum's rule was that she gave unprecedented importance to educating the girl child. By doing this she bestowed the priceless gift of literacy to future generations of women. Though back in those days, men were not that well-read either, but at least work in that direction had already begun. There were quite a few schools and colleges for boys across Bhopal.

Sarkar Amman had paid close attention to the academic and religious education of her older sons, the late Nasrullah Khan and Obaidullah Khan. Despite this, their free time was spent indulging in decadent activities common amongst male members of the royal families, such as hunting, consuming alcohol and enjoying the song and dance of nautch girls, almost on a daily basis. The youngest, Nawabzada Hamidullah Khan, lived with his mother in Ahmedabad Mahal and it is rumoured that he treated the women residing in the palace and those from royal families, as a mere means of entertainment. The talk was that sometimes even young married women managed to catch Hamid Miyan's wandering fancy. We often heard stories of envy and jealousy, of open confrontations as the ladies were constantly anxious that a more attractive rival might gain the Nawabzada's attention.

Nawabzada Hamidullah Khan had three daughters, Abida Sultan, Sajida Sultan and Rabia Sultan. Through the year, various ceremonies were held at the palace on important occasions such as when the princesses kept their first roza and for nashrah – when they finished reading the entire Quran. Whenever Amma received an invitation for any of these delightful parties, I threw a major tantrum and insisted on going with her. I loved visiting Ahmedabad Palace as it gave me the opportunity to play with real princesses. Also because, the festivities included musical events during which female singers regaled guests with their splendid voices. I thoroughly enjoyed listening to their melodious songs. Now all this was going to be a thing of the past – the gotes of Bhopal, our enjoyable hunting trips, gadding about freely around the Ladies Club. An entire way of life had come to an abrupt end.

Whenever I went back to Bhopal during my summer holidays from Lucknow, the days passed in the blink of an eye. I met my old friends, chatted endlessly with them and spent an extremely pleasurable vacation doing those things in our leisure time that only children fortunate enough to live in Bhopal could enjoy back then. Lost in this fun and delight, I forgot that I was now living permanently in Lucknow. I often thought, 'Can it be possible that I finish my tenth grade from Karamat School and somehow or the other come back to live in Bhopal? After all this is my real home. We have been residing in Bhopal for God knows how long. Lucknow has, for no particular reason become a part of my life. My roots are still right here in Bhopal.'

Over the course of time, other aspects of life in Bhopal came to light. Compared with men, women within this society had always been in a far superior position. Slowly the effect of this dominance reared its ugly head. We heard stories of lesbianism, of fierce competitiveness between women as they vied with one another for the favoured spot at the palace and how this manifested itself in the form of jealousy and spite. There were cases of women shooting each other with pistols, committing suicide and even going so far as to perpetrate murder; of their merciless attitude towards servants and how some of them completely ignored their husbands and treated them in a cold, callous manner. This kind of imbalance happens in society when the equilibrium between ignorance and power goes askew. Behavioural maladies such as these are mostly evident amongst high society ladies. This sort of chaotic restlessness is not seen in middle-class women or even the general public as they remain busy keeping a strong grip on social values that lie at the core of humanity.

4

Lord Harcourt Butler's Lucknow

The social milieu in Lucknow[18] during Lord Harcourt Butler's time had reached rock-bottom; men and women in this decadent world were speeding towards impending disaster, completely clueless that behind the seductive glamour and rosy charm of this aristocratic society lay nothing but doom. This was one aspect of Lucknow society. And there was another. Due to the large presence of East India Company officials in Lucknow, residents of the city increasingly came under the influence of western culture and thought. They were witness to the fastidiousness the English had for cleanliness, punctuality, order, discipline and the immense importance they gave to education. Slowly, the western way of life began to spread its liberal roots within our orthodox society.

To some extent, in every era, it is women who play the role of being silent spectators. Here we were, keenly observing the open-mindedness that was so evident in Lucknow society during Lord

---

[18] Situated on the calm banks of the river Gomti, Lucknow is the capital of the north Indian state of Awadh, formerly known as the United Provinces of Agra and Oudh. In the eighteenth century Awadh was ruled by nawabs, who were formerly from Nishapur in Iran. Despite being extremely powerful, literate and wealthy, by the early 1800s officials of the British East India company had reduced these nawabs to mere titular heads with little say in matters of governance. By the mid-nineteenth century, the British gained direct control of the grand state of Awadh and sent its then nawab, Wajid Ali Shah to exile in Calcutta.

Between 1918–1922, an English officer by the name of Lord Harcourt Butler governed Awadh, initially as the Lieutenant Governor of the United Provinces of Agra and Oudh and later as its first Governor.

Butler's time and comparing it to the conventional environment in our own homes, where unjust atrocities and outdated customs were being enforced rigidly, brilliantly camouflaged behind the joy of wedding celebrations and the hustle-bustle of living in a joint family setup. But for how long? For instance, women soon became aware that outside the confines of purdah, members of their own sex led unrestrained lives. Young girls found this freedom very attractive. Those who were bold raised their voices for the right to an education – a western education.

Among men too, there were many who wanted to liberate women from the shackles of ignorance but most lacked the courage to break the barriers of orthodoxy. Some, however, did step forward, inspired perhaps by the women's efforts to change the situation. As more schools for girls began to open, the number of girl students also went up. The issue of female education became a regular subject of discussion. Schools and colleges for boys already existed, and now a number of institutions for girls also came up. Within Muslim homes the practice of educating daughters was not so common, but this too had begun to change. When I joined Isabella Thoburn College several girls I was personally acquainted with had already completed their Bachelor's and passed out of this institution. Tara Kuruvilla, Cecilia Philip, Kaneez Bano Sanober, Nurunisa were some of IT's star students.

At the time, the popularity of the college was at its peak. The architecture of its exceptional façade, designed in an American style, was symbolic of knowledge and wisdom. The very atmosphere radiated an air of intelligence and awareness; the girls studying there reflected this modernity and self-reliance in their appearance and personality. All of our professors and teachers were American women. After me, the ace personalities that graduated from IT included Prema Khanna, Attia Hosain, Sharda Rao, Sakina Zaheer, Quratulain Haider, Waheeda Bano, Shakuntala Jaspal, Maya Ratna. Young people had by now grown passionate about acquiring a good education and well-to-do families had even started sending their children abroad to study.

The social structure of Lucknow society at this time was feudal and the taluqdari system was prevalent. Landowners or taluqdars[19] were rewarded with property for their services to the Crown and were given the title of Raja, Maharaja and Nawab. There was no dearth of Ranis, Maharanis, Begums and Lady Sahabs in the Lucknow of my days. All these women were in purdah. When British ladies visited the homes of Indian nobility, they made a concerted effort to try and speak with them in Hindustani – an erudite blend of Urdu and Hindi. As interaction between the angrez ladies and Lucknow's elite increased they started entertaining one another. Grand purdah parties were organised where the women could mingle freely with each other and yet maintain complete purdah from men. These gatherings were extremely delightful. Ranis and Begums socialised with each other, enjoying themselves, chatting eagerly with their English counterparts. Someone spoke English, another chose Urdu, a third spoke in Hindi. Part of the conversation was understood by a few and the rest artfully dodged with a quick laugh and a timely smile. This is how, slowly and steadily, Indian women became influenced by Western culture and the feeling that, 'if only we could also go around as freely as these women do,' began niggling at their minds.

Those who were older and gutsier felt that despite purdah they could make a substantial difference in society. Begum Habibullah,[20] Rani Mandi,[21] Rani Bam Bahadur Shah,[22] Lady Wazir Hasan,[23]

---

[19] Feudal landlords in Mughal and British times who were responsible for collecting taxes.

[20] Begum Hamida Habibullah was a pioneer of women's empowerment, an educationist and a Rajya Sabha member. First President of the Women's Cricket Association of Lucknow, she died in 2018 at the age of 102.

21 Rani of Mandi was President of the All India Women's Conference (AIWC) in 1929. The organisation was dedicated to the upliftment and betterment of women and children.

[22] Rani Bam Bahadur Shah Kalawati Devi was married to Rai Bahadur Bam Bahadur Shah of Khairigarh Estate. She was an active member of the Lucknow Women's Association and donated her own personal land to start the Pramodini School which is still in existence and is located on Wazir Hasan Road, Lucknow.

[23] Lady Wazir Hasan, Sakinatul Fatima was the wife of Sir Wazir Hasan, Chief Justice of the Oudh Court in Lucknow. Despite her husband's rank and position, she was legendary for her outspoken fiery nature. She bluntly told Lady Wellington at an official function that she would not learn the English language, 'When we

Begum Wasim,[24] and many such enterprising ladies got together and decided to start an organization. Though all the women I have mentioned here were in purdah, they were bold and fearless. After some ten or fifteen meetings, the Lucknow Women's Association was formed. After running about and doing a bit of leg-work, these ladies even managed to induct other women as members of the Association.

Every week the Lucknow Women's Association would meet to plan out welfare projects for underprivileged women. One group was appointed to visit the jail and educate female criminals. Those who knew how to knit and stitch worked three days in the week making clothes and sweaters for the poor. Two or three groups were given the responsibility of visiting various mohallas across the city to teach poor children how to read and write. These were minor jobs but they gave these women who had been locked within their homes a deep sense of satisfaction that they were doing something much more meaningful with their time.

Society was on the cusp of change. Little by little the practice of purdah came to an end. Indian women appropriated Western culture with such confidence that some became even more anglicized than the British.

I had left my cherished childhood and adolescence in the carefree world of Bhopal and was now living permanently in Lucknow. All those awkward characteristics that are part of a girl's growing up years were still there in me. But the time had come to shut down on them. There was a strange sense of suffocation in the very air one breathed in Lucknow. I was constantly expected to behave in an exemplary manner while meeting people. It was a blessing that I finished Matric (Grade X) and was admitted in IT College as it gave me the opportunity to get away from home and breathe freely.

---

rule you, we will learn your language.' Influenced by Gandhiji's Civil Disobedience movement, she is believed to have defiantly burnt Manchester cloth in Lucknow's Hazratganj area. She was against the purdah system, polygamy and child marriage. After independence, she was nominated to the UP legislative assembly.

[24] Begum Mohammed Wasim was a Standing Committee member of the All India Women's Conference (AIWC) from Lucknow who supported joint electorates and spoke strongly about women's suffrage.

Then it so happened that the searing heat of Lucknow became unbearable for my father and he decided to spend the entire summer in Mussoorie. Much like its pleasant weather, the socio-cultural environment in this hill town was very different from that of Lucknow. Since my father was fundamentally a broadminded man, he ignored the conservative rules of Lucknawi society and allowed us to be quite free in Mussoorie. The strong values with which Miyan had himself been brought up, such as honesty, truthfulness, tolerance, respect towards elders, the importance of maintaining relationships, living in a friendly yet cordial manner with neighbours, all these had been instilled in us. He trusted me completely. Within the blueprint of freedom he had sketched for us in his mind, we had his permission to roam about, shop around, go on picnics, watch movies and gad about with our female friends as much as we liked, as long as we avoided the company of men.

In any case, in that society girls and boys were hardly ever seen together. In our small family we didn't have any male cousins either. We were constantly surrounded by girlfriends. So Miyan's stipulation didn't really bother us. If on some occasion we were outside with my brother and he happened to bump into his friends, he would simply cross the road and meet with them by himself. This may sound like a strange, hypocritical thing to do, but this is how life was in our days and we were quite happy living like this. Attending sumptuous dinners and amusing purdah parties was entertaining enough.

There was a premium hotel in Mussoorie called the Savoy[25] where the latest western dances including cabaret and fox-trot took place. We were extremely keen to visit this luxury hotel which was frequented by top officers of the British Raj as well as the crème de la crème of Lucknow society. One day our wish was fulfilled. Some of us girls, and some women from the family, went to the Savoy and were made to sit in the upper balcony of the ballroom. When we looked down from there we could see men and women dancing with one

---

[25] Visiting Mussoorie in 1926, the famous American writer, broadcaster and traveller, Lowell Thomas wrote, 'There is a hotel in Mussoorie (Savoy) where they ring a bell just before dawn so that the pious may say their prayers and the impious get back to their own beds.'

another on the smooth dance floor. Most couples were British though there were some four to six Indians strutting about elegantly as well.

My attention was caught by a young Indian girl dancing nimbly in high heels. She was wearing a gorgeous red sari. As she swayed expertly with her partner, I watched her glide across the wooden floor, mesmerized. I was so envious of her. I also wanted to dance and I loved wearing red! But in our society unmarried girls were not allowed to wear crimson. Nor could we decorate our feet with henna or wear a nose pin. I couldn't care less about the latter two, but I was burning with desire to wear a flaming red sari!

I asked around and found out that the lady-in-the-red-sari had just returned from Oxford after completing her studies, that she was not married and belonged to an affluent family from Lahore. Apparently their lifestyle was heavily influenced by Western culture. But I was hardly impressed with any of that. I was simply obsessed with the desire to own a red sari of my own. I began pleading with Amma to get me one. For a couple of days she skirted the issue, then finally she relented on condition that I buy it with my own money. I used to get ten rupees as pocket money and always managed to increase this amount by adding a few extra bucks from here and there. If I saw my brother's money lying around, I helped myself to it and never once thought of returning it. I wangled some out of Amma and this way, by the end of the month I managed to increase it to fifteen rupees!

An excellent French crêpe cost five rupees per yard in our days. I borrowed another fifteen or twenty rupees and somehow or the other bought myself a gorgeous red sari. But from where was I to get the money to buy a decorative border? I thought of stitching an inexpensive gota[26] on the sari as that would cost only a few rupees. This is how I finally got my very own red sari. I already had Amma's permission to wear it, so as soon as I was invited to a purdah party, I draped my new sari and tottered off excitedly. My sister, who was staying at the Savoy hotel was also invited. When she saw me entering wearing red she was aghast. Almost immediately she started scolding me, albeit in a hushed tone.

---

[26] Gold or silver ribbon or lace of varying width, woven in a satin or twill weave.

'How besharam, how shameless are you? You've come here wearing a red sari…! Who gave you permission?'

'Amma did,' I whispered back angrily, refusing to look at her.

'Amma is too *seedha,* too naïve,' she hissed back. 'But at least you should have had some sense! You should know how indecent this is!'

I moved away from her and went and sat with some other women under the pretext of mingling with them. But every time Beevi spotted me, she would move in closer and start admonishing me. I was also extremely obstinate and stood my ground. The sad conclusion of this sari episode was that my sister magically made it vanish from my cupboard. She had it embroidered and stashed away for my trousseau. My ego was hugely bruised.

In Lucknow, my father had chosen to live in a small independent house located within the compound of Niyamat College. A certain Begum Aley Raza lived in half of a bigger bungalow within the same premises. She was the oldest daughter-in-law of Justice Mohammad Raza and the wife of advocate Syed Aley Raza sahab. She was also a close friend of Beevi's and since our homes were close by, I started visiting her house often.

Begum Aley Raza was an affectionate lady. She was kind-hearted and took a keen interest in listening to the problems of us young people, no matter how inconsequential they were. She would sympathise with us and even try to help resolve our problems, if possible. Exceedingly generous, she was always giving gifts or preparing delicious food and sending it over to our place. Quite often she would drop by, sit and talk informally with my mother as though she had all the time in the world. Since we had just arrived from Bhopal and knew only a couple of people in Lucknow, we enjoyed being in each other's company. During the endless boring afternoons, I would wrap a thin sheet around myself and walk over casually to Bhabhijaan's bungalow, which was barely 100 yards away.

One day I heard I had received a proposal from Justice Raza's house to marry his third son, Abbas Raza who was a munsif or Judge in the Judicial Service. Munsifi sounded like a rather insignificant job to me. The designation was later changed to Civil Judge. When I heard this news, I felt extremely anxious. I had a razor sharp imagination and could envision just about anything except how two complete strangers could be thrown into an intimate relationship with one another, just like that, for their entire life. I immediately shot off a letter to my father expressing a desire to study further. I wrote that I was also keen to learn how to play the piano and mentioned briefly that I was absolutely not ready for marriage. I did not even receive a one-line reply in response to my four page rant. My wedding was fixed by my sister Begum Ali Zaheer and Begum Aley Raza.

In 1930 my father had suffered a heart attack and since then he wanted to be free from the financial and moral obligation of getting his second daughter married. He knew, just as well as Beevi did, that I was not like other girls, that I was carefree, outspoken, daringly bold and extremely mischievous. He knew too that my heart was set on playing sports and reading books. I used to devour anything I could lay my hands on, novels, encyclopaedias, autobiographies of famous personalities and even philosophical treatises. I had read Hume, though I couldn't understand much, still I was keen to read him. I had started learning piano and I played hockey. Both of them knew it wasn't going to be easy, fitting a girl with such a strange blend of complicated traits in her personality, into a conventional marriage. But back in those days, the thought behind arranged marriages was simple, the man should be from a good family, he must have a decent enough job, he should be able-bodied and he should be a Syed.[27] That is all. Abbas Raza sahab ticked all the boxes.

My letter was lost like a parrot's squawk in a noisy marketplace. On the evening of 14 November 1932 I was married off to Abbas Raza. I cried all night long and woke up with throbbing pain in my head. Prior to this I had never had a headache. Sometime afterwards, sitting behind the sheer purdah curtain at a poetry symposium, I turned to look at a gentleman when one of ladies seated nearby remarked rather loudly, 'Look, look, an Englishman wearing a sherwani!' That is when I learnt that this was the man I had married! Abbas Raza sahab was extremely fair. From December to the 5th of February Abbas Raza wrote me a couple of letters expressing his love. By way of a reply I told him the names of the novels that I was reading.

---

[27] Title borne by descendants of the Prophet Mohammed (PBUH).

5

My Husband's Home

―――――⚜―――――

The protest I launched against marriage was purely emotional. My rebellion lacked substance, had no soul and was basically just a pathetic remonstration. I was simply acting on this overwhelming feeling that I did not want to be married at the time. Especially because it had been arranged. At the same time, I had no idea what I really wanted to do with my life. Within the socio-economic strata of society to which my family belonged, there was no question I would ever have to live independently or earn my own living; not even a vague possibility. We were counted among the liberal families of that time. But this broad-minded, socially progressive tag we had appropriated was strange in that it was a totally undecided phenomenon.

Back in 1917 when my sister passed her Matriculation exam it was unheard of for a girl, that too from a Muslim family, to have studied till Grade X. But educational opportunities were opening up for women and that made it possible for me to attend college. Despite this, the attitude of our community towards female education was somewhat ambiguous. We could not so much as dare to even think of acting on what we felt. Neither were we capable of objectively carving out a balanced middle path for ourselves, something that was different from the traditional environment we were brought up in and the ultra-progressive milieu we were witnessing around us. As a result, our confused thoughts and repressed feelings manifested themselves in the form of constant rebellion and a persistent edgy restlessness.

My four-page letter against marriage had been disregarded. The wedding preparations were in full swing. I was constantly in a foul mood. As part of the 'manjha', the haldi ceremony, I had to have a thick yellow paste of turmeric, sandalwood and rose water applied on my skin to make it glow before the big day. The barber's wife would enter my room gingerly to do the needful, see my enraged face, dab a few blobs on my hands and feet and run out of the door hurriedly. She didn't dare to so much as say 'Bitiya, the ubtan has to be applied all over your body.'

On the 5th of February, 1933 the groom's wedding procession arrived at my gate. It was accompanied by a dazzling display of fireworks, so impressive it seemed as though gigantic waterfalls were flowing from the sky as sparkling rockets made their way to the firmament for a fiery conversation. A group of enthusiastic dancers were leading the parade. Nautch girls had been called to perform a traditional mujra in a shamiana within the compound. I was in my bedroom on the first floor along with my niece and my friend Masood Bano, who had come all the way from Bhopal to attend the wedding. I had locked the door from inside. The girls kept insisting I come to the window and see the grand procession, the splendid fireworks as well as the lively mujra. I was lying with my face buried in my pillow, crying hysterically.

An elderly American acquaintance called Mrs Williams came to my room to meet the 'bride' with one of her friends. Seeing me weeping Mrs Williams said, 'Come on Saeeda, you should be happy. Have you not met him?'

'No!' I shouted furiously and began howling even louder. She immediately started consoling me. I'm sure she must have wondered about this strange Indian custom of arranged marriages. The noise and ruckus of the celebrations continued all night long. In the morning I was dressed up like a bride and brought downstairs to the drawing room.

The bridal dress in those days was designed in the most peculiar fashion. Bright red in colour, it was made with either silk, cotton or a thick muslin cloth called *tol*. The entire tiresome outfit – kurta, pyjama, dupatta – was stitched together without the use of scissors! Cutting the cloth was considered inauspicious. The logic was that the relationship of the bride and groom should be protected (like this garment) from the snip of a sharp scissor. Their union should be as smooth as milk and sugar. The way the bride was made to sit, all huddled-up, cramped and absolutely still, like a bundle of clothes, completely superseded the discomfort of wearing this ridiculous outfit! I was also placed like a sack on a takhat in the drawing room. The bridegroom was seated comfortably in front of me. We both had our sehras[28] on: the custom in my family is for both bride and groom to wear the sehra. A long red shawl was then draped over our heads. Under this mini-canopy our fragrant sehras were lifted. Along with a large ornate mirror the Holy Quran was placed between us open to the 112th Chapter of *Surah-al-ikhlaas*. I heard someone say, 'Banno Begum, open your eyes, read the *Surah-al-ikhlaas*, then look at your husband.' The same words were repeated to the groom. I didn't have the courage to do justice to this age-old custom called *arsi-mushaf*. Perhaps he saw my face. I heard the ladies around us teasing him, 'Now stop staring at her dulhe mian or else people will say the groom is so besharam, shameless!'

This kind of playful banter went on till someone suddenly started singing '*Babul...*' the soulful song of separation.[29] The poignant lyrics of this classical Hindustani song brilliantly capture the intense emotions an Indian bride feels when she is being sent away from her father's house after the wedding ceremony. '*Hare har baans katao babul*' is another traditional folk song written almost 700 years back by the poet Amir Khusro. Its emotional lyrics and soulful tune aptly capture this heartbreaking moment. But try and imagine the plight of the bride. She has absolutely no idea where she is going once she leaves the familiar surroundings she grew up in as a playful child and a carefree young girl. What kind of family will she be with? What kind of person will she have to spend the rest of her life with?

---

[28] Headdresses, usually made of flowers or beads or golden tassels, that fall like a veil across the face of the bride and bridegroom.

[29] '*Babul mora naihar chhooto jaye...*' is a thumri in Bhairavi raga written by Nawab Wajid Ali Shah, the last Nawab of Awadh who uses the metaphor of '*bidai*,' a bride's farewell from her '*naihar*' or father's home to express his own anguish at leaving his beloved Lucknow. Bidai is also called rukhsati.

There's never a dry eye when these slow mournful songs are sung as everyone identifies with this emotional moment. My father was not keen on prolonging this sad moment. We heard his voice, 'Stop singing *babul*... it will delay the bride's departure.'

At the time of rukhsati, my father did not come to see me off. I have no idea who lifted me physically into the groom's car. Begum Aley Raza, my jethaani (eldest sister-in-law) came and sat next to me. The shehnai[30] began to play. It was the sorrowful notes of *babul* once again. The curtains on the car's window were drawn, the bridegroom slid into the front seat next to the driver and off we went to my husband's home.

The wedding procession reached Redichi Road. As our car pulled up under the porch, people came running with yards of cloth to hold as makeshift curtains of purdah for us. The bridegroom stepped out of the car, but before he could move towards me, I heard an excited voice shouting, 'I will carry my dulhan bhabhi (elder brother's bride) into the house... in my arms.' That was my sister-in-law Aqila. (Sixty long years since then and it still feels like yesterday!) I had asked Begum Aley Raza to ensure that the groom does not lift and carry me into the house, as was the custom. Bhabhijaan had alerted Aqila. This is why she bounded forward insisting, 'I will carry my dulhan bhabhi out of the car in *my* arms.' Her words instantly won me over and made me feel a bit more comfortable.

What wonderful people they were!

'Come here bhai sahab,' Aqila said, turning to address her elder brother. 'I will cover your head with this end of my sari pallu, you put your hand on top of dulhan bhabhi's head. Prem,' this to her friend Lucknow's famous surgeon Dr Bhatia's daughter, 'you go on bhai sahab's other side, your pallu should cover his head.'

Once out of the car I was made to sit on a masnad[31] in the aangan (courtyard). Suddenly a woman came, lifted my sehra, stuffed paan in my mouth hurriedly and said, 'nibble a bit.' The remaining half of the paan was fed to the hapless groom. A maidservant holding a silver

---

[30] Wooden musical instrument made with a double reed commonly played in India, Pakistan, and Bangladesh.

[31] A throne like structure made for the bride.

jug and washbasin then came and stood next to us. The jug was filled with milk. With great ceremony, my feet were found and extracted from under the strange bridal dress. The groom was given orders, 'wash her feet with milk.' He then had to dry them with his kerchief. The significance of this custom is that the husband should remain obedient to his wife and the bride should be prosperous enough to bathe in milk and have lots of children. Basically the couple should be happy, get along well with one another and their house should be filled with children. Bhabhijaan was sitting patiently behind me, supporting my back. She whispered in my ear, 'Don't open your eyes Saeeda, a group of ladies is heading this way to see you.' Then, one by one, the women lifted my sehra, and scrutinised my face. I heard them say, 'Oh, what an innocent face, Mashallah, Mashallah.'

In our days, at the time of the bride's muh-dikhayee[32] and during the groom's salaam-karayee,[33] guests gift money to the couple in fancy hand-stitched bags or envelopes. Gradually a large number of colourful envelopes and red bags began gathering in front of me. After about an hour Bhabhijaan announced loudly, 'the bride is very tired now.' Aqila was given orders to reach the bride to her room which was on the first floor. She lifted me in her arms and carried me till the staircase. I whispered in Aqila's ears, 'you can put me down now, I can climb the stairs myself.' She agreed. We raced up the stairs together as fast as we could and on reaching the room I immediately took off the sehra and flung it on the sofa.

'Arrey arrey… what have you done!' Aqila cried. 'Bhaisahab must remove your sehra.' The bulky veil of flowers was fitted back onto my head. Dear God, I had completely forgotten about Bhaisahab! So much had happened that morning, it totally slipped my mind that all of this hullabaloo was for Bhaisahab's benefit. Well, just then he arrived and Aqila fled.

Abbas Raza sahab lifted my veil, placed five hundred and one rupees in my lap along with ten gold coins and pulled me closer. That very moment, thank the good Lord, we heard a loud male voice saying, 'Bhaiya it is two in the afternoon, lunch is served.' It was the

---

[32] A wedding tradition that allows people to lift the bride's veil and see her face.
[33] Money given by the bride's family to the groom when he greets them.

Raza family servant informing us that Bhabhijaan was waiting at the dining table. Abbas Raza sahab quickly moved away from me. The storm passed; I breathed a huge sigh of relief.

'Abban, the food is getting cold.' This was Bhabijaan's voice.

'I'm coming, Bhabijaan,' Abbas Raza replied. He turned to me, 'Come, let's eat.' Without any coy hesitation I was ready to go. Bhabhijaan was waiting for us in the dining room. We ate lunch together. I didn't show any signs of being a shy, newlywed bride and chatted with her informally over lunch. Unfortunately the meal ended. Bhabhijaan made some excuse or the other and left. I was taken back to my room. It was around half past two in the afternoon.

Abban sahab lay down on his bed and casually invited me to do the same. 'Come, why don't you also lie down?'

I was aghast. 'Good God,' I thought to myself, 'how can I lie on the same bed... right next to him?'

I sat where I was, mute.

He stretched across, held my hand and said, 'Come... lie down.'

'*Dekhiye...*' I said, releasing my hand from his, 'See... I don't know you at all... I have never even seen you in my life... and...'

Abban sahab seemed shocked to hear me speak in such an outspoken, forthright manner. 'What are you saying...What do you mean...?' He replied aghast.

'I want that you and I stay together like two friends,' I said and regurgitated the conversation I had been rehearsing all this while in my mind. 'Then when you and I get to know each another better... well... then... then we will see...!'

Abban sahab was visibly shaken at hearing my rant. He did not say a single word and turned his back to me. He may even have dozed off. I remained on the sofa next to the bed.

I had mustered up a great amount of courage and had managed to express my feelings. I'd thought it would be extremely difficult. Now that I had said what I wanted to, it all seemed so futile. I sat there thinking, 'Perhaps this is what has been happening for years. The disgruntled groom goes to sleep while the apprehensive bride tries to sort out her tangled thoughts in a strange new environment.'

And what was I supposed to do now?

All around us there was silence. There was only one bedroom up here and that was ours. Everyone in the family wanted to leave us alone, hence not a soul could be spotted. I sat all-bundled-up in one place. I couldn't spot a single book in the room to seek refuge in. My self-confidence had just been dealt a violent blow. Shocked and confused, I kept asking myself, 'What should I do now?' I was extremely tired since I had been up all night. Sitting right there on the sofa my eyes closed and I fell asleep. When I woke up Abban sahab's bed was empty. Aqila was standing next to me. 'Dulhan bhabhi please change your clothes, guests have already arrived to see you. They are waiting downstairs for the muh-dikhayee.'

I changed and went downstairs. Once again several ladies came to see the bride. They lifted my veil, they lowered my veil. A group of mirasins (folk singers of Awadh) sang at the top of their gravelly voices. Some of the newly-wed women and young girls teased me, giggling and gossiping. But I was lost, drowning in a sea of my own thoughts. I couldn't understand what had just happened. Yes, I had come up with a novel way to start off my married life, but it was not out of malice. Neither was it my nature to sulk at the smallest provocation, cover my face and brood.

My father was an extremely broad-minded man. He gave me the opportunity to study in a liberal and progressive college such as Isabella Thoburn, where not only did I gain the confidence to think for myself but I also learnt the value of discipline and how to respect rules and regulations. Along with this another thought that had subconsciously started to bother me was that a grave injustice was being done to women. After all they are also human beings. Why should they be treated like chattel? Why weren't women being given a say in crucial matters such as their own marriages? On the basis of this I found courage to speak with my husband candidly. But his reaction left me stumped.

Surrounded by a constant flow of relatives and guests, I sat still and quiet in the same place till night fell. Whoever wanted to do so, came, removed my veil, gently lifted my chin with their hand, looked at my face, showered some blessings or said a few words of praise and left. At dinner-time, I was once again taken upstairs. Food had been laid out on the table, Bhabhijaan was already there along with Abban sahab. We finished our meal in a congenial manner. Then the bridegroom turned to me and said, 'Come let's go to the terrace and listen to Benazir Bai's songs.' Benazir was a famous courtesan of Lucknow.

Bhabhijaan quickly interjected, 'Don't make that mistake Abban, a large number of ladies are already there. If they see the bride they will start gossiping. If they see you they will wonder what a man is doing up there in the first place. You know they are all in purdah.'

Oh well, that was that! Back the two of us came to the bedroom. I was wearing a lovely crêpe dupatta delicately embroidered with star and moon motifs. Abban sahab came, sat down close to me and said, 'Your duppata is extremely beautiful… how did they make this design?'

'With a needle!' I retorted cheekily, looking the other way. Though pithy, my saucy remark was completely uncalled for. Abban sahab found it extremely distasteful. He got up quietly, removed his sherwani turned his back on me and lay down. I don't know if he fell asleep or stayed awake. I kept sitting like a shocked criminal in the very same place for a long, long time. That entire night my bridegroom didn't so much as turn one single time towards me.

Then slowly and gradually the reality of my situation began to dawn on me. I said to myself, 'Come on dulhan begum, get wise, no one is going to pamper you here, whether you get up and change your clothes or you don't, nobody cares. Your bed has been made, if you want to rest, sleep, if not, you can keep sitting where you are.' I began sobbing uncontrollably; a few loud sniffs escaped my lips, but that human being continued to sleep. After crying my heart out, I got up, changed and went and lay down quietly on the same sofa. It was the month of February, winter had set in, at some point I must have dozed off.

When I woke up Abban sahab had left for the mardana. Aqila was standing next to me with some of her friends. She lovingly helped me finish my morning rituals and ordered some breakfast for me. Both Abban sahab and Bhabhijaan were at the breakfast table.

I was taken back to the same drawing room where the scene was much the same as yesterday. Mirasins were joyfully singing wedding songs, guests were merrily socialising with one another, young girls were chatting, laughing and teasing each other. Now my bridal veil was not as long as on the earlier day. I was to sit demurely, in a decent manner, with my dupatta draped loosely over my head. The walima (wedding reception) was scheduled for later that evening. I was dressed up and made to sit in the drawing room. Guests started to arrive. This time, some of the ladies went as far as to fold back the corners of my dupatta to admire the jewellery I was wearing! A few of them even asked whether this or that piece was given by my in-laws or by my parents!

According to custom, on the second day after the wedding, the bride goes back to her parents along with her husband. Her brother comes to get them. With an array of delicious dry fruits and fresh seasonal produce, the groom leaves for the bride's house. He is accompanied by his sisters, his sisters-in-law, brothers, friends and together they celebrate the most enjoyable of all functions of a traditional Muslim wedding, the chauthee ki rasam. The newlyweds are made to sit opposite each other on a takht or on the floor, surrounded by their respective family members. The two sides then create near pandemonium playing a strange kind of Holi, tossing fragrant flowers, soft fruit and tender vegetables at each other.

Last in the line of ceremonies, the chauthee is a sort of ice breaker that helps the bride and groom, as well as their extended families, to shed their inhibitions and get to know each other informally. Boys and girls from both sides of our families thoroughly enjoyed the event and made a huge ruckus till the entertainment finally ended.

Wedding celebrations had been going on for weeks. We were all completely exhausted so dinner was served early. After my in-laws left, I was sent off to my room. In a short while Abban sahab came in. He was staying at my place for a few days. The little bit of vivacity and sparkle I had been allowed to nurture in my personality proved to be a source of trouble for me. My situation felt similar to what Burq has described in this Persian couplet: 'Ai roshani tabah tu barman bilashudi.' (The spark of my nature has become a curse for me.)

The thought that kept niggling at me was how unjust and unfair it was to force two complete strangers to marry one another. To make matters worse, I did not have enough emotional strength to know how to react to the situation I was in now. The thoughts I had expressed so confidently and candidly earlier were really those of a young immature girl who lived in a world far removed from reality.

The two of us were alone once again. Along with the anxiety I felt the previous night, I was also extremely shaky and unsure of myself now. All my confidence and boldness completely vanished. Nonetheless I went to the dressing room, changed my clothes, cried a little, tip-toed back quietly to my side of the bed and lay down. The unique solution I thought I had found and expressed so bluntly on our wedding night, was nothing more than childish ignorance on my part. I was married now, this was my world and it was up to me to make my life a bed of roses or let it all turn to dust.

I have mentioned earlier that I was not sly or cunning, neither did I have the tendency to simmer with rage or be envious; nor had I forged any enmity with my husband. I was simply clueless about the biological needs of a man. Now my state of mind was such that I had completely forgotten I had an outspoken mischievous side to my personality. Through the day younger women and newly-wed girls kept teasing me. I played along, pretending to look coy and happy. Every single day I was given new clothes to wear, decked from head to toe in bridal finery and made to sit amongst relatives. The entire time all I really wanted to do was cry. But I had been taught to smile when I felt sad and miserable. And that's exactly what I was doing now. The only difference was, I had lost all my self-confidence.

From my mother-in-law to my sister-in-law, along with all the other women in the house, everyone was constantly trying to pamper and entertain me. Aqila and Begum Raza were so affectionate and understanding, it didn't feel as though I had just moved in with them. I was completely unaware of the innate nature of men and the importance of conjugal relations for them. Now when I think of it I understand to what extent my attitude was unacceptable for Abban sahab. Emotionally he must have also gone through a difficult time.

The success of an arranged marriage in our society and its future well-being rested squarely on the sexual relationship the couple shared with one another. Because the restrictions imposed on men and women only ever allowed a husband and wife to meet at night. During the day the bride was kept busy amongst relatives, or doing some chore or the other. Hence the foundation of a good marriage was based on the conjugal relations and the sexual satisfaction they shared. The need for the young bride and groom to know each other or make themselves worthy of one another's everlasting affection and companionship had been completely overlooked. With the passage of time when the novelty of marriage wore off, differences would arise between the couple and it would become extremely difficult to maintain harmony in the relationship.

During the day in front of everyone, Abban sahab would be courteous and pleasant with me. At night he would become sullen, turn his back on me and go to sleep. I would lie awake feeling tormented and frustrated. Then one night, God knows how, but our unfamiliarity ended. We consummated our marriage. Now Abban sahab seemed very happy and content. He made it part of his routine to stay on in the zanana after breakfast. During this time the most difficult problem was our relationship. Sometimes right after extreme intimacy I felt as though I had suddenly been flung from the sky straight into hell. All at once he would turn his back on me and I would lie there feeling miserable and lost. When there was no visible reaction from him, I would burst out crying, but my new husband never took the trouble to console me. He had taken deep umbrage at the way I had behaved on our first night together.

The stories I heard from young brides were that after marriage they would be coquettish, throw tantrums and their eager groom would constantly be trying to win them over by flattering them and demonstrating his undying love for them. When the women narrated these incidents their faces radiated with delight. The absolute opposite was happening with me. The gist of the matter was that we were two extremely ignorant individuals who had been married off to one another. And I had to atone for the mistake I made on our wedding night, when I insolently drowned his manly desires with my bold, candid remarks.

If only he could have laughed it off, made fun of me, or simply just reacted – even if it meant fighting with me. Instead he turned the entire situation into a sort of 'cold war' between us. On my part I failed to understand his psychological temperament.

I had never been outright rebellious but I was a carefree playful sort of girl. During my wedding, I managed to act like a coy bride, sat quietly in one place with head bowed meekly, but fundamentally I could never be a blushing docile woman. Neither was I a domestic goddess, when it came to housework. Abbas Raza was an uncomplicated, simple-minded man with a good solid character. He needed a wife who could, from get-go, merge her personality into that of her husband's, nourish his sense of self-respect and cater in every way possible to his ego. Like one of my older sisters-in-law, who would often be heard repeating this phrase to her husband, 'whatever pleases you, pleases me.' This, I couldn't do.

The days passed and gradually I became familiar with the other members of the Raza household. Every now and then Abban sahab would fall into a blue sulk and then unexpectedly get out of it as well. We were still quite formal with one another. I did not have the courage to ask, 'What's wrong? Why are you so angry?'

The first few months passed in this formality. Yes, when he got into one of his bad moods it affected me deeply. I would find it difficult to eat anything or even to socialise. But in front of others I would try and remain as normal as possible, keep with the routine and fulfil all my daily responsibilities. It is possible that seeing me act normal Abban may have thought I was completely indifferent to his emotional state of mind. That was far from true. When he switched off from me, I would be upset and frustrated and would often cry in solitude. In retrospect sometimes I wonder what would have happened if I had been a bit more dramatic, sulked (like he used to) or perhaps talked about our personal problems with others and created a big scene.

But what is the use of thinking all of this now? At that time life was turning into an unfathomable puzzle. I was not well versed with the art of coquetry, the guiles and tricks women use to get their way with men. It's a precious skill that comes quite handy in married life. The first three or four months passed in trying to understand the customs, rules and social etiquette of my new family, aside from attending numerous parties. Bhabhijaan was extremely affectionate and generous; she was like a friend. She helped melt the tension I was facing by making the home environment as pleasant as possible. Aqila was constantly trying to make me feel comfortable at home, so I could get along well with everyone. The truth is all members of the

Raza household were good people. They were dignified, law-abiding, honest and genuine.

Mohammad Raza sahab had initially been appointed as Civil Judge in the District Courts of Lucknow. His reputation as an extremely able and honest man, preceded him. It wasn't long before the foresighted British officials recognised his potential, assessed his worth and as a gesture of their appreciation offered to nominate him as Judge of the Awadh High Court. Mohammad Raza sahab graciously accepted this prestigious high-ranking post. But he never fawned in front of any angrez nor did he show his gratitude for the appointment by kowtowing in the court of the Governor Bahadur. Throughout his tenure, he did not accept a dinner invitation from any Englishman, nor did he entertain any of them at his place. He would go to court, pronounce decisive judgments, come back home and get busy with his hobbies. Now and then a couple of close friends would drop by, other than that he led a simple, spartan life.

Attached to his bedroom was a lounge, on one side of which there was a small dining-table where Mohammed Raza sahab usually took his meals. Adjacent to these two rooms, was another which doubled up as his office and library. Entry to these areas was sacrosanct; only his Begum and private butler Annu had the honour of having unlimited access to the esteemed Judge sahab's living quarters. This does not mean Mohammad Raza sahab was arrogant or vain, on the contrary he was an extremely modest human being, compassionate towards people, tolerant and easygoing. He just chose to live his life pretty much to himself.

I called him Abbajaan.

Justice Raza usually took his breakfast, in fact, most of his meals, in his lounge. While he ate, Begum Raza would sit with him, patiently shooing away annoying flies from his plate with the free side of her pallu (loose end of dupatta). The loyal Annu stood on one side, alert, fulfilling the duties of a butler. He would serve Abbajaan his food, remove his plate when he finished eating and would place the sweet in front of him or offer him some cut fruits. Nobody kept purdah from Annu.

I have no idea what Abbajaan's early years were like, but within Indian society at that time, a formidable chasm of propriety and etiquette had deliberately been created between the older and younger generation. In order to effectively maintain control over children, parents consciously cultivated a method of upbringing that involved allowing their offspring to come close to them from time to time and then handing them orders. 'This must be done,' 'do it like this,' 'sit like this,' 'get up like that,' 'read this, not that' and so on. This method was practised widely throughout north India, especially in Awadh.

Mohammad Raza sahab never spoke directly to his sons. He always communicated with them through his wife.

'Dekho sunti ho, listen do you hear me, call Hashim to see me.'

Their fourth son would be summoned.

Hashim would enter, stand dutifully, head bowed, next to his mother.

'Hmm… Allan ki walda, tell him he should not keep reading till past midnight, it will have a bad effect on his eyes. I have seen the light of his room – it is on till late at night.'

Mohammad Raza always referred to his wife as Allan ki walda or Allan's mother. Allan was Justice Raza's oldest child Aley Raza's nickname. Another peculiar custom back then was that husbands never called their wives by their names. It was considered disrespectful.

Begum Raza would then address her son. 'Bete, your father is saying you should not stay up till late at night. It can strain your eyesight.' Standing head bowed in a gesture of respect, Hashim would obediently mutter, 'Ji, very well.' And that was that. Meeting over. Hashim miyan would run off to seek shelter in his room. The extent of a man's role as father was limited to keeping a strict eye on the children's education and upbringing. The entire responsibility of discipling them, reprimanding them as well as imparting good values rested on the shoulders of the mother.

Justice Raza and his wife had suffered the loss of two grownup girls. One was approximately 18 when she passed away and the other only 15 years old. Both fell prey to the life threatening disease, Typhoid. They now had five sons but only one girl, Aqila. They doted on her and she did have the most lovable personality. Justice Raza was an exceedingly family-oriented man. To top that he had taken on the financial responsibility of looking after a couple of destitute girls as well. Perhaps to provide his only daughter with some female company and keep his wife adequately entertained at home. As a result, one would see women of almost every age hanging around in the house. Judge sahab's doors were always open for needy relatives – men or women. These people would stay on at the Raza household for months on end, every need of theirs taken care of. When they left, another group arrived. This went on through the year.

Later I got to know, that aside from this endless cycle of hospitality, Abbajaan kept approximately eight hundred rupees aside every month for charity. No one had any inkling what Mohammad Raza sahab actually earned or spent. This is how he chose to lead his life.

My husband, Abbas Raza had two older brothers. They were married and lived on their own. He was the third son. At the time when I became a member of this family, Abbas Raza had successfully cleared the munslfi Judicial Services exam and was waiting for his appointment. Hashim had passed the Indian Civil Services examination and been sent to London on probation. Masud, the youngest, was studying for the Imperial Finance exam. The sons kept busy with their studies. They played hockey and tennis and went to the cinema once or twice a week.

An unusual thing happened during the initial days of my marriage. Justice Raza, my father-in-law, who was a man of few words, would send for me, make me sit in his lounge and hold informal talks with me on a wide range of topics. He would speak in such a comfortably familiar manner as though we had known each other for years. Our meetings were never long but thanks to them I attained a position of respect in the house. Gradually he grew even more interested in our discussions and whenever he had free time he would ask me to come over. He would talk about books and express his opinion on subjects such as history and geography. He was extremely well-read. Our chats were rather enjoyable and led to an increase in my own knowledge. During our discussions he told me about the Raza khandaan, their family and the lifestyle they had chosen as theirs. He wove these vital bits of information so subtly into our discussion, as though the topic just happened to come up during the course of our conversation. I was not a highly educated woman but the appreciation I was receiving from Abbajaan made me happy and confident about myself. Life seemed worthwhile.

During those early days, Abban's behaviour towards me was quite gracious. He had been appointed Civil Judge in Lucknow and would usually leave for court by 9.30 in the morning. When he got back at around 5.30, we would sit and take our evening tea together. We always served some interesting snacks along with tea such as matar phulkiyaan, puri-kabab, namak-paare.[34] These sort of wifely duties I executed with great delight. Our lives fell into a rhythm. We were still not very free with one another, Abban did most of the talking, I would sit and listen. If I didn't disagree with him, there would be no unpleasantness.

In my day-to-day behaviour I was demure and respectful. I behaved with everyone in a proper fashion. That outspoken, playful girl who chattered nonsensically, laughed uncontrollably for no apparent reason and indulged in silly antics with friends, had simply vanished. The only time I felt like my old jovial happy-go-lucky self was when I spent time with Aqila. In fact my behaviour often reminded me of these lines by Mirza Ghalib, *'phir waza-e-ahteyaat se rukne laga hai dum.'* (I am so consumed with the anxiety of being discreet, I feel suffocated).

In those early years of marriage I have no clue what mistakes I made without realizing it, but what happened almost every night is that we would be intensely passionate and loving with each other, then for some unknown reason his demeanour would suddenly change. He would appear angry, turn his back on me and go to sleep. I would lie awake for hours or get up and go outside or walk up to the roof. The veranda there had large spacious niches, sometimes I spent the entire night sitting or lying there.

If one doesn't try and delve into the nitty-gritties of what life should be like and focuses on simple facts – such as you wake up, wash-up, have breakfast, make some pleasant conversation for a while, do some household chores (perhaps stitching) a friend drops by, then later you go attend a dinner, come back home and go to sleep – things are much easier. Yes, during the day you make

---

[34] Different kinds of savoury snacks.

sure your husband's clothes are ironed, there is no button missing from his shirts, his shoes are polished and his hookah ready and bubbling. All your wifely responsibilities are, in a sense, complete. Your husband then says some confusing things that offend you or he just stops talking. You should simply overlook this as long as the day is going according to routine. After all what more can a wife want?

But when a person stops focussing on this simple predictable pattern and gets trapped by the whimsical demands of their ego, difficulties begin to raise their ugly heads. You have unrealistic expectations. You start questioning if a certain behaviour is appropriate or not. Deep within, you wish desperately that someone would pamper you. You get cranky, accusations are flung and stories fabricated to justify one's reaction and behaviour.

There was strict purdah in my sasural. I couldn't play the games I once enjoyed; Tennis and badminton had become a thing of the past. All I had now were books. I read voraciously. If I compared Abban's way of life to the environment in which I had grown up, the most glaring difference was that aside from going to court and reading law books pertaining to work, Abbas Raza had no other interests. Then after some more time passed, I started feeling that I was repeatedly committing an extremely grave mistake. Without warning, Abban would become quiet and his dense spells of silence would keep growing in intensity and duration. I should have dealt with this issue rationally, by simply ignoring it. Instead after two or three days I would lose my temper and flare up.

'Why are you not talking?' I would ask agitatedly.

'No… it's not like that….' would be his standard reply.

Then he would withdraw completely.

Afsurda dil, afsurda kunndd, anjuman-e-raah' (One sad heart makes the entire gathering cheerless.) I was sad, unhappy and felt overwhelmingly depressed every time I thought, 'what should I do?' The Razas were used to seeing Abban angry and withdrawn. They did not know what to do either. But no one dared to disturb him. During these phases, he ate when he felt like, fasted when he wanted to. The mistake I made now was that I started quarrelling with him.

'Why are you behaving like this again? What is bothering you?' I would argue angrily in the hope of convincing him to snap out of it.

'It's wrong to stop talking with everyone. Do you even know the effect your silence has on us? It makes everyone unhappy. If I have made a mistake, tell me. Let's talk and get this over with.' Sometimes my efforts paid off; he would bounce back to normal and appear cheerful again. A few days would pass. Then once again he would get ticked-off about something and I would be left dealing with his radio silence.

I started observing him closely to see what it was that set him off and realised he didn't like my reading books. I made a concerted effort not to do so while he was around. Though of course this was pure conjecture – I could never tell for sure what triggered off his mood swings. When we got married, he had not spoken with his mother for six months. With Aqila's help, I managed to get them to patch-up.

I was definitely not in love with Abban sahab, but as a wife I felt a strong sense of duty towards him. If he complained of a headache, I happily massaged his temples. I would press his feet for hours on end. He often complained of pain there. I never sulked with him. I was cheerful, I got along well with the other members of his family. The entire issue was that he was a simple, good-natured man, naïve in that he did not know how to impress a woman and win her over. And I wasn't such a naïve woman that I would easily get charmed by the closeness I shared with a good-natured man. Not that I was complicated. I was feisty and playful, straightforward and sincere, a strange combination of different personality traits. When Abban was not prey to his silent-spells, we spent several enjoyable days with each other as a couple. Abban miyan was a simple man. His way of thinking was pretty straightforward and conventional. I suppose I was at fault, but what could I have done about it, I was so young at the time. I lacked both tact and diplomacy.

I have mentioned earlier that my father was a rather sensible man. He took a keen interest in our studies, as well as our extra-curricular activities. During the many informal chats we had, he would give good advice on simple practical matters such as the value of discipline, punctuality, cleanliness. He taught us good manners and proper etiquette. In our house we'd never seen anyone sulk, clam up or lie about feeling angry all day, bedsheet stretched over their head. We were ordered to eat whatever was served, without any fuss. We couldn't say, 'we don't like the taste of this' or 'we won't eat that'. Secondly we had to eat on time, not munch whatever we could lay our hands on all day long. These were the rules laid down in our house.

There were several fundamental rules in place within the Raza household as well but the circumstances there were different. The lady of the house, Begum Mohammad Raza, was constantly surrounded by countless relatives and spent her time running her home as best she could while having to maintain several other relationships at the same time. She had received a basic education, given birth to 14 children and had shouldered the grief of losing eight of them. Mohammad Raza sahab had, from the start, carved a separate niche for himself and drowned himself in his law books and legislative work. Under these circumstances the children were brought up, to a large extent, according to their own sensibilities and judgement.

Abbas Raza was their third son. As a child he contracted the dreaded chicken-pox, which very few people survived back then. Thankfully he did. Then he got typhoid. He recovered from this life-threatening disease as well but his immunity was badly affected. Compared with his four brothers, Abbas Raza's job was not as high ranking. He worked at the district level whereas three of his siblings were employed by the Imperial Government. The fourth was also a lawyer.

Their house was constantly filled with at least a dozen relatives. They would be sitting about in the veranda or in the rooms laughing and joking, gossiping with each other endlessly.

'Ooee, have you heard Abban Bhaiya has also got a job?'

'Hahn, but how will he work? He doesn't keep well.'

'I have heard Hashim's got a very high-ranking job.'

'And Masud I hear is working with the Imperial government.'

'Kazim Bhaiya is already such a big police officer.'

'Well at least Abban miyan has a job.'

When talk such as this took place regularly how was it possible that it would not scar the mind of a young man? Abbas Raza was deeply affected. This irresponsible banter and comparative praise of his siblings' achievements gave him a severe inferiority complex. It was the responsibility of his father and his older brothers to stop this toxic chatter and re-instil faith and confidence in him. If they had given one stern warning to these illiterate women, they would have been intimidated into silence. There were a few men in the family as well who indulged in such careless talk. They would come by to meet Begum Raza in connection with some property matter and end up trying to flatter her with their damaging gossip.

I was completely clueless about the hierarchical structure of government jobs and neither did I suffer from any complex. But there were several people within the Raza family who did. Though they were extremely good people with high values and ideals. It was after about a year of marriage that I realised that quite unknowingly some members of their family could end up causing irreparable damage.

It was my second Muharram after I'd been married. We had gone to Neotani village where the Razas have their ancestral home and imambara.[35] According to Shia custom the bride spends her first Muharram with her family and the second with her in-laws. In Neotani, Muharram was celebrated with great enthusiasm and fanfare. Grand preparations were made for the majlis which would end with a generous serving of pulao (aromatic rice cooked with meat) sheermal (saffron-flavoured traditional flatbread) khameeree roti (flatbread made with yeast) kababs and more. Generally, Bade-bhaijaan my oldest brother-in-law, Syed Aley Raza, addressed the majlis and recited the soz khwaani or songs of lamentation. Along with the Razas, the entire village of Neotani attended the event. We women sat on the rooftop of the Imambaara and listened to the majlis.

I was sitting in this special gathering of women, listening attentively to Bade-bhaijaan's recital of the marsiha (an elegiac poem) He finished and started giving a small talk. 'We are immensely proud to be associated with Neotani which we consider our motherland. Many residents of this village have made a great name for themselves.' Saying this Bade-bhaijaan started narrating names of the members of the Raza family, Kazim Raza, Hashim Raza, Masud Raza... but

---

[35] Large hall where Shia Muslims pray.

he forgot to mention Abbas Raza's name. Other than the fact that Kazim, Hashim and Masud had successful jobs there was nothing special about them. In front of the entire Raza clan, and the older as well as younger generation of Neotani, Bade-bhaijaan had made it clear that Abban's job was not as important. Almost immediately Abban came to me and said, 'Come on, I want to go back to Lucknow right away.'

After a lot of persuasion I managed to convince him. 'If we leave right now everyone will gossip and say we left as you are over sensitive. And the truth is Bade-bhaijaan has actually shown himself in a rather poor light by making such a statement.' This incident took place on the ninth day of Muharram. We spent the tenth day in Neotani and came back to Lucknow the day after that. But Abban felt extremely disheartened. The only way to fix this would have been to find the courage to communicate to Bade-bhaijaan that he had made a grave mistake. And this would have been a lesson for everyone in future, that such thoughtlessness causes deep pain. It must never be repeated. But that is not what happened. For Abban, these small hurtful lashes gradually grew into a deep wound.

In my parents' house we led a comfortable life. Though we were middle-class, not overtly wealthy, we did not lack anything either. We never faced any social pressure in Bhopal regarding our class or rank within society. The citizens of this city were focussed on observing the Begum sahiba of Bhopal, not one another. In Lucknow and Uttar Pradesh however it was the opposite. We often heard people talking about each other.

'Ayy… he works for the Indian Civil Services….'

'Ohh… So and so is a Deputy Collector?'

'Well, he is a Tehsildaar or Tax Inspector….' etc.

Even at social gatherings, the socio-economic status of a person would come up by way of conversation.

Then the long hot summer began. Courts in Lucknow were shut from the beginning of June. It was decided that we would spend our vacation in Mussoorie. I was extremely delighted when I heard this as almost every year I used to visit the hill station with my parents. I began preparing for the trip excitedly since I knew from experience what had to be taken on the journey.

Back in those days travelling was not what it is now. For a two or three month trip we had to pack and carry every single item of daily use, from utensils and beddings to comforters, cheeni ke bartan, bone-china crockery, teacups, spoons and cutlery. We would take all the things we needed and used with us, along with at least three servants. We usually hired a five or six bedroom house in Mussoorie for the entire season for around Rs 1700. Abban and I rented a one-bed cottage which had a huge bedroom, one dressing room, a bathroom and veranda. It was called Sedborough Nest.

I personally wrapped and boxed the bone-china crockery and got the rest of the paraphernalia packed efficiently in large sandookhs (trunks) under my critical supervision. My in-laws seemed quite impressed with my organisational skills and watched me prepare for our holiday with great admiration. We reached Mussoorie on the 6th of June along with a cook and an old maidservant who had been sent with me from my parents' home.

Our cottage was located strategically on a scenic bend on Mussoorie's famous Camel's Back Road. From here, the stunning view of the majestic mountains and the lush green valley was absolutely breathtaking. It was everything the romantic in me was yearning for. I was delighted to be at Sedborough Nest and got engrossed in setting up my new home, though I had still not developed any strong attachment for my husband. Neither was his behaviour such that I felt drawn to him. But since I was married now and was leading the life of a married woman, I had started to long for someone who could love me passionately, whose love I would reciprocate with equal intensity.

I was bold, mischievous and happy-go-lucky; I never let the minor distasteful annoyances of life get the better of me and leave their mark on me. I decided I should try and adopt the same approach towards my married life. After all, I asked myself, 'Is there any problem that cannot be resolved? Perhaps, there is something lacking in me? Why don't I try to understand my husband's temperament?'

After reaching Mussoorie, Abban appeared cheerful. I would often hear him whistling to himself. I liked this. Mussoorie was packed with people at this time of year. Almost the whole of Lucknow was visiting and since there was no dearth of acquaintances we began to socialise. Radha Krishan, one of my father's dear friends was staying at Sedborough Cottage with his wife. I used to call her Radha Bhabhi. The Cottage was a stone's throw from our Nest and we began meeting regularly. One day I went and hired a folding table as we needed some additional furniture. One could expand and collapse this amazing piece of furniture in three simple steps. The shopkeeper had carefully explained the dynamics of this mechanism to me. But when I got home I clean forgot what he had said and for the life of me, could not figure out how to open the table!

When they saw coolies coming in and out of our house both Radha Bhai and Bhabhi walked over. Even they tried to expand the table but to no avail. Then quite by accident, almost simultaneously, both the maid and I reached our hands under the table, felt a piece of wood, moved it slightly and voila the folded table opened up.

'Saccda, your maid is smarter than you!' Our guests said teasingly.

I went along with the joke and laughed. Abban was completely silent. Radha Bhai and Bhabhi sat for a bit and left. By this time Abban's mood had grown quite grim. The enthusiasm with which I had set up the table, vanished. I started to wonder, 'What could have happened? What can cause someone's mood to change so suddenly within a split second?' At the age I was, I did not have the wisdom to get to the root of the matter. Perhaps in my ignorance, unintentionally, I was doing something wrong.

For a day or two, Abban remained aloof. Then he was all right and our lives returned to normalcy. I had promised myself that no matter what, I will stay happy and keep him happy. We were roaming about, shopping, going on picnics and attending various dinner parties, almost every day. Throughout this time I was clueless that I may have been committing a grave mistake. I was not conditioned to think that men are inferior or that I needed to exert my superiority over them.

Abban slept late. I was an early riser. We used to have breakfast together around 10 in the morning. Quite often I would get up, walk across to Radha Bhabhi's place, spend an hour or so with them, then come back before Abban woke up so I could supervise breakfast. One morning when I returned from Radha Bhabi's place, Abban was awake. In an extremely harsh tone he asked, 'Did you go to Radha Krishan's place?'

'Yes, I did.'

'Why did you go there?'

'I went to see Radha Bhabhi,' I replied.

'Why don't you tell the truth…' he said angrily, 'that you went to meet Radha sahab!'

I was shocked at the allegation. Reaching my hand out I took support of the wall and stood rooted to the spot. What should I say? What reply do I give him? Dear God, he knows I tie rakhi on Radha Bhai. I even get a gift for it every year. Radha Bhabhi is so dear to me! Despite this, is my behaviour so utterly deplorable that I can be made to feel shameless and vile? Everything was spinning. I felt as though I was being buried alive. But that did not happen. Neither did the earth swallow me, nor did the sky burst open in fury. Instead I heard my maid's voice.

'Breakfast is served Begum sahab.'

In my head I thought, 'Aah yes, it's time for breakfast. The world is moving the way it has been. Everything seems exactly the way it was just a few seconds back. Get up Saeeda Bano, straighten out those shoulders. Go face the world. Your food is on the table. It is getting cold.'

I came to the table and sat down.

'Sahab is sleeping Begum sahab, he says he will not eat.'

With great difficulty I had breakfast. The aaya served me.

Then I went and sat down in the veranda. I wanted to run away, far away from here. Break free from this so-called enchanted existence, but my feet wouldn't move. I just sat. I wasn't angry, but the thought that paralysed my mind was, 'How can one build a life together on such a hollow foundation?'

Then it was lunch time. Abban did not come out of his room. I had been taught to honour the demands of time. I gave food to the servants then went and sat in the drawing room. 'What should I do now?' I thought to myself. 'Should I go back to my maika? But what will I tell my parents? Everyone usually looks to blame the woman. How will my parents overcome this accusation? Yes I was bold and playful but I am not promiscuous.' I knew I had the self-confidence to battle these hideous accusations. I had barely been married three or four months. My in-laws were extremely fond of me. Especially my father-in-law, who was a reserved man and didn't speak directly to his own sons. While no one in the family had the courage to even enter his room, I was often called to his private lounge to sit and chat with him. On his way back from court Abbajaan often stopped at Lucknow's famous Kashmir Fruit Mart and bought fruit for me. He'd find me sitting in the veranda, come from behind, put his hands over my eyes lovingly and place the fruit basket in my lap.

'Abbajaan?' He'd take his hands away. 'See I got you fruit, now go get some snacks for me.'

Because of this informal interaction with him I had acquired a favoured position in the family. 'Judge sahab is very fond of his third daughter-in-law.' Could I be the cause of his dishonour? Oh Lord how do I break free from these shackles?

Racked by such perturbing thoughts, I felt intensely restless. I got up from my chair, sat back down, walked to the veranda, stood, came back, held my head in my hands and sat down again. I didn't know how to lie about and sulk with a bedsheet pulled over my face. Around four in the afternoon, Abban came out, took me by the hand and led me into the bedroom. He hugged me tightly. I began to sob uncontrollably. When he tried to get more intimate with me, I asked cautiously, 'Do you really think I am that shameless? Then do one thing, don't have anything to do with me.'

'How can you say that I think you are shameless? I was angry when I said all that. When I woke up, you were not there. I waited for you for a long time...' Now his tone of voice and his style of speaking was soft and appeasing.

'So you can completely lose control when you get angry?' I asked.

Abban put his hands over his head and began to cry. 'Please forgive me Saeeda. I should not have said all that. God knows what happens to me when I get angry. I am a bad person. You be the sensible one – forgive me.' Abban kept repeating this and crying. I had never seen a man cry. In a flash, my anger and sadness disappeared. He kept crying and trying to assure me that he loved me and in my helplessness, I sought refuge in his efforts of assurance. Once again the two of us were back on the straight and narrow path. We stayed in Mussoorie for another twelve or fifteen days. Abban had to be back in Lucknow by the beginning of July as the courts were reopening. It was decided

I should go and stay with my parents in Dehradun for a couple of days. I reached Dehradun on the 2nd of July. My father had bought a house on Pritam Road.

Barely two days after my arrival, I woke up one morning feeling extremely unwell. My head was spinning and I was feeling nauseous. I told Amma. Without giving my illness any importance, she handed me some chooran.[36] When that did not work, she made some excuse and got busy doing her household work. I had never seen my mother sitting idle. She was always doing something or the other. The next morning I woke up feeling worse. The doctor was called. Even he did not give a clear diagnosis and left saying, 'Oh, you will be fine.' By evening I did feel better. But next morning, once again I was unwell. My head was spinning; I couldn't even look at breakfast. I hated the sight of food. This became a regular feature. I couldn't eat a thing and started feeling very weak.

Then gradually I was told I was having a baby. Ya Khuda, O dear God, mentally I was not at all prepared for this. The birth of a child is in itself a miracle for which a woman has to be in the right frame of mind – of peace and acceptance. Psychologically I had some basic shortcomings which I could not even fathom myself. Regardless of this I handled the issues I was facing with sincerity and honesty. Which is why I was attentive and sincere in my day-to-day interaction with my husband. But he was so immature that my sincerity was not enough for him. In his own way he loved me intensely and wanted me to love him with equal emotion. After marriage the foundation of love is based on sexual compatibility between the couples and the woman's ability to cater to the male ego. I failed at both; part of the reason for his frequent mood swings was this. Though he was in the habit of sulking as well. Anyway, at the time, I didn't quite understand any of this.

At the end of July, Abban took two days off and came to Dehradun. I was not well and had become quite weak, as I was not being able to keep any food down. That night he was extremely loving and affectionate with me. He spoke about almost everything under the sun. In my own way, I also tried to keep him happy. Then

---

[36] A digestive powder.

I don't know what we were discussing, but I disagreed with his point of view. I can't recall exactly what the topic of conversation was but it wasn't anything serious. Abban got really angry. As his temper started rising, I said, 'If anything I say, no matter how small, displeases you, what was the need for you to come all the way from Lucknow?'

I had barely finished speaking, Abban got up from the bed, put on his slippers and walked out. We were sleeping in the veranda. I sat on the bed, shocked. Half an hour passed, he didn't come back. I got up and started looking for him in the compound. I couldn't see him anywhere. I opened the gate and walked out on to the silent street. The moon was shining bright. Everything around me was intensely quiet. It was probably one o' clock at night. I crossed the length of the road outside our house, turned onto the adjacent street and saw someone standing under the dim light of the lamp post. As I walked closer I realised it was Abban. I suddenly felt extremely sad and also very very angry at the same time. After fighting, arguing, pleading and God knows what else, I finally managed to get him to come back to the house. By now it was almost two in the morning.

I wish I had wept hysterically that night and made myself sick. Abban would have had to come back by himself. My parents would have found out what had transpired between us. In his own way Abban would have had to take responsibility for his actions. If only I had not been gutsy enough to go looking for him at that hour of the night.

This was the fundamental difference between us as a couple. It could not simply be overlooked just because we were married now. I was fearless and strong-minded and he reacted without considering what the consequences of his actions could be.

After we got back, both of us lay down in our beds quietly and fell asleep. A couple of days later he left for Lucknow and I kept thinking, 'what should I do with my life. I have never been rude or bitter to my husband. I get along so well with everybody in the house, I am not an incompetent housewife, I make a conscientious effort to take care of his day-to-day comforts, unlike the wives who keep gadding about all day. When he gets back from work I was always there and when I go out to socialise it is always with him. In fact I am extra attentive when it comes to respecting him as a husband – more than some of the other wives I know. Then what mistake is it that I keep committing, which allows him to become so indifferent to me that he can leave the house and walk out in the middle of the night? He knew I wasn't well, he knew that I was pregnant with his child. He didn't even stop to think for a split-second that 'So far this woman hasn't complained to anyone about the way I behave, I am at her parent's house, I should not cross my limit here at least.' I don't know what used to come over him and I didn't know what attitude I should adopt. When he reached Lucknow he wrote me a loving letter in which he informed me that he had been transferred to Gorakhpur.

My health remained poor during those initial days of pregnancy and kept deteriorating steadily. Because of the immense weakness I was finding it painful to even walk about. At the end of September I was brought back to Lucknow with great difficulty. My mother-in-law and Aqila came to receive me at the railway station. They insisted I go straight with them to Redichi Road. My father agreed and I went to my sasural straight from the station. Everyone was extremely attentive to my needs. They made a concerted effort to make me feel as comfortable as possible. My condition remained much the same. I was completely disinterested in eating anything though a wide variety of delicious food-items would be cooked especially for me. I could barely take a bite. In fact it was difficult for me to even keep water down. As was his habit, Abbajaan would get delicious fruit for me on his way back from court. It would be placed in front of me but I wasn't able to enjoy any of it.

After a while I was confined to bed; bathed in bed and even my hair was washed in bed. Ultimately a nurse was hired to look after me. Basically I created such a huge sham that all kinds of doctors would constantly be on call to come and see me. They would prescribe some medicine or the other as consolation and leave. The entire Raza household was worried sick and my parents were consumed with anxiety. When I look back now and think of my behaviour I feel it was so sanctimonious and hypocritical. Because in our days, people tried to solve psychological issues by trying to impose the pressure of customs and social expectations on to the person suffering. Subconsciously, my ill health was probably a desperate call for help. A direct result of the unpleasant relationship I shared with my husband and the severe shock my ego received repeatedly because of his thoughtlessness.

By early November my mother got me to her house. My health remained much the same. But by early December I started to feel a bit better and my interest in food resurfaced. Slowly I got back to my normal eating habits and the debilitating weakness began fading. During this phase of my life, I realized, for the very first time what a tremendous blessing it is to have a mother. My mother was a woman of few words, yet she looked after everyone in the family in a dedicated loving manner that is hard to describe. She kept track of even the smallest needs of each person.

My father had rented a villa on Clandar Road. On the night of 31st December we had finished eating and were sitting around the dining table chatting. My brother, Mehdi, (whom we fondly called Machchan Bhai) had gone to spend New Year's at Valerio's, one of Lucknow's exclusive restaurants. After dinner Miyan liked to sit comfortably and engage us in discussion. Suddenly his head slumped on to the table. I quickly got up and lifted it. He was sweating profusely. He put his hand on the left side of his chest and said he felt excruciating pain. With some difficulty, Amma and I managed to get him to lie down in his bed. I reassured Amma, told her to look after Miyan, ordered the servant to sit with her and not move an inch from there, threw a coat hurriedly over my shoulders and started walking towards Carlton Hotel. It was a short walk from our house. From Carlton, I made a telephone call to the civil surgeon and asked him to come to our house immediately. Then I dialled Valerio's and requested the manager to tell Mehdi sahab to go to his house as quickly as possible. Finally I made a call to my sister and told her Miyan had had a heart attack. The civil surgeon was always an Englishman. After making the calls, I walked home as fast as I could. Machchan Bhai's car passed by, he stopped, I hopped in and as we pulled into our driveway, the civil surgeon's vehicle entered at the same time.

Miyan was in extreme agony. The doctor straightaway gave him a morphine injection. It's effect was immediate, the patient felt relief and began to doze off. The doctor informed us that Miyan had suffered a severe heart attack. There was nothing to worry about if he remained well after the injection but it was imperative he stay quiet and not move about. He needed complete rest. By this time my sister also arrived. Miyan spent the night comfortably but woke up feeling extremely weak. We followed the doctor's orders to the 'T' and after four days the debilitating weakness reduced. When he asked us details of what had happened, we narrated the entire incident. That evening when Abban came to visit Miyan, my father said to him in Persian, *'Zauja shuma karey kard.'* (Your wife has done wonders.) Even now when I hear the echo of his words they comfort me in so many ways.

It was the 14th of January, I was at my parents' place, when all at once, around three in the afternoon we felt as though a dozen road-rollers were roaring into the house. Amma, who was sitting on the corner of her bed in the veranda stitching a piece of cloth screamed, 'Arrey... I'm falling, I'm falling!'

I looked up and saw gigantic eucalyptus trees with thick intertwined branches being uprooted, falling on the ground right in front of me. I pushed Amma instinctively under the bed. It was an earthquake. Then I pulled her out and ran with her into the open compound. Miyan came out of his room hurriedly. All the servants had congregated outside as well. The massive trees in the compound, the buildings across the road and even our house were all shaking and moving like a ship in a stormy sea. The earthquake lasted three and a half minutes. That is a lot of time for such a terrifying experience.

This earthquake of 1934 lasted ten full minutes in Quetta (now in Pakistan) and created a lot of destruction in Bihar. The ground right under our feet was trembling uncontrollably; we managed to steady ourselves with a lot of difficulty. It felt as though, any minute now, the earth would simply split apart. When the tremors finally stopped, we stood shocked and silent for a couple of minutes. Then each of us began narrating their own peculiar experience of the disastrous event at almost the same time. Later we found out several old buildings had been badly destroyed and quite a few of the old trees had fallen. Other than that, on the whole, the city did not suffer much damage.

Shortly after this incident, in January 1934, my father-in-law, Justice Mohammad Raza, retired. Prior to this he had shifted out of the huge bungalow on Redichi Road and moved into another on Shahnajaf Road. I had been given orders to decorate the drawing room with sky blue curtains, matching upholstery and befitting furniture. This was going to be Abbajaan's gol kamra, his exclusive drawing room.

I managed to fulfil Abbajaan's wishes and by the end of the month his private drawing room with sky-blue interiors was ready. My health kept improving. I had come back to live with my in-laws. Doctors had advised me to take regular walks. Every day, before dark, I would sit in Abbajaan's official 7-seater Fiat and go till the bridge on the banks of River Gomti.

On the 30th of January, Abbajaan sent for me. He seemed to be in an extremely good mood. 'See,' he said cheerfully, 'yesterday I received a letter from the Viceroy. I want you to read it and tell your Chachijaan what is written in it.' I read the letter, then translated it and told my mother-in-law that the Viceroy had made Abbajaan an offer to become a member of his Legislative Council. After discussing the matter with his family, Abbajaan decided to accept the honour. He wrote a reply to the Viceroy informing him that he would arrive in Delhi on the 1st of March 1934, to take up this official responsibilities.

Abbajaan was suffering from prostate problems. The remedy suggested was an operation. He decided to get Lucknow's famous surgeon Dr Bhatia, to do the procedure on the 2nd of February. Dr Bhatia was our neighbour and also one of Abbajaan's close friends. One room in the house was thoroughly sterilized for the surgery. Two private nurses were hired and it was decided that Dr Bhatia's older son, Raj Bhatia would stay at our house, morning to night for Abbajaan's post-operative care. This way he could attend to any emergency and effectively supervise the nurses as well. After taking all necessary precautions the operation was conducted with great care and proved to be successful. Both nurses fulfilled their responsibilities efficiently. Dr Raj Bhatia's presence was a great source of comfort to us.

Fourteen days later Abbajaan's health began to deteriorate. Within minutes we got to know he had developed tetanus. The disease is caused by using dirty, rusted operating tools. But we had left no stone unturned to ensure there was no negligence. Then how was it that Abbajaan got infected with this dreadful disease, for which, at that time there was no cure?

Abbajaan passed away on the 25th of February. I was with him till he breathed his last. I had not seen anyone die before this. Chachijaan fainted. I didn't know what to do. The entire house, which was filled with relatives and close friends, was in a state of shock. Then Aley Raza Bhai and Masud Raza came and took charge of their mother. They led Aqila and me into another room. I don't remember how each of us managed to deal with this colossal tragedy. Both Aqila and Chachijaan were beside themselves with grief. A daughter had lost her loving father for ever and Chachijaan was now a widow. For the family, their pillar of support had fallen.

Within minutes the news that 'Raza sahab Judge is no more' spread across the city like wildfire. Justice Raza was a highly-respected man, much loved by those who knew him. There were many anecdotes and stories about the just and sound judgments he gave in court and the deep long-lasting friendships he had cultivated through his lifetime. People used to imitate the style in which he pronounced his decisive verdicts. I heard close to 2000 people turned up to attend his funeral procession, and many wanted to shoulder the bier on which his body lay. Affected by this immense loss, Aley Raza Bhai recited a few verses at his father's funeral which he had written himself. I can recall two:

Baithe theyy ghani chaun mein kya uski khabar thee,
badh jayegi dhoop aur ye saaya na rahegaa.
Wiraan ghar ko dekha, rokar salaam bheja,
ujde huey makaan se bichde huey makeen pur.

Sitting in the vast shade of your love who would have thought,
One-day the blazing heat would destroy the comfort of this cover.
I look at our deserted home, weep and pay my last respects
to this empty house and the beloved patriarch who once lived here.

Time doesn't stop for anyone. We were now finding the house on Shahnajaf Road too large for the needs of our family. After looking around we found Chanderpore House on La'toushe Road and shifted there. It met with all our requirements and was not too expensive either. Abbajaan's letter to the Viceroy was left forgotten in the alcove of time.

6

No Bed of Roses

According to Indian custom, a woman delivers her first child in her maika, her maternal home. I went back from Chanderpore House to stay with my parents. A private ward had already been booked for me at Dufferin Hospital, along with a private nurse. The month of March was almost over. It was getting warmer and we had started sleeping outside on the lawn. On the 4th of April, around 10pm, I felt a slight pain in my stomach. I got up, went inside, popped some chooran, came back and lay down. The discomfort did not subside. I waddled back inside and had some more and then lay down again. The cramps refused to die down. I sat up and wondered what I should do. Amma's bed was next to mine. She heard me move about restlessly, and woke up. 'Why are you sitting up?'

'My stomach is hurting.'

She sat up hurriedly.

'Since when?'

'Ummm, about half an hour or so.'

'You didn't wake me up…!' She rushed inside and began making preparations to take me to hospital. Around midnight we were at Dufferin. By three in the morning, Bhabhijaan also arrived. The pain was getting intense and the lady doctor kept insisting I should walk around.

'How can I do that doctor,' I asked, 'I am in a lot of pain.'

'This is hardly anything,' she said jovially, 'right now you can still do it.'

This went on till six in the morning. Then they knocked me out with chloroform. I have no idea what happened after this. When I regained consciousness it was daytime. I saw Amma, Bhabhijaan and a nurse sitting in the room. I closed my eyes. I don't know how much time passed but when I woke up next, it was night. I could see lamp-lights flickering in the distance. I looked around, concentrated and saw a dark skinned woman standing by my bedside. She was swabbing my forehead with a wet cloth.

'What's the time?' I asked.

'Two in the morning Begum sahab.'

I racked my groggy mind, tried to figure out what was going on, then remembered I was going to have a baby and that they had given me chloroform. 'Surely the baby must have been born?' I thought. 'This woman must be the new maid. It's two in the morning, she is looking after me. She will get scared and run away.' Scattered thoughts kept playing in my mind. I turned to the aaya and said, 'Go and sleep now.'

'Very well Begum sahab,' she replied calmly and kept applying cold compress on my forehead. I saw the nurse coming towards me, then I fell unconscious again.

When I opened my eyes, it was daytime. I saw a lot of people sitting around here and there in the room. The nurse came, put her hand on my head, checked my pulse and said, 'you had us all very worried. After delivery your fever went up rapidly and you fainted. You were completely unconscious.'

'How much is it now?' I asked.

'About 100.'

'Where is my baby?'

The nurse brought the baby. 'He weighs six and a half pounds,' she said.

I stared in amazement at the little soul before my eyes. When I placed my hand on him, my hand looked humongous. My husband walked up to my bedside. He kept gazing at our child with immense love and a deep curiosity. I was feeling extremely overwhelmed. Shutting my eyes I said a silent prayer in my head. 'Dear God, for the sake of this baby, please let there be happiness and understanding in our married life. Let this awkward distance between us vanish.'

Seated in the chair next to me, Abban reached out and held my hand. This miracle of our union, this tiny little creature, this baby of ours, all the joys and sorrows of the world are now going to be associated with him. Our emotions and responsibilities will forever be focussed on him. Both of us instinctively felt this in the touch of our hands. Silently we raised our hands in prayer, may this child bring peace and harmony between us. 'You still have fever, please, try and get some rest.' That was the nurse's voice. Abban continued to sit next to me. She started applying strips of wet cloth on my forehead. After a few days the fever began to subside and a fortnight later I came home with baby Asad in my arms. The maid who was taking care of Asad in hospital, proved to be as efficient and alert at home. She was experienced in looking after new-born babies and was neither lazy nor a slacker. I felt content and peaceful at the thought that a wise and capable woman was helping me raise our child.

The hot dry summer had become unbearable. We wanted to leave for Mussoorie as quickly as possible. Miyan had suffered a severe heart attack in January. It was not practical for him to travel to the hills. We consulted several doctors and after a thorough check-up, their collective opinion was that he could travel as long as he took the necessary precautions. Under no circumstances was he to strain himself. Miyan was eager to escape the Lucknow heat. He was also extremely concerned and over-protective about the baby and me and insisted we stay with him in Mussoorie.

Under Miyan's benevolent guidance we left for the hills on the 1st of May 1934. We rented four rooms on the first floor of a nine bedroom bungalow, the other half had been hired by Radha Bhai and Bhabhi. The house had a huge glazed-roof veranda which had been converted into a massive drawing room. We settled in comfortably. The holiday spirit was palpable in the air. The month of May passed in the blink of an eye.

Asad was almost two months old and my father was enjoying spending time with him. Every morning around 9am, while we were having breakfast, the nanny would bring Asad to us. Miyan would hold the baby lovingly in his lap and give him small licks of tea with his spoon. I didn't like this. Whatever little knowledge I had as a new mother pointed to the fact that this was not good for the infant.

But I didn't have the courage to dare suggest this to my father. After breakfast Miyan usually went off for his walk. Seeing him at the door, Amma would say, 'take a dandi[37] on the way back.' That day she forgot.

Miyan left, we got busy with our household work. Before we realised, it was noon. Then the clock struck one, still no sign of Miyan. We were waiting for him when we heard the loud bang of a dandi being lowered on the floor of the compound. Someone yelled, 'Machchan Miyan come fast.' I ran out behind my brother and saw Miyan sitting doubled-up in the dandi. He was almost unconscious, completely soaked in his own sweat. Supporting Miyan on his shoulders, my brother got him inside and made him lie down. He was writhing in pain. Radha Bhai's brother Kamla Babu was a doctor. He came over immediately, administered some medicines and gave my father a few sips of brandy. A heavy downpour started outside. Within minutes, its force increased with such ferocity it felt as though, after today, it would never rain again.

I dialled one doctor after another. Finally I found two, one was a specialist in Mussoorie called Dr Bucher and the other was Lucknow's well-known physician Dr Abdul Hameed. Around 2.30-3.00pm both reached our house. They gave Miyan a few injections and by four in the evening his condition stabilised. We finally ate lunch which was still lying on the table. Amma went and sat with Miyan. His eyes were closed. He looked peaceful and tranquil.

It was time for Asad's feed, the nanny brought him to me. I had barely sat down with him when I heard, 'Ya, Ali, Ya, Ali… what is happening…?'

It was Amma's voice. Thrusting the baby hurriedly into the nanny's arms I ran to the other room. Amma was holding Miyan and sobbing. I pulled Amma off and placed my head on my father's chest. I could hear the sound of his heart beating. I felt for his pulse, it was moving. I turned to Amma and said, 'No, don't cry, Miyan is alive.' I kept repeating, 'Miyan is alive,' again and again in my state of shock as people began to gather around us.

---

[37] A reclining chair with a coarse rug in the middle used by hill porters to carry a single passenger to their destination on foot. Similar to a litter or sedan chair.

But Miyan was not alive. He had left us and was gone forever.

When the truth dawned on me, I hugged my father's body and wept uncontrollably. I can't remember how or when I was removed from his room. Neither was I conscious of what happened after that. When I did get my bearings I realised it was morning.

Bhabhijaan, Mrs Aley Raza, Bhabhi Radha and some other ladies were sitting in my room.

'Where is Amma?' I asked Bhabhijaan.

'In the other room,' she replied.

'I want to go to her.'

'She's been up all night. In fact she just left from here. Let her rest a bit... if she sees you she'll be anxious again,' Bhabhijaan explained.

I grew quiet.

Gradually I learnt that Sir Sultan Ahmed, one of Miyan's friends, had rushed to Mussoorie on hearing the news of his demise and had taken complete charge of everything. On his advice, the body had been taken to the masjid. Arrangements for the funeral were being made. The men of the family had already left for the mosque.

A large white bedsheet had been spread across the floor of the house, women arriving for the condolence meet were being seated here. Around 11-12 in the morning I saw Amma. She was sitting quietly in a corner of the room. Holding back my tears I went to her. I felt like throwing my arms around her and crying hysterically but seeing her brave silence I controlled myself. Though from time to time I still kept losing my self-control. Somehow that God-awful day ended. On the third day, my sister and brother-in-law arrived from Nainital. Once again the pain of our loss grew fresh. It was Miyan's soyam – the third day after his burial. As part of the functions there was a majlis for women at the house and another at the imambara for men.

When my father passed away I was probably 21 years old. I couldn't come to terms with his death. I would keep crying all the time. Amma saw that I was finding it extremely difficult to deal with my grief. I overheard her telling a lady who had come to offer her condolences, 'I am fine my dear, but please go and help Saeeda, she has lost the love and protection of her father.' Were these my mother's words? A woman who had just lost her only support in life? Miyan took care of everything for Amma. All household chores beyond the limit of purdah were Miyan's responsibility. Amma had never even travelled without him!

From grain to groceries, if anything needed to be bought and re-stocked, it was Miyan who would be informed. If we needed new clothes, it was Miyan who asked the cloth merchant to bring his stock home. Our maids carried these heavy bales of cloth inside the house. Amma would select what she liked and send back word that she wanted this much cloth of such-and-such print. What I am trying to say is that the house ran smoothly because Miyan was there to handle everything. Amma's job was simply to keep the house lively and cheerful, which she did to perfection, sitting contentedly on the takhat, busy doing some chore or the other.

When Miyan came home, the atmosphere of the house changed. The ladies would quickly cover their heads with their dupattas. We'd cast a cursory glance to make sure nothing looked dirty. I would make an innocent face and come running to greet him. Basically we made a concerted effort to ensure things appeared the way Miyan liked them to be. And here was Amma, sitting and worrying about me. That I had lost the security only a father can give his daughter. It's then that I realised how utterly selfish I was being, nursing my own grief when my mother, whose entire world had turned upside down, was more worried about me. From that moment on, I started controlling my emotions. If I felt like crying, I either held back my tears or moved off to my own room.

Now the issue we had to tackle was: how could we let Amma live all alone by herself? My brother was working in Bhopal, he was settled there. I decided that when we got to Lucknow, I would go stay with Amma. We came back by the end of July: without Miyan the house was so empty, it must have been really hard for Amma. But although she was clearly going through a great deal, she never made it obvious to any of us.

When Miyan was alive, whenever we sat down to eat, he placed whatever had been cooked, whether it was kababs or vegetables or daal and rice in front of Amma. She ate only what he put in front of her. If he forgot to offer her a particular dish, she would not help herself to it. This was not a case of her being coquettish or trying to seek attention, it was just a private understanding the two shared, which reflected the unspoken feelings they had for one another. Not that we ever saw them being romantic or affectionate with each other. But neither did we see them quarrelling or arguing. There was, instead, an atmosphere of love and affection in our peaceful and harmonious house. God knows how deeply this husband and wife understood each other, but till the end of their life together, the environment at home remained pleasant.

Now Amma was left holding the reins of her own life. She didn't complain, or heave a helpless sigh and we did not hear her mention Miyan's name again. Stoically and quietly she got busy handling the endless work around the house. Asad became her biggest distraction and her full-time occupation. He was, by the grace of God, five months old by now and had begun to gurgle and coo. His babyish antics were adorable and became more enjoyable as time passed.

I had been dealing with acute pain in my backbone for a while. It made me feel listless and weak. We consulted the famous Dr Abdul Hameed. He took several x-rays and gave his diagnosis: that I had Tuberculosis of the bone. 'Stop moving around too much. Lie still on a wooden bench, as much as possible. Then we will wait and see what the next protocol will be.'

Ya Khuda, I have a small child, how is it possible for me to lie supine all day? There are so many things to take care of when one has a baby. Plus I have to be there for my mother. I can't possibly do any of this lying down. But it was imperative to follow the doctor's orders. I was made to lie in bed for most of the time. My mother and our maid took on the task of looking after both Asad and me. This was an extremely trying period in my life, but nonetheless, I had to bear it.

By September Abban was transferred back to Lucknow. He wanted me to move to Chanderpore House. I also realised that looking after Asad and me was taking its toll on Amma. Though she was the kind of woman who could handle any situation, but physically it was tiring her out. Before I moved we had to find a solution to the key issue at hand: Amma could not be left alone with just the servants. My sister came up with a suggestion that she would construct a small two-three bedroom cottage for Amma next to her house. It would give her privacy, plus my sister would be there and could watch over Amma as well. This is what we did.

I came back to Chanderpore House. We had a large joint family; there were several relatives to help nurse me back to health and several more for company. Two big rooms, one dressing room, a bathroom and an office were given to us for our use. Asad's ultra-efficient nanny was looking after me and taking care of the baby. She was extremely proactive and had several amazing qualities. If she found time she even helped with the housework. Having her around gave me the respite I badly needed. Four months passed, but the soreness in my back did not go away. The doctor's opinion was that I should get an orthopaedic cast made with plaster of Paris fitted onto my torso. This would help relieve the pain, ensure my backbone remains straight and help heal the wound faster.

I was taken to Lucknow Medical College for another x-ray. During the physical examination when Dr Raghunandan Lal touched the part of my spine which hurt, I clenched my teeth tightly and said, 'It's not hurting anymore, Doctor.' When he gave his report, it read, 'The wound in the bone is showing signs of healing.' Dr Hameed studied it, nodded his head in satisfaction and said, 'But to be on the safe side, as a precautionary measure, we should still fit a cast on your torso.' In those days the plaster of Paris frame was made in Bombay and usually took 15 days to arrive. I implored Dr Hameed to allow me to move about freely for a fortnight. 'After that you can bury me alive in this plaster, Doctor.'

He agreed. Immediately I called my family physician, Dr Lahiri and narrated the entire sad story to him; including the lie I had just given Dr Hameed. I also told him we had just 15 days to deal with this matter. Dr Lahiri was always sceptical of other physicians and their new-fangled diagnosis.

'You are not running a constant temperature, nor are you losing weight. You don't have TB of the bone. This pain is probably from the hurt you got when you fell while skating.' Dr Lahiri's fee was five rupees while specialist doctors charged Rs 32 for a home visit and Rs 16 for a hospital consultation. To cut a long story short, I felt confident after hearing Dr Lahiri's words and at the end of 15 days, flatly refused to get a cast put. Dr Hameed tried his level best to convince me. He scared and intimidated me by saying I would double up in pain in a few days or might even develop a hunchback, if I didn't take his advice. 'We'll see then doctor,' I replied cheekily. 'Right now I can move about. When I can't, I'll go lie down.'

Till 1937 we stayed in Chanderpore House. During this time, our personal differences as husband and wife remained dormant. Asad was growing up. We hosted a grand purdah party on his first birthday. It was attended by the who's who of Lucknow society, from prominent begums to wealthy ranis. Asad was extremely fond of cars and could identify different models at a single glance. He knew a Ford from a Chevrolet, a Fiat from an Austen – and this when he was barely a year old! As a gift we gave him a kiddy car. He was simply overjoyed and immediately learnt how to drive it. On this special occasion my sister, Begum Ali Zaheer composed and recited several couplets,

> Tum anjuman mein sitaron ke maah ban ke raho,
> nazar mein khalk ke noor-e-nigah bann ke raho,
> saeed-o ba-adab, honahaar bann ke raho,
> Raza ke ghar mein hamesha bahar bann ke raho.

In a galaxy of stars may you shine as radiantly as the moon,
In the eyes of the world may you be as lustrous as light,
May you be happy, courteous, and accomplished
Like spring may you always blossom in the Raza household.

Chanderpore house was always abuzz with activity. Several relatives from Begum Raza's side of the family would come and stay with us for months on end. This kept my mother-in-law busy and gave Aqila the opportunity to be with girls her own age. The house was quite large. One bedroom was always reserved for Kazim Bhai and his wife. When they came to Lucknow they stayed with us at Chanderpore House.

A major blessing of being in a joint family set-up is, that thanks to the constant presence of people, unpleasant incidents get ignored and forgotten. Abban would be in one of his bad moods, Asad would come running, he would start playing with his son. Masud Raza would suddenly burst in saying, 'Bhaisahab, where are you...'. They would start discussing something or the other and Abban's attention would get diverted. But human-beings are strange creatures. When they are at peace, for no apparent reason, they will suddenly start growing restless. They create their own storm.

I was living comfortably with absolutely no responsibility. The headache of running the house was entirely my mother-in-law's, I was being looked after and fed. Both Chachijaan and Aqila constantly made me feel loved. I was leading a carefree life. Despite this, in 1937, when Abban said he had been transferred to Sitapur, I was overjoyed as I had for long nursed a desire to run my own home.

My saas was not too happy. 'Sitapur is a small town bahu, you will not like it there,' she said. But I was dreaming of setting up a house of my own, where I would have a say in everything. We had two servants, Abban's bearer Ibrahim and Asad's nanny. I just had to find a cook, which I managed to do. We already had enough dishes and other household items.

By mid-September we rented half of a huge kothi (bungalow) in Sitapur. The other half was occupied by a Civil Judge by the name of Tofail Ahmed. Abban was already acquainted with him. Our side of the house had four rooms and a zanana. We decided to share the rather large drawing-dining area. Adjacent to the zanana were five or six servant's quarters. The compound itself was massive – just looking after the garden was a full day's work. When I reached Sitapur with Asad he was, Mashallah three and a half years old. Immediately I got busy setting up and decorating my new home.

There are a few things worth a mention about the three of four years I spent with my in-laws. My second oldest brother-in-law, Kazim Raza sahab, was a rather fun-loving colourful character. A brilliant hockey player, he had been selected as Captain of the provincial team. He had a good singing voice and used to learn Hindustani classical music from a certain Ustad Muravat Khan. Aside from these hobbies, he was keenly interested in playing bridge and enjoyed a game of golf as well as tennis.

Over and above all this, the single most endearing quality about him was that he was a flirt. Almost constantly he would be infatuated with some lady or the other. His wife knew all of this and was his partner in crime! When he visited the homes of his lady-loves his begum went along with him. There, Chottey Bhaijaan Kazim Raza sahab sat comfortably on the floor, a harmonium in front of him, and began to sing romantic songs such as *'yaad piya ki'* in his melodious voice. Often, his beloved's husband was right there, sitting next to him, and enjoying the song! These parties went on till the early hours of the morning.

Chottey Bhaijaan was a high ranking officer in the Police Department. If he had a day off the next day, how he spent it can best be described by this Persian couplet: *'Allus subha cho mardum, ba karobaar rawand, bala kushaan-e-mohabbat ba qooey-yaar rawand.'* (Early morning, while people leave for work/Those smitten by love make a beeline for their beloved's home.)

At the crack of dawn, Chottey Bhaijaan would be at his beloved's house and would spend the entire day there. The merrymaking continued well into the night. Most of Chottey Bhaijaan's sweethearts were either married women or the wives of his friends and colleagues. The affairs carried on with great intensity for three or four years, then his benign attention would drift in the direction of another woman. But whatever he did, he did openly. Secret glances were sometimes exchanged as fragrance would be dabbed artfully on the beloved's dupatta, the restlessness of love would be apparent, and the whole time his wife would be sitting right there next to him.

'Whatever my husband likes, I like,' was the one phrase she repeated all the time.

For about four years, from 1934 till 1938, Chottey Bhaijaan was smitten by one of my close relatives. One day I asked her, 'What are you doing? Does your husband know all this?'

'Haan, he knows,' she replied casually.

'... And what does he think?' I enquired, shocked.

'Nothing. He said don't ask me for a divorce, I have no objection to you meeting him.'

Ya Khuda! The strange shenanigans of middle-aged people! According to me, such a huge deception was taking place right in front of my eyes. The result could be disastrous! But when I expressed my views, I was told I am making a mountain out of a molehill. The entire Raza family seemed shocked that I had even mustered the courage to speak up. Meanwhile, the couple in question carried on with what they were doing while we watched the fun. What did however happen was that I started maintaining a distance from these people and stopped attending their parties. I was young and could only understand that two and two make four. That the answer could be five, was beyond my comprehension. After a while Chottey Bhaijaan's attention got diverted. By that time I had also started understanding that two and two can easily add up and make a five.

Chottey Bhaijaan was a multifaceted person. No matter what the topic of discussion, he would impress you with his vast knowledge. He was well-versed in the finer nuances of music and painting. He could throw light on the life of any world class painter. And was there any Hindustani poet whose verses he could not recite verbatim? If the conversation turned to history or geography and the 1857 Sepoy Mutiny was mentioned, Chottey Bhaijaan would floor you with his extensive insight on that as well. He was extremely well-dressed and looked even more handsome in his police uniform. Basically, his entire persona was so striking, he could even get away with murder. He romanced his women openly with panache. But in my opinion, no matter how intellectually stimulating these relationships might have been, they were merely platonic. He never crossed the line of propriety.

As far as his job was concerned, he had a stellar reputation. He gave unbiased judgments. If the Police Department received information that bandits were causing havoc in a certain area, that they had formed a stronghold and were harassing the common man, looting travellers in broad daylight, Kazim Raza would head off on an 'encounter' with them. Senior officers preferred to send their juniors for these 'encounters' as facing hardened criminals was dangerous. Kazim Raza sahab would go alone on these missions and come back victorious. He was also famous for his humanity. Grand words have been written about him in a book called *The Men Who Ruled India*.

Sometime in 1935, Kapurthala House on Rotrum Road was being auctioned. Beevi went and placed a Rs 80,000 bid for it. To her surprise, the bidding closed right at that moment. She gave Rs 20,000 as down payment and came back home. When she told my mother the story, Amma said she had only Rs 20,000 to give. Beevi then narrated the entire incident to Chottey Bhaijaan. He went to Begum Raza, got Rs 40,000 and gave it to my sister as a loan.

Kapurthala House was surrounded on all sides by approximately 10 bighas (approximately 4 acres) of prime land. It was decided that Kapurthala house along with 4 bighas (1.6 acre) would go to my sister while the rest of the 6 bighas (2.4 acres) would be sectioned into smaller plots, two of which would be given to Begum Raza at cost price. Begum Raza always wanted to have a home of her own. She liked the sound of this arrangement and immediately agreed. By mid-1935, she had the land.

Who would help her build a house was now the problem. Bade Bhaijaan Aley Raza was a poet at heart. He found it difficult to juggle his time between his favourite hobby and his intense schedule as a lawyer. Chottey Bhaijaan Kazim Raza was appointed as Superintendent of Police in Banaras. Hashim was posted in Ahmednagar and Masud Raza was studying for the Imperial Finances exam. My husband, Abbas Raza was a Civil Judge in Lucknow, so naturally everyone looked in his direction. But where did he have any time? After a full day's work in Court, it was not possible to supervise the construction of a house in the few free hours one got in the evenings. But then I was there and I enjoyed executing challenging projects. Everyone knew that if I took on the responsibility of getting something done, I would get passionately involved in it. Expressing complete faith in my abilities, my mother-in-law said, 'I know Saeeda dulhan will get my house made.' I was thrilled to hear this. Her words filled me with self-confidence.

We began by sketching basic designs on paper. The house should be the best architectural example of Begum Raza's style of living.

Lucknow's renowned architect at that time was Hamid Husain sahab. We knew his entire family well and used to socialise with them quite regularly. I went and met Hamid sahab, told him our requirements and showed him our incomplete sketches. Keeping these in mind, he drafted some blueprints. The entire family sat together, scrutinised these and then collectively selected one of them as our future home. A Bengali contractor by the name of Mitra Babu was hired to start work. The auspicious ritual of laying the foundation stone was done by Bade Bhaijaan and construction began in full swing.

One day we heard an American architect by the name of Walter

Burley Griffin[38] was visiting Lucknow. I quickly took an appointment to see him and got him to our site. After he surveyed the work he said, 'The foundation has already been dug, I won't change the layout, but I can design a new façade for the house.' Hence the credit for creating the impressive exterior of Begum Raza's house goes to Mr Griffin.

By early 1938 the house was ready. It had an exceptionally striking appearance and the spacious interiors had been planned keeping the needs of each family member in mind. Since it was located on Clyde Road (now Rana Pratap Marg) bang opposite the National Botanical Gardens, Dr Lahiri called it 'Garden House'.

The name for the house was also suggested by me and a plaque with the words 'Kashana-e-Raza' or Abode of the Razas went up on the gate outside our new home. I was living in Sitapur while the house was being built and used to drive down from there to supervise the construction.

I have described the layout of the Sitapur house earlier. We had settled down in this city and our lives were moving in a normal predictable pattern. Each morning, Abbas Raza would go to Court. When he got back in the evening we would have tea together. In our days, a lot of preparation went into serving an eclectic array of delicious snacks with evening tea, as most people left for work after breakfast and skipped lunch altogether. The same custom prevailed amongst the English; they called it 'high tea'.

In the evenings we went to the club which had a swimming pool, tennis and badminton courts and some billiard tables. All of the clubs in the district were equipped with almost the same recreational facilities. Abban enjoyed swimming and playing tennis. He would head off towards the pool or the courts while I made my way to sit and chat with the ladies. Back then it was easy to make friends.

One day I remembered I was also good at playing tennis and thought to myself 'I have the opportunity, perhaps I should start again.' I asked Abban. His answer was an immediate, 'Of course,

---

[38] Best known for designing Australia's capital city Canberra, Griffin came to Lucknow in 1935 after he won a commission to design the library at the University of Lucknow.

you must play.' I hadn't so much as touched a tennis racket in five years. I started paying close attention to the game and gradually, my confidence along with my preferred style of playing, came back. People began talking about my game. 'Mrs Raza plays such good tennis.' Our routine also changed. Abban would walk with the men towards the tennis courts. I would walk in the same direction with a couple of ladies, two of whom were British. I began playing mixed-doubles. Four to six months passed, when I realised that on the way back home from Club, Abban's mood changed and he often became quiet. When we reached home Asad came running to meet us, and then we'd get busy showering him with attention and Abban's silent spell would end.

A couple of days later I noticed that he began to pick fights with me before we went to bed, and they'd be about all kinds of small inconsequential things. The next morning he'd wake up completely uncommunicative. But between getting ready for Court, playing with Asad, having his breakfast, there was no time to sulk. In the evenings we took Asad and his ayah with us to the Club. Other mothers joined us with their children and Asad played happily in the compound.

In Sitapur we had hired a nanny for Asad who was actually a mughlaani. Within Lucknow society a mughlaani's position was ranked among the highest as it involved organising the household as well as handling the other responsibilities. She was quite similar to what the English call a majordomo. Extremely resourceful and accomplished, these women knew exactly what it takes to run a home efficiently. Unlike other servants, mughlaanis did not have a villager's accent, they spoke perfect Hindustani or Urdu. Aware of the culture and lifestyle of those times, they were also extremely well-mannered and knew, with experience, how to gauge the temperament of the people they worked with. With time, some mughlaanis lost these skills, though one could still find a few with these traits.

Our mughlaani was a bit too cheerful and too mischievous. She would keep looking for opportunities to sit and make small talk with me.

One day she said, 'Begum sahab you must be in your sweetest year?'

'What is the sweetest year?' I asked.

'Ayy Begum... you must be 18 years old?'

Amused at her flattery, I laughed and replied, 'I'm way older than that.' She used to get along famously with our bearer Khurshid. Every time we heard a big loud guffaw coming from the zanana, we knew Khurshid was there. One bathroom in our house had a curtain but no door. During the intense hot summer days my husband often bathed there. As soon as the mughlaani heard he was inside, she would walk quietly right up to the curtain and ask in a soft polite pleasing tone, 'Nawab sahab do you have soap in there? Should I get it for you?'

Extremely flustered Abban would retort angrily, '*Lahaulawilla qoovat illah billah....* God give me strength to ward off this evil...! Yes, yes, I have everything.' He would come out fuming from his bath and say, 'Stop this woman from coming near the bathroom when I am in there. And for God's sake tell her I am not a nawab!' I would call her aside and say, 'Why do you go and ask if he has soap? Sahab gets very angry. We have a bearer in the house. That is his job.'

When food was laid on the table the mughlaani would saucily announce it, using grand words, 'Begum sahab, your khaasa is served. *Tanawal farmaiye.*' In Urdu, khaasa is the word for top-class gourmet food. Tanawal farmaiye is a grand elaborate way of saying, 'please come and eat, your food is served.' Lucknow is known for the charm of its language which has a refined elegance to it.

I was an eager home maker; I thoroughly enjoyed running the house and bringing-up my kids. Before Asad was born and later as well, I voraciously read-up books on child development and would follow the advice given to a 'T'. We had no personal hands-on experience in raising children but were not ready to accept the know-how of our elders. It is strange, that as youngsters we are convinced the advice of our elders is passé and we readily embrace the new-fangled suggestions of our contemporaries. We don't have enough sense to realise that the experience of our elders is tried and tested, it doesn't need to be validated, that one day the new ideas will also be disregarded as they will become outdated. By the time we understand this complicated cyclical truth, it is almost always too late.

Our days passed along smoothly. I was not highly educated or some grand degree-holding intellectual, but I thoroughly enjoyed reading books. Initially, I read just about any book. Whichever English novel I could find, I read. There was no maturity in my taste. Then I started enjoying detective novels, and grew interested in philosophical treatises. There was a time I read David Hume though honestly, I couldn't understand a lot of what was written. Then I took to reading historical books, biographies, autobiographies and even books on geography, just about any and everything I could lay my hands on. I started noticing that my husband did not like me reading.

If one analysed our relationship, then the fact was that Abban simply wanted to treat me like a devi, a goddess. But a devi is made of stone; she is a statue. You can adore her, prostrate yourself in prayer before her – she will stand there motionless, silent, watching this spectacle unfold. When angry, the priest can dethrone his beloved idol from her pedestal and when his rage subsides, he can reinstate her in the same niche and starts worshipping her again.

Perhaps my analysis is not a hundred percent perfect, but this much is certain, a man wants his woman to submit herself completely to him; she should have no identity of her own. Unknowingly, I was not able to do this. Though it was not like I gave my needs or my desire for free time priority over that of my husband and children. Nor was I ambitious to do some outstanding work or stand-out at social gatherings. There was nothing like that. I was simply a cheerful sort of woman from a normal middle class family who enjoyed life thoroughly. For years I lived within a joint family and got along well with all of them. Till date I share a close relationship with relatives from my sasural.

My husband liked me a lot. He also disliked me intensely. He didn't like the fact that I had my own individuality. But I had not gone about trying to create this for myself purposely, it was just who I was; I was born with it. If my husband had accepted this difference in me and said, 'this woman may have some good qualities as well, let me focus on these' then those character traits would simply have dissolved and merged with the good qualities in Abbas Raza's personality. But Abban's bruised ego, the pain of which he had been nursing for a long time, was slowly turning into a chronic wound.

My father-in-law was a worldly wise man. He felt he could brighten the light of his house with the sparkle I had in my character. He was always friendly and affectionate towards me and appreciated who I was as a person. Perhaps if he had lived a few more years, his positive influence would have brought some degree of balance to the emotional upheavals Abban and I witnessed in our marriage. Then perhaps my story would not have been what I am writing now. At the time of my proposal, my father told Justice Raza, 'Raza sahab, I want to tell you my daughter is a chingaari, a spark.' Raza sahab promptly replied, 'Don't you worry Majid Husain sahab, my son is also an angaara, a red hot coal.' I did not see myself as a spark, nor did Abban see himself as a burning coal. His over-sensitive nature seared his personality and as for me, I wasn't that fierce a flare that my intensity could not be tamed.

A spark does after all get extinguished.

We barely spent a year in Sitapur when Abban got transferred to Barabanki. It was during our stay in Sitapur that we came to Lucknow and bought a brand-new Opel Cabriolet for only Rs 2200! We drove it straight out of the showroom and showed it eagerly to everyone. The car moved as though it were gliding. Its effective shock absorbers hardly allowed us to feel the bumps and potholes on the road. The hot summer months, now felt as breezy as spring. Since the Cabriolet was a convertible, we would fold down the roof and drive around for miles, the wind playfully blowing my red voile dupatta in the air. The car was an absolute beauty. All this seems like a dream to me now. One cannot buy so much as a two-wheeler scooter in this much money today.

Barabanki was a mere 17 miles away from Lucknow. We started making frequent trips back home and would stay at Kashana-e-Raza. We had already rented half of a huge bungalow in Barabanki. Just half of these massive homes were way bigger than the largest apartment one can find now. We were leading an exceedingly comfortable life with a cook, a bearer and a maidservant.

Asad was Mashallah five years old. We started thinking about his education. A new primary school called St Mary's had just opened in Lucknow. Along with imparting knowledge it offered fun-filled recreational activities for children with proper supervised care. The classrooms had small colourful desks and the playground was equipped with swings and seesaws. The school also had experienced nannies and pleasant good humoured teaching staff. I plucked up courage and decided to leave Asad in Lucknow with my sister so he could attend school. I also left our reliable servant Khurshid with Beevi to help take care of his needs.

There was only one major problem. Asad had already had two attacks of appendicitis. The doctors had no cure for it, except to make the child lie still and put him on a liquid diet. Imagine suggesting that a four year old lie inert all day and then not give him anything to eat either! It required immense patience. But Asad was an extraordinary child. He was in so much pain that he could not move of his own accord. If I asked 'Asad beta should I make you turn on your side?' he'd respond, 'No Bibi I'll lie like this.'

And he would; motionless, on his back, 15-17 days at a stretch. When the pain subsided he would have to watch what he ate. Basically we spent several anxious weeks in this manner. Then someone advised us to consult Hakim Abdul Moeed, a renowned doctor of Unani or traditional medicine. He gave a concoction for Asad to drink, a glass full of which had to be taken morning and evening mandatorily. I explained to Asad, 'Beta Hakim sahab says if you have this medicine it will help you.' He looked at me and asked, 'Bibi then will the pain go away...? Will it stop hurting?' I hugged him and said consolingly, 'Inshallah, it will definitely help and the pain will vanish.' Then Asad showed the strength of his character. Without a single protest, without making a face or creating any fuss he would drink the entire glass of this bitter brew. My heart ached, but I tried to hide my feelings and instead showed my appreciation for his effort. The medicine tasted awful. This treatment lasted two full years.

Asad started school and he came to us every weekend. His presence helped make the home environment pleasant. Though my husband was highly educated, he preferred to adhere to old-fashioned conservative values. His personality was moderate and predictable. As a creature of habit he chose to take the tried and tested path and stick to it rigidly. He was, to add to this, highly sensitive and whimsical when it came to looking after his own health. He could get offended over the most trivial thing and not speak with his mother for six months at a stretch. During these phases he would avoid the rest of the family as well.

We lived in a strange world. When bringing up children, parents went to great lengths to stress the importance of propriety, discipline and courtesy. Strict instructions were handed out that rules of etiquette had to be adhered to at all times. But if their children suffered from any psychological complications or emotional anxieties, parents simply ignored these saying, 'It will go away automatically once they grow older.' Or, 'these problems will vanish after marriage.' However my main concern at this time was only Asad. We were still in Barabanki and he was studying in Lucknow. In 1938 I was pregnant again. This time though I had no morning sickness or nausea and on 24 January 1939 gave birth to my second son. Bade Bhaijaan suggested we name him Saeed. Abban and I both liked the name. Kashana-e-Raza was almost ready, a few finishing touches were left, hence after delivery I took the baby from St Mary's hospital straight to my sister's place. By this time, my mother was living near Beevi's house.

7

Kashana-e-Raza: Ancestral Home of the Razas

By 1939 Kashana-e-Raza had been constructed and was ready to be occupied. Begum Raza was beside herself with joy. She happily shifted out of Chanderpore House and began setting up her own home.

Certain areas of Kashana were always abuzz with activity, her bedroom, the spacious veranda in front of it, the small prayer room and huge yard it opened on to, the zanana kitchen and restroom. A number of Aqila's friends from Neotani often visited us, aside from several relatives who were constantly coming and going from the house.

These women could be seen sitting about, smiling and chatting with one another in the zanana. Some shelled peas, another group prepared ladoos or carrot halwa, a maidservant sat relaxed sewing lace on a dupatta. New recipes were always being tried in the zanana kitchen. Our daily meals were prepared by male chefs. There was a separate kitchen in the house for that.

A frequent guest to the house was Begum Raza's close relative Hamid Dada. He used to manage the mango and guava orchards, and other cultivable land they owned, for the Razas. One could see Begum Raza herself, sitting taking accounts of income and expenditure from him.

Our bedroom in Kashana was on the top floor. There were two more rooms up here. We converted one into a drawing room and the other into a bedroom for the boys.

Asad was attending proper school and had been admitted in La Martineré. Saeed's nanny, Khanum was an extremely intelligent, hardworking and experienced woman. She had taken on the responsibility of looking after him rather well.

Saeed had a sweet innocent face but his eyes simply gave him away. Not only was he extremely naughty, he was also quite fearless. He must have been around two years old, when a street entertainer with a large black dancing bhaloo (bear) came to Kashana. Midway through the performance, Saeed asked the man, 'Can you put me on the bear's back?' The bhaloo wala man was delighted. 'Haan bhaiya, come… I'll put you on his back,' he replied. And then, there was young master Saeed sitting fearlessly astride the bear's back as the animal danced and performed various tricks. Our servant's children (who lived within the compound itself) gathered around to see this spectacle. Even the servants decided to stop their work to watch the show. The bemused bhaloo wala kept reassuring all of them, 'Don't worry, he's a trained bear. He won't hurt bhaiya.'

I had gone out for some chores. I entered the gate and what do I see, Saeed sitting on top of a bear and the bear is dancing away! When he saw me, Saeed slid off sheepishly and came and stood next to me quietly. I called out angrily to Khanum. 'Take him and give him a good scrubbing.… And wash his clothes immediately.' The bear's back was caked with a thick layer of dried filth. After being bathed and cleaned, Saeed was brought to me. I tried to explain why he should not have climbed onto the bear's back, 'See *beta*, that bear had mud all over him, you know all sorts of diseases spread where there is dirt, etc. etc.' God knows how much he actually understood.

Both brothers got along famously. Asad's naughtiness was that of a typical boy. He was always jumping about, playing and getting hurt. Saeed was completely different. He came across as a calm and serene boy, but he was extremely mischievous. One day a tonga (horse carriage) came and stopped in our porch. I was standing holding Saeed's hand, waiting to greet the gentleman who had come to visit us. In a flash of a second, Saeed let go of my hand, dashed under the belly of the horse and came back to where we were standing. He must have been two or three years old.

I never hit my kids. Instead I would try and reason things out with them. I did threaten them at times and have even gone as far as to say, 'If you don't listen to me, I will throw you out of the house.' A few minutes after the tonga incident, we realised Saeed was missing.

Everyone in the house was worried. Since the Botanical Garden was bang opposite Kashana, one servant was hurriedly dispatched to look for him there. Another was sent in the direction of Banarsi Bagh (where the Lucknow Zoological gardens are located) towards the right of the house and a third to the left, towards Carlton Hotel. A couple of hundred yards down the road to Carlton, the servant saw a small boy ambling along seriously on the dirt track, both hands behind his back. It was Saeed.

'Bhaiya, where are you going?' The servant asked in his villager's dehati accent.

'Carlton Hotel,' Saeed replied seriously. 'Bibi has thrown me out of the house.' The servant quickly brought him home. I never repeated that threat again. One time, Saeed was found wandering about in Narahi, a good twenty minute walk from Kashana. Aley Raza bhai's older son Qamar saw him and asked, 'Saeed beta, who are you with?'

'I've come by myself to buy a kite.' Qamar brought him home. He must have been four years old.

Another incident I remember clearly is that a certain gentleman by the name of Mr Sapru lived in a bungalow next to my sister's place. One day Beevi and I strolled down together to meet them. Saeed was with us. The Saprus had a pet monkey. While we chatted, Saeed played happily with the simian. The layout of their house was such that as soon as you enter the gate, there was a straight pathway for about 200 yards which passed in front of the porch and led to a round lawn. It was a small lawn, one side of which opened on to the porch and veranda.

A few days after our visit, Mrs Sapru saw a small boy walking down her pathway. She assumed he would be followed by some adult. But the child was alone. Walking up straight to her he said, 'I have not come to meet you. I want to meet your monkey.' That boy was none other than Master Saeed.

There is a saying in Hindi '*poot ke paon palne hee mein nazar aa jaate hain*' which translates roughly as 'one can guess the characteristics of a child's personality right from the crib.' This wandering was clearly written in Saeed's fate.

He was born in Lucknow. For the most part he went to school and college there. He had a home of his own in this city, in fact his father's ancestral property was spread around Lucknow. When he started work, Saeed's first job was in India and after being transferred across various cities in the sub-continent, he got posted back to Lucknow as Assistant Manager in the Indian Oil Corporation. Basically, aside from his family, Saeed's own existence was firmly rooted within India. No one could have imagined that one day he would suddenly break these everlasting bonds to go settle in America. Such are the games of destiny.

Meanwhile Asad had been staying with my sister for two years studying at St Mary's Nursery. He was dutifully drinking a glass full of the concoction Hakim sahab had given and had not had another appendicitis attack. I thought, 'Let me stop giving the poor child this awful stuff, perhaps the problem is over.' We barely stopped and within a month or so the pain reared its ugly head again. As before he had to lie down and remain still, this time for fifteen straight days, without eating any solid food. Then Abban and I decided to go for a surgery. This was the day and age when the mere mention of the word 'operation' sent chills down one's spine. Asad was barely six years old. The entire family congregated in Balrampur hospital before the procedure. By the grace of God, the surgery was successful. Asad made a complete recovery and was soon busy playing games and attending classes like other children.

The days that I am writing about were some of the most peaceful in my married life. Both my children were going to school, Khanum was earnestly and tactfully handling not just their work but had also taken the responsibility of running the entire house in her efficient hands. So much so that for anything we needed, it was her name that we called.

Aqila had been married to a certain Syed gentleman, Hussain Naqvi from Amroha, Uttar Pradesh. He had a good job in the Agriculture Department. The wedding went off very well; most of the arrangements were my responsibility. Her stunning dowry was almost entirely chosen by me. I enjoyed doing such things and excelled at them. These activities also kept my focus off the unpleasant moments in my personal life.

Masud Raza, my youngest brother-in-law, had successfully given his Imperial Finance examination and was posted in Kanchrapara, West Bengal. One day, while visiting us during his December holidays he came to my room around 6 in the morning and tried waking me up.

I got up, startled. 'What is it Masud?'

'Please come to the other room, I need to speak with you.'

I followed him and then in a tone of utmost secrecy he said, 'Bhabhi, I want to marry Sughra... what is your opinion?' Sughra was Masud's first cousin; his maternal uncle's daughter. Masud used to joke around and say, 'I wonder which poor unfortunate soul will marry Sughra.' Wondering what could have transpired to bring about this change of heart, I said, 'Masud if you have made up your mind, then may God bless this marriage. If you want my opinion, take the evening train back to Kanchrapara.' After a brief pause Masud said, 'I have made up my mind, but I don't know how to tell Amma.'

'I will tell her,' I replied. 'If your mind is made up, then don't worry about these things.'

Masud seemed somewhat relieved. Finding an opportune moment I informed Begum Raza about Masud's wish. At first she was silent. Then after a long pause she said, 'Sughra is my brother's daughter; what better match could there be for my son? May God bless my child.'

This was the kind of wisdom women had back then. These uneducated women, who were considered illiterate, handled the most complicated of issues with such patience, forbearance and tolerance that they kept their families together.

In December of 1942 Masud came back on vacation and we began making arrangements for his marriage with Sughra. Most of the responsibilities were once again handed over to me. Aqila and I got busy with the shopping. The main incident I can recall from this time that's well worth a mention is that Begum Akhtar was called to do a mujra at the bride's house from our, that is the groom's side. She was still a courtesan at this time and went by her former name, Akhtari Bai. Akhtari had a unique character, vastly different from that of other courtesans. Despite performing mujra her body language did not reflect the vulgarity or cheapness one associates with women from this profession.

Around 1938 a radio station was set up in Lucknow. Everyone was extremely interested and started listening to the programmes. Shows for women and children were also being broadcast which used to be hosted by women. Listening to a radio discussion or radio play, we would often hear the names of these women being announced on air. Some of us began to wish we could also hear our voices booming across the air waves. At the same time we realised this would not be possible since women from good families kept purdah from courtesans.

Slowly executives at the radio station also got to know that most women from traditional families of Lucknow, maintained purdah from courtesans and because of this, would never visit the station. The radio station was in need of educated women to participate in various on-air programmes such as debates, interactive discussions, dramas as well as several other Urdu and English shows.

The officials made a concerted effort to become friendly with men from the most conservative of families and gradually succeeded in convincing them to change their minds. They informed them that though courtesans visit the station (as it would be next to impossible to have any programme on air without them; after all they are accomplished singers and it is essential to have good music on air) the entrance they use and the studios they work out of are completely separate from the ones used by the other employees.

After managing to create a good impression of themselves with various families of Lucknow, the officials started sending out invites to their friends and the women in their homes to come and participate in a talk or discussion at the station. I also received a letter from the Director in which he politely suggested, I should come to the station with my relative Huma Baji to take part in a discussion, on so and so date. I showed the invite to my husband. His response was, 'of course... you must accept it.'

I don't quite remember now what the topic of the on-air discussion was but my deepest desire was being fulfilled! A day prior to broadcast, we were called in for rehearsal. The next day as we were heading out for the live broadcast, my four year old son insisted on coming along. We explained to Asad that he could come but that he would have to stay in the car. He promised to do this. When we reached the station, one of the officers was enthusiastically waiting in the portico to welcome us. He insisted on taking Asad out of the car and along with us. On the way to the studio he kept explaining to him eagerly, 'Beta, listen, when we start talking in the room, you must remain totally silent.' I did say, 'Let the child be in the car.' But the officer, who was hell bent on being the epitome of virtue, kept insisting, 'No, no let the child come to the studio. He has understood what I am telling him. He will sit quietly.'

We reached the studio, a microphone was placed between Huma Baji and myself and the discussion started. After seven odd minutes we heard a tiny voice saying, 'Let's go home now....' It was immediately followed by a loud, '*Shhhhhhhhhh.*' Anyway, there were only three more minutes of the talk left. We exited the studio scolding Asad and got back home. Those who heard our discussion liked it immensely and the officers at the radio station were all praise for my voice.

Now every second week or so I would receive a request to give a talk on some topic or the other or to narrate a story for the children's show or compere a ladies programme on radio. I already had Abbas Raza's permission. After a while, one of the officers by the name of Haseeb sahab suggested I start compering a woman's programme regularly. When I asked for details, he said, 'Just come once a week to the radio station for a couple of hours. Whatever has to be broadcast will be scripted and handed over to you.' Saeed was around two years old and by the grace of God I had a fabulous maid. I accepted Haseeb sahab's offer. Once a week I drove down to Lucknow, read out details of a woman's programme for radio and returned to Barabanki by evening. I used to drive myself.

During our stay in Barabanki we became quite friendly with a District Magistrate by the name of Mr Abbasi Wahajuddin. Abbasi was a member of the Indian Civil Services (ICS), one of the highest ranking posts within the British government. Executives working within the administrative department came directly under the District Magistrate, hence the DM could not socialise with them. The official protocol for a Civil Judge was different. They were answerable to Provincial Judges so if Abbasi sahab hobnobbed with us, he would not be accused of favouritism.

Eight miles to the north of Barabanki there is a small town called Dewa Sharif. It is famous for the mazar, the shrine of an early 19th century Sufi saint by the name of Haji Waris Ali Shah. Every year to commemorate his death anniversary, a grand celebration is held for an entire week at Dewa. The town pulsates with activity.

The district officers set up elaborate camps in Dewa, as musicians from across the country congregated here to showcase their talent. After paying tribute at the shrine, these musicians gave private performances in the evenings, within the camps of the district officers. During these melodic gatherings courtesans, well-known qawwals and experts from the field of music regaled guests with the magic of their art. This had been going in Dewa for ages. The year we visited Dewa Sharif a renowned qawwal by the name of Moharram Ali, from Mehmoodabad, was all the rage. We turned many a night into day listening to his pulsating voice belting out devotional qawwalis passionately.

One such night, the tawaifs (courtesans) were invited to sing. Special arrangements were made for us to sit behind a chilman, a thin cloth curtain, and see them perform since women from good families kept purdah from tawaifs. How strange and how very hypocritical! When it came to hearing the qawwals perform, we sat with the men. And to listen to a courtesan, who was after all a woman, we had to sit behind purdah! What can one say about such hypocrisy? But then these were the customs of that world. Anyway, we were simply delighted to be attending the event. From behind the chilman what do we see? A white spotless sheet spread out across the length and breadth of the large hall stretching in front of us; several plush carpets rolled open near the walls on top of which gautakiyas or bolsters had been placed strategically. Reclining comfortably on these, were the privileged listeners, the audience of men. Lounging regally on a gautakiya with an extremely beautiful razai (quilt) thrown over her feet sat the famous courtesan Benazir Bai. On either side of her, at the opposite end, inside the same razai, sat two of her ardent admirers. Another tawaif was seated in the same andaaz (style). She also had a gorgeous quilt covering her feet. To one side of her sat Akhtari Bai.

She was wearing a simple sari, pale grey with beautiful silver zari embroidery. Her face looked radiant, without a trace of arrogance. She did not have a razai, nor was she lounging on a bolster.

After a short while, Munni Bai finished her song and Akhtari Bai picked up the tanpura (a long-necked, plucked string instrument) She hummed a few stray notes to tune the instrument to her voice, smiled, looked at the audience and started singing. What a magical voice! Within seconds, the entire gathering was mesmerised. The tone of the evening was set. Then one after another, guests started making requests for her to sing their favourite songs. She kept obliging, tirelessly. If she looked at someone and so much as smiled, the person would be captivated. She was not doing this deliberately to entice her listeners, it came naturally to her. Her mannerisms were simple and unaffected. The mehfil ended around 4am, but we didn't feel as though we'd had enough. I felt a woman who can sit in a gathering surrounded by all sorts of men and present her talent with such dignity that everyone seems hypnotised, must have an amazing personality; one should say a prayer at the hem of her skirt. I was young and deeply impressed by Akhtari Bai Faizabadi's simplicity.

Every Friday I used to drive down from Barabanki to broadcast a women's programme on All India Radio. One day, after rehearsals as I was sitting alone in the studio, Akhtari Bai suddenly walked in. Greeting me warmly with a quick salam she said, 'Begum sahab I would like to speak with you.'

I was shocked to see her to begin with, but her second sentence had me stumped.

'Bittan, please get me married to Ishtiaq Abbasi sahab.'

'Ya Allah, what sort of woman is this?' I thought, keeping my feelings to myself. I can't recall what I said in reply but I clearly remember that she talked nonstop. Then she apologised and said, 'What do I do Bibi, I can't live without him.' Then she left as abruptly as she had walked in. I finished recording, went home and narrated the entire episode to Abbas Raza. He was most amused and said, 'Let's call Ishtiaq Bhai and tell him he has received a proposal.'

'I just want to see his reaction,' I replied, laughing.

Both my father and Justice Raza were well acquainted with Ishtiaq Ahmed Abbasi's family. Ishtiaq Bhai was married to Asha

Begum, whose father, Mateen-us-Zaman sahab was Special Advisor to Nawab Sultan Jahan Begum in Bhopal. Asha Begum had passed away two years back. My husband and I had known Ishtiaq bhai for decades. He was an extremely interesting person with a great personality. Whenever he was at a social gathering, he became its very life. We invited Ishtiaq bhai to our place for tea. He entered in his usual jolly manner, narrating jokes, calling out to the kids and then came and sat in the drawing room. Tea was served. When he was sitting comfortably enjoying his cake and pastry I said, 'Ishtiaq Bhai we have called you for something specific.'

'Hahn Bittan, is there something I can do for you? Tell me quickly... what is it?'

'You should marry Akhtari,' I said without any warning.

'Ayyn...? What? What did you say...? Saeed bete... have you tried this cake? Come here, come to me... let us play Akhtu-Bakhtu.' Saeed immediately jumped into Ishtiaq Bhai's lap. Ishtiaq Bhai held his tiny hands and began to recite a local Indo-Muslim poem (like Incy Wincy Spider) about two friends named Akhtu and Bakhtu. (It was all the more amusing since Akhtu sounded similar to Akhtari!)

> *'Akhtu ne pakayee badiyaan, Bakhtu ne pakayee daal,*
> *Akhtu ki badiyaan jal gayeen, Bakhtu ka bura haal,*
> *Sayyan phir bhi ladenge, Sayyan phir bhi ladenge.'*

Akhtu fried some fritters, Bakhtu made lentil soup,
Akhtu's fritters got burnt, Bakhtu didn't know what to do
The two kept fighting, the two kept fighting.

He had smoothly skirted the issue. But I was not one to let go that easily. When he was about to leave, I once again repeated my sentence.

'Hahn Hahn, achcha achca, yes, yes, we will see. I have some work Bittan, I must leave now.'

I couldn't understand his reaction. I had mustered up quite a bit of courage to ask him directly to marry Akhtari. I stated it as candidly as possible, without beating about the bush. I was a bit apprehensive, after all he may get offended, may even turn around and say, 'how dare you... etc etc.' But instead I got this feeling that he was somewhat flustered and wanted to avoid the topic.

Now what started to happen was that every Friday, after the ladies programme, Akhtari Bai would come to the studio to meet me. Since, for me, she was already someone to look up to, I felt quite elated seeing her. Gradually she started opening up with me. She told me the story of her life and how she hated the profession of a courtesan.

'My mother left me to live as a "keep" in some rich man's house. That's how it all started. I was very young. I couldn't rebel. Then somehow, after a lot of difficulty I managed to get out of there. Now I am in Nawab sahab Rampur's court, but I am constantly restless, and keep trying to figure out how to run away from here. I adore Ishtiaq miyan. Only you can help me now.'

I believed every single word she uttered, blindly. In my mind, the picture I drew was that she is a victim of her circumstances. Sick of the world she is living in, she is desperate to lead a respectable life. I should definitely try to help her. I convinced my mother and mother-in-law that Akhtari was actually very decent. Both of these ladies had been brought-up in an extremely protected and traditional environment. They were amazed to hear about the life of a courtesan and all its complexities. One day I suggested, 'You should also meet Akhtari.'

'Ayy nahi dulhan, I don't think we should, we keep purdah from prostitutes,' my mother-in-law said.

'But she is not a prostitute, Chachijaan,' I replied. 'Despite staying in that environment, she is still so pure. If you all meet her, it will have a positive influence on her, the respectability in her character will emerge.'

A few days later once again I asked them, 'Should I call Akhtari to meet with you?'

Neither responded. They changed the subject.

During this time, one day Akhtari said to me, 'Why don't you and Abbas Raza miyan come for dinner to my place?' I said I would ask Raza sahab and get back to her. When I went home and told Abban, he grew thoughtful. To go to a courtesan's brothel, and that too with his wife was unheard of. It was considered a dishonourable thing to do. Abban had never gone to a brothel by himself before. Thus far he had led a chaste life though he thoroughly enjoyed reading good books, listening to poetry, music and qawaali. Whenever he got the opportunity he gladly attended such functions.

I used to discuss everything that happened with Akhtari, with Abban. He was a simple gullible man. I had presented her case to my entire family in such a convincing manner that my mother and mother-in-law almost agreed to meet her. Abban also started enjoying listening to the stories I told him about Akhtari. In fact sometimes he would even ask about her. Now when I said she has called us for dinner, despite being uncomfortable with the idea, he agreed. And so it was that one fine day the two of us went to Akhtari Bai's kotha.

The floor was spread wall-to-wall with the finest of Iranian carpets, gautakiyas placed here and there across them. While welcoming us Akhtari almost flew towards us in delight. Her mother was also there. After making some small talk, a table cloth was spread on the floor and food was served. It was sumptuous and delicious. Akhtari was making interesting conversation but with a conscious effort at remaining respectful.

God knows what my poor husband was going through. This was the first time he was speaking with a courtesan. Abban was well-versed in the intricacies of sher-o-shayyari poetry and was quite passionate about music. Both of them talked about these subjects endlessly. Words of some thumri were hummed. Then Akhtari gently asked, 'Raza miyan do you not like my songs?'

'Nahi bhai, no, no, it's not like that, I like your singing a lot,' Raza miyan replied, startled at being asked such a straightforward question.

'Then just give the order… I'll come any evening and sing at your place.'

'*Basar-o-chashm*' Abban replied. 'Your wish is my command. I will let you know which evening you will have to take the trouble to visit our home.'

The next time we were in Lucknow, we invited Akhtari to come and delight us with the magic of her music. Everyone in the family attended the function. From amongst our friends we also called Ishtiaq Bhai. That night the raw intensity of her melodious voice was a result of his presence. With her beloved sitting in front of her eyes, Akhtari's voice sounded ethereal. The entire gathering was bewitched by the mellifluous quality of her voice. As dawn broke, she finished with a befitting finale in raga bhairavi, a morning raga. Everyone was spellbound and people showered praise on her. Akhtari kept bowing gracefully and accepting their appreciation with a courteous adaab. We gave her two hundred rupees as nazarana, a special token of our gratitude, and saw her off, thanking her profusely. For a long while after that we sat about as though hypnotised, reeling from the after effects of her melodious voice and talked about her.

One day while driving past Wala Qadar Road in Lucknow, I impulsively turned towards Akhtari's house. Stopping the car outside I blew the horn. A couple of minutes later a strange looking man appeared. 'I'm here to meet Begum sahab,' I said. He looked at me oddly, then without uttering a single word, went back inside the house. I waited a couple of minutes. There seemed to be some commotion going on behind the door. Then it opened and who do I see but Ishtiaq Bhai. He came out saying, 'Aao Bittan aao... come, come... what brings you this side?' I was foxed. Anyway I went inside with him. Akhtari appeared smiling and almost hugged me over-enthusiastically saying, 'Oh how nice of you to drop by to my humble house... Where is Abban miyan? Will you have tea? Good Lord, at least sit down. You must have lunch with us.' She was being extremely courteous and affectionate. I sat, made some small talk and then escaped from there after explaining, with difficulty, that I had to have food at home and they should please excuse me.

Gradually I started to learn details about their relationship. Ishtiaq Bhai had been meeting with Akhtari regularly; they had known each other for years. The acquaintance had now blossomed into an irrepressible love and both were really worried as neither knew what to do about it. How could Ishtiaq Bhai marry a courtesan? It would bring dishonour to his entire family. It wasn't easy, in the early 1940s, to try and create a tiny little crack in the impenetrable wall of social conventions. Not like it is now. Today well, there is no wall; it got broken a really long time ago. Times change, old-fashioned norms fall by the wayside as new laws take their place. This is how our ancient world has always operated. And so it was in the case of Akhtari and Ishtiaq. They were meeting almost every day and finding it difficult to control the flames of their love.

One time when I came back from Barabanki, Ishtiaq Bhai came to see me and said, rather hesitatingly, that he wanted to marry Akhtari and that Abban should be in Lucknow at the time. I felt immensely happy and proud to hear this and informed him that we were both going to be in Lucknow by the end of the week. Ishtiaq Bhai had taken a flat in Qaiserbagh which he used as his office; we were both asked to come there. A maulvi priest was already present along with Gulab, Ishtiaq Bhai's personal servant. I carried my nikaah dupatta (wedding shawl) with me and draped it over Akhtari. The maulvi read out the marriage vows, mahr[39] was fixed for approximately Rs 25,000. Abban and Gulab signed the marriage document as witnesses. We congratulated the newly-weds, ate dinner, left them to be by themselves and drove back home. And that is how Akhtari Bai became Begum Akhtar.

The year was 1943.

I hosted a purdah party in her honour where I introduced Akhtari to the crème de la crème of Lucknow society, the begums, ranis and the maharanis. She became a regular invitee within Lucknow society and Abban and I started visiting her place quite freely. Society opened its doors to Begum Akhtar.

The boundary wall of my home, Kashana-e-Raza and my sister's, Kapurthala House, were next to each other. Our children used to come and go freely between the two places as and when they felt like. It was also convenient for the elders.

One day while I was sitting in my brother-in-law Ali Zaheer's drawing room, chatting with my niece Kamman, their servant entered and handed her a taar (telegram). Kamman was still reading it when her father, Allan Bhaiyya (Ali Zaheer sahab) came in and asked, 'Who is it from?'

'It's from Jamila,' Kamman replied.

'What does Jamila begum have to say?'

'She is arriving with her husband Brijbhushan and will stay with us,' Kamman said.

---

[39] A mandatory payment made to the bride at the time of the marriage, that is legally her property.

'Such people should be boycotted! She will not stay at our place,' Allan Bhaiyya replied. After a short pause he added, 'we should also boycott Saeeda. She meets with Akhtari.'

'Why did you take so long to say what was on your mind?' I said, at once adding, 'Let the boycott start from today. And one more thing, if someone you loved immensely did what Jamila has, would you stick with your principles and boycott them as well?'

Turning to Kamman I said, 'Kamman, make Jamila and Brijbhushan stay at my place.' And I walked off to my house. I found Allan bhaiya's remarks highly distasteful. These so-called broad-minded people projected themselves as progressive thinkers and then showed their narrow-mindedness. I have no clue what was said about me after I left his house. The next day Allan Bhaiya came to Kashana to make up with me. Jamila and Brijbhushan were sitting there, he left without entering!

For the next three months he did not come to my place nor did I go to his. The other members of our family, my sister, his kids, my kids, my husband – they continued to meet with one another like they used to.

Jamila was Kamman's childhood friend. Her mother Jannat Apa was my sister's friend. The men of the two families were also related to one another. Jamila divorced her first husband and had married her classfellow Brijbhushan who was a Hindu Kayasth (A caste within the Hindu religion) Marriages between Hindus and Muslims were considered highly improper in those days and rarely ever happened.

8

Catastrophe

———— ❧ ————

Sometime in 1942 we were driving back from Lucknow to Barabanki at the end of the week, Abban was at the wheel, I was sitting next to him, the children were in the back seat with their nanny. Suddenly a large insect flew straight into Abban's eye and disappeared. He immediately stopped the car. His eye was badly hurt. I took his handkerchief, tied it over the injured eye, got behind the wheel and drove rest of the way back home.

As soon as we reached, we washed his eye with boric lotion and did hot fomentations. He felt no relief. The next day I got him back to Lucknow to see an ophthalmologist. After examining his eye thoroughly the doctor informed us that the sting of the insect had penetrated deep into Abban's cornea and that the wound would take time to heal. Medication was started, the pain reduced substantially, but unfortunately Abban's vision had been impacted. What could have been a minor eye injury became an endless affliction. Even when the pain stopped, we had to continue the treatment.

After pulling a few strings we had Abban transferred to Lucknow. He began to attend Court, but was not able to drive by himself any longer. So I dropped him and picked him up from work. My day began by leaving the children to school, then I would come back and take Abban to Court. In the afternoon, I brought the kids home, fed them lunch, left them with the nanny for two hours or so to play about in their room, sleep or read and go lie down for a bit myself before heading off to get Abban from office. This became my routine.

To begin with, temperamentally, Abban was irascible, now he became extra irritable. Though I was trying to be even more attentive to his needs and took extra-care not to trigger his mood-swings. But a person who feels so utterly dejected that he makes his own life miserable over the smallest of things, every single day, how could someone like that have the patience to smile and bear constant physical discomfort?

I often tried to talk to him, 'See you have two adorable children, be strong, keep courage, Inshallah your eye will get better. You are always sitting about feeling sad. Don't be so ungrateful… and I am not such an awful wife either… If I have said or done anything to upset you, let me know.' I began these conversations with great optimism, but more often than not, they went in the wrong direction. He accused me of things that were completely baseless and tried to hurt me as much as he possibly could. Even prior to his eye injury he had done the same thing. At that time I often lashed out at him and a hideous chasm would open up between us. By now I had understood that some fit of madness comes over him and at such times he forgot that words cause wounds that never heal.

We had already started drifting apart even before the incident with his eye. I used to warn him, 'for God's sake don't let this happen.' After his injury, I learnt to heal my own hurt and putting all the unpleasantness behind me, would genuinely try to attend to his needs as best I could. If he said his head was hurting, I would sit to massage it; if his stomach cramped, I would rush to get him a hot water bottle. And for hours on end, I sat and pressed his feet. He was making himself weak and brittle by the day. No matter how I tried to boost his flagging spirit – nothing worked. The only way it would have is if he had told himself, 'yes this is an extremely difficult phase of my life, but I have to stay strong.'

I had thought that sometimes during a time of extreme crisis a person undergoes a radical change. They become more flexible, compassionate and learn to compromise, to reconcile to facts. I hoped desperately, that this kind of transformation would come over Abban, that he would rid himself of the suspicion and bitterness he had been harbouring in his heart. But that is not what happened.

By 1944 doctors in Lucknow suggested we go to Bombay for Abban's treatment and consult with an eminent ophthalmologist by the name of Sir Duggan.[40] At once we sent off a letter to Sir Duggan and in the month of October, after fixing a day and time for the appointment, we left for Bombay. An alert and capable orderly was sent with us. We stayed in Dadar with Abban's cousin, Mohsin Bhai. I left the children under the watchful care of both their grandmothers and their aunt, my sister. This was the first time I was leaving them and going away to another city.

On the day of the appointment we reached Sir Duggan's clinic. He did a thorough check-up of Abban's eyes and gave his diagnosis, that Abban had developed Choroiditis (a potentially blinding condition caused by inflammation in the choroid, a layer behind the retina of the eye) in his injured eye. The ailment usually flares up if there is infection in any part of the body – the teeth or the tonsils. But if a proper treatment protocol is followed, the infection can be contained, otherwise it gets worse. Sir Duggan advised us to meet with an Ear Nose Throat specialist by the name of Dr Gandhi and get Abban's tonsils operated. After coming out of Sir Duggan's clinic, I turned to Abban and said, 'Now that we have the right diagnosis, let's go back to Lucknow. There are brilliant doctors there, we have our own home, it will be a lot easier for us to get you operated there. We might face all sorts of problems here.' Abban did not agree. He was adamant about having the operation in Bombay. I was anxious. Various unpleasant thoughts kept troubling me. Abban had already had two attacks of colic, during which, along with intense pain he would also throw up. I was worried. What if his stomach pain starts after the tonsil operation? What will I do? If a patient starts bleeding from the throat after this procedure, it is difficult to stop the flow of blood. The situation can get extremely dangerous. In Lucknow we have so many relatives to help us out. Here we have no one. I discussed my doubts with Abban but he refused to change his mind. I'm also the sort of person who is ready to face a challenge at any time. I rolled up my sleeves and thought, 'Okay, so be it.'

---

[40] Sir Jamshedji Nasarwanji Duggan was a prominent Indian ophthalmic surgeon, magistrate and the Sheriff of Mumbai in 1942.

We went to meet Dr Gandhi. He was very matter-of-fact, didn't speak much, fixed a date for surgery, told us his fees, gave some relevant information about the operation, then grew silent. That was the end of our meeting. Abban did not like his cut-and-dried approach. 'Let's look for another doctor,' he said. 'I will not get operated by Dr Gandhi.'

I did not argue. It is absolutely crucial for a patient to be operated by a doctor he has complete confidence in. The problem however was that Sir Duggan was our consulting physician and advisor. How could we reject the doctor he recommended?

We took Cousin Mohsin's advice, made some further enquiries and found another ENT Specialist by the name of Dr RAF Cooper. He was as qualified as Dr Gandhi, in fact, more so. We went and met him. He turned out to be the absolute opposite of Dr Gandhi. Dr Cooper had an attractive personality and was literally courtesy personified. He welcomed us graciously into his cabin speaking perfect Urdu.

'Please come in Nawab sahab. How may I help you?'

'Dr sahab, we are not Nawabs,' I informed him. 'Just ordinary people. We've heard so much about you, that's why we have come for consultation.'

Dr Cooper smiled, apologised, made some polite conversation about Lucknow and its impressive culture and then asked, 'Raza sahab what is the problem with your health?' Abban told him the entire story. Dr Cooper picked up the phone, dialled St Elizabeth Nursing home and made the necessary arrangements for Abban's operation, from fixing a date, appointing a dedicated nurse to selecting an operation theatre. Sitting right there in front of us, in that one call, he organised every single thing.

On the appointed day Abban and I reached St Elizabeth Nursing home and checked our room – the nurse had already arrived. Everything seemed absolutely perfect. The premises were impeccably clean and the staff, unusually polite and respectful. Next morning, around 10am the patient was taken to the operation theatre. I was made to sit in a room some distance away from the OT. After 45 mins Dr Cooper came and reassured me in that the procedure was a success, there was nothing to worry about. The nurse, whom we had hired the previous day, would stay twenty-four seven with the patient.

By evening Abban was wheeled back to his room. He was conscious, but had been asked not to talk. The nurse got busy with her duties of looking after him. She was efficient, knew her work well and was a pleasant sort of woman. When it was night, the patient dozed off. He had probably been given some medicine. The nurse pulled her chair closer to his bed, made herself comfortable and sat down. A bed had been made for me in the veranda attached to the room, I went and lay down and went off to sleep. Around two in the morning, the nurse suddenly woke me up and said, 'the patient's stomach is paining, I have given him a hot water bottle, go call the doctor immediately.'

'Oh my dear God....' I started to panic. Then collecting my thoughts, I got up, rushed downstairs to where I remembered I had seen a telephone. I have no words to describe what I was feeling. What I had been most apprehensive about had just happened. When I reached the lobby, God is my witness, I was told the telephone was out of order. I froze with fear. I went up to the guard and asked, 'Is there any place nearby I can make a call?'

He thought for a moment, then said, 'There is a bungalow in front of the hospital, you can ask there.' I crossed the road and saw an enormous gate. In the veranda, situated considerably behind the gate, a dim light was flickering feebly. I banged on the gate loudly. A guard appeared, holding a lantern. He raised it to my face, looked suspiciously at me and asked, 'Who are you? What do you want?'

I told him my story. 'My husband is admitted in hospital, he is not well I need to call a doctor immediately – the phone at the nursing home is not working.'

The watchman opened the gate reluctantly and led me to the veranda. There was a telephone kept there. I hurriedly dialled Dr Shirodkar. We had already fixed up with him to help us in case of any emergency. He was at the hospital by 2.45am and quickly gave the patient an injection. It took immediate effect, Abban's pain started to subside. Gradually he fell asleep. The next morning, Dr Cooper came and reassured us that there was nothing to worry about, they were already treating Abban's colitis. He added that since the surgery had been successful we could take the patient home after three days.

While coming out of the bungalow from where I had called Dr Shirodkar that night I had asked the guard, 'whose house is this?' 'Sir Duggan's.'

Ya Khuda, What divine intervention! In my hour of need, I reached the doorstep of the same man whose very name brought us all the way from Lucknow to Mumbai. Being completely unfamiliar with the localities of Bombay, in the nervous jittery state I was, for me to find Sir Duggan's house in front of the hospital was nothing short of a miracle.

The next day I went to meet Sir Duggan and told him the entire story. I also apologised for not taking his suggestion and for getting Abban's operation done by Dr Cooper. Sir Duggan was extremely kind and praised Dr Cooper. He added, 'Don't be formal. If you need anything, I am here.' Sir Duggan was an elderly man. During our four months in Bombay he was extremely kind and sympathetic towards us. In fact his mere presence filled us with confidence. After Abban was discharged, we went back to consult Sir Duggan and did all the treatments advised for Abban's teeth. Then because we knew complete recovery would take time, we headed back to Lucknow.

Time went on. I had come to terms with his mood swings. I was not happy but despite that, was managing to do whatever I possibly could. The house functioned according to routine. The children went to school and got busy after that playing games or doing their homework. Whenever Abban felt up to it, he would join in. He enjoyed playing with them. In the evenings we mostly went to Akhtari's place.

Life would probably have gone on like this but time was not on our side. One day Abban was working with the gardener pruning a shrub. He held one side of the thorny branch down to instruct the gardener where to cut, when all at once the branch slipped his grip and its long sharp thorn pierced through the cornea of Abban's good eye. Exactly the way the insect-sting had damaged his other eye earlier.

Ya Allah, why did this unforeseen calamity have to fall on him? On such a good soul? He was already doubling under the weight of the challenges life had thrown in his direction. He lacked the patience to deal with simple day to day problems. Why did God have to put him through this gruesome test?

But divine purpose is beyond the understanding of man. To begin with, Abban was his own worst enemy. There was no need for the world to turn against him. Once again, treatment for the injury commenced. Slowly, the wound started to heal but Abban's vision was impacted in this eye as well. Abbas Raza's pessimistic nature found new ground to flourish.

In October 1944, a few months before we left for Bombay, a new Director had been appointed at AIR Lucknow. His name was Jugal Kishore. When we returned, he started socialising with us and visiting us at home. Jugal Kishore was extremely sympathetic towards Abban, made friends with my children and completely floored both Begum Akhtar and Ishtiaq bhai with his impeccable manners.

We formed a sort of group and started meeting every evening at Ishtiaq Bhai's place. During our get togethers, Akhtari would lavish Abban miyan with attention. If he gave even the slightest hint that his head was aching, she would immediately start massaging it. Deep down inside, Abban liked this sort of attention. She kept the rest of us equally entertained with her attractive mannerisms. Ishtiaq bhai would make us laugh, narrating one hilarious anecdote after the other. Jugal sahab also had a rather impressive personality. He had a thick Punjabi accent, knew Urdu well and when he spoke, it further enhanced the atmosphere of our informal get-togethers.

At the radio station, Jugal Kishore sahab would often come and sit in my room. If he couldn't make it, I would find a cup of tea sitting waiting for me. Often when I drove into the porch, Jugal sahab would immediately step forward and open my car door for me. I didn't quite like this attention, but he was a suave man as far as women were concerned. If I said anything, he would come up with such a witty remark that I was often amused!

When we met up in the evenings at Kashana-e-Raza or at Begum Akhtar's place our time passed pleasantly. This was one side of the picture and on the other, Abban was still sad and dejected with life.

We lived in a joint family, my mother-in-law was on the ground floor. In the evenings or in the mornings, Begum Raza would climb up the steep stairs to meet her son and ask him how he was feeling. If she came in the morning, he wouldn't come out of the bathroom. When he finally did, there would just be enough time to have breakfast, before he rushed off for work. Meanwhile, his mother sat, waiting for her son.

He would come out, say adab and go back inside.

If she asked, 'How are you feeling beta?' there was no reply.

I kept my focus on the need of the hour and made sure the children were kept entertained and busy. And every morning I went downstairs to say adab to my mother-in-law and the older ladies of the family. On days we were not socialising with Begum Akhtar, Abban would go to his room and go to sleep. The kids would eat dinner by eight and head straight to bed. This was their daily schedule.

Gradually, Abban sahab, started avoiding having breakfast or dinner with me, as far as he possibly could. In front of the kids, for the sake of decorum, he tolerated my presence with great effort. He would behave the same way with his mother. The other relatives were of course of no consequence. Two of his older brothers were in Lucknow at the time, they never showed any interest or sympathy towards him. They did not come to spend any time with Abban or express concern about his condition to either their mother or me. Everyone was engrossed in their own lives. It was just Abban's mother and I. And we were both emotionally drained.

My sister and mother, who lived right next door at Kapurthala House, were also anxious. Beevi would drop by to see him often. Abban did not mind her coming over. They were affectionate and genuine with each other. I felt relieved, at least he is meeting someone happily. What's worth mentioning here is the back story. Abban knew that my sister often got irritated with me and scolded me. I was used to being reprimanded by her. I knew she loved me immensely, despite the fact that there were several things about me that Beevi deeply disapproved of. For example, according to her I was not worldly-wise. She would constantly keep telling me I was not a good home maker, that I didn't keep the kid's clothes properly and that I was too lenient with the servants, etc. Right from the beginning she had been very attentive towards Abban and genuinely wanted my marriage to work out. Both Amma and Beevi were

worried sick about my relationship. What I am trying to say is that
the reason behind Beevi criticising me constantly was nothing but
love. There was no complex or sibling rivalry between us. When we
were in Bombay, I had run short of money for Abban's treatment
and had called my mother. She sent Rs 2,000 to me. I was never able
to repay her.

With time the atmosphere at home became so dismal, I began to
lose courage. Overwhelmed with sadness, I could barely eat or drink
anything. I spent many days without eating anything substantial at
all. In front of the kids I would nibble a toast or have some tea.
Then, one fine day, Abban's mood would suddenly change for the
better. He would come to me of his own accord, apologise and keep
repeating this one line again and again. 'I don't keep well... that's
why I have become like this.' He would cry, I would cry, we would
make fresh promises and pledges to one another and a few more days
would pass off pleasantly. Akhtari, Ishtiaq, Jugal Kishore, Abban and
I would once again start socialising. Isthiaq bhai used to call Abban
'pehli mulaqaat ka badshah' or 'a person who makes a very positive
impression, in the very first meeting.'

Meantime at work, Jugal sahab's over-attentive kindness towards
me was on the rise. When I went to office, having been on the verge
of starvation for several days, it obviously reflected on my face. Now
what started happening was that the watchman would come and say,
'Bade sahab, the Director is calling you.' And when I went in to his
office, I'd find a lavish spread of delicious food, cakes and pastries
laid out for me along with tea. Jugal sahab also ate and called in his
Assistant Director to come relish the goodies as well. A small tea-
party of sorts, would take place and I would end up snacking on at
least something or the other. At home I starved and in office Jugal
sahab hosted mini parties for me, replete with samosas, pakodas
and cakes.

During this entire time I had not opened my mouth about
what I was going through. I didn't cry on anyone's shoulder nor
mention to Jugal sahab what was happening in my married life.
But Jugal was a shrewd man. He used to visit my house. He could
assess the circumstances there. Even in the evenings when we met,
he was constantly trying to put two and two together. Then one fine

day he finally declared that he adored me. I was stumped, gaining back my composure I said, 'See I am a married woman... I have two children... Our paths can never meet. I respect the friendship we share. Please let us leave it at that.' Jugal sahab was a mature experienced man, he never spoke on this topic again.

However there was no let-up in his kindness or his attention towards me in office. When he came home, he was as polite and congenial with Abban as well. Abban was a simple man, it was beyond him to see more than what was obvious.

After some time passed, Jugal sahab expressed his feelings once again rather cautiously and tried to give me some advice. By now somewhere deep down I was starting to get convinced that his feelings were sincere. I was no longer averse to the importance he was showering me with in office. The atmosphere at home was so dismal, unpleasant and suffocating it felt nice to be able to breathe freely. And if that wasn't enough, here was someone actually offering me their attention.

But my heart was not in it. (Though strangely I was starting to feel guilty and I would question myself 'what am I doing...? How outrageous that I have feelings for a man who is a stranger... I am not worthy of showing my face in society!') With all the troubles I was facing, my strength of character was also weakening – that one thing that had allowed me to live with my head held high all this time!

I had been brought up to adhere to the rule, that no matter what you may be going though emotionally, you must fulfil your responsibilities. If you feel like crying, learn to laugh. It was only because of this rigorous discipline that I managed to do what I was supposed to every single day. Otherwise my condition was such that I felt thoroughly defeated and was finding it difficult to face the world. Abban must have sensed this change in me. Whenever we were alone, he would lock himself in the room. The distance between us was growing nightmarishly wide.

One day Abban came to me and said, 'I want to resign.'

'Don't do that,' I replied, shocked. 'Because of the loss of sight you have been asked not to strain your eyes reading and writing but you can get a munshi. He can write your judgments for you.'

He heard me out but didn't reply. Later I found out he had resigned from his job as Civil Judge. I didn't say anything. What was there left to say? It was all useless now. But I was worried. When he was attending Court he used to be busy, now when there was nothing to keep him occupied, what would he do? Within a few days of early retirement, my apprehensions proved right. He became extremely over-sensitive. In anguish he preyed on just two people – his mother and me. The other residents of Kashana-e-Raza were anyway distant relatives who lived in the house as guests. They could gossip all they liked amongst themselves but were petrified of Abban sahab's temper and avoided any interaction with him. The brothers did not share the kind of relationship that allowed them to make our problems, theirs. But my sister started coming over to Kashana more often. She would take Abban and go to her place. Begum Akhtar and Ishtiaq Bhai also started dropping by frequently and with them, Jugal sahab would also land up.

I was finding it extremely difficult to reciprocate Jugal sahab's feelings, though I was enjoying the attention I was getting from him. I couldn't get myself to see the rosy picture he was trying to paint. Jugal had this habit – he would not look you in the eye when speaking. His advice to me was, 'take the kids and go away to Bangalore, I have a friend there. You stay there, I'll come join you later.'

I was aghast. I looked at him and thought to myself, 'Good God what kind of woman does he take me to be? I want to sort my problems and resolve differences with my husband, I am not looking for a way out!' Like a soldier at battle, I was constantly fighting the feelings I was starting to have for Jugal sahab. I had not considered, even in the remotest recess of my mind, that I could leave Abban and go away. I barely went for two hours to the radio station and even that was proving difficult now that Abban was home all the time.

Then once again my husband and I made up. We made a fresh resolve to handle this new phase of our lives in a different manner. He started showing interest in taking charge of Begum Raza's orchards. The groves were being looked after by Hamid Dada who used to fudge accounts and show less profit. Abban felt the two of us should go ourselves, inspect the place and get an idea of how we could improve profits. Some days passed peacefully, but then his innate nature got the better of him.

Dropping me from heaven into the darkness of hell after intimacy was an old habit. I had discussed this particular issue several times with him. 'Don't do this… when you switch off and become indifferent, I feel insulted. You try and make up later… you apologise… I forgive you and make up with you but if such storms keep rocking our relationship, they will eventually leave a trail of destruction… we will move apart, the informal bond that exists between a husband and wife will end.'

But a man's ego and the right society has given them allows men to humiliate a woman as and when they please. The woman on her part must bear it all and remain silent, like an impassive pillar. She must never ever dare raise her voice and say to her Lord and master, in Mirza Ghalib's words: *'Main bhi munh mein zubaan rakhta huun'* (Well even I can speak, even I have a tongue in my mouth).

I tolerated everything because of my children and also in the hope that maybe Abban would change; that he would realise the moody storms that surge through him every now and again are harmful for him as well, that these were affecting the entire family. The kids were growing up, they must have sensed there was constant tension at home.

Then by some stroke of luck there was divine intervention! In August 1945 Jugal Kishore got transferred to Delhi. Prior to leaving, he tried once more to persuade me to run away to Bangalore saying he would follow soon. But despite the fact that I had developed a soft spot for him and would listen to him spewing advice as though in a daze, the minute he left Lucknow his words lost their effect. I felt 'I must stay where I am, I cannot break these bonds. I can never leave my children.'

Meanwhile at home the situation was such that Abban's anger and irritation towards his mother and bitter resentment with me was becoming glaringly obvious. But life went on. There would be days he was absolutely normal and I would feel, 'these testing times will pass somehow or the other. Life will smile on us again.' But my situation was similar to what has been expressed beautifully in this Persian phrase, *'mann darjaa khayaleen wa falak darcheyy khayal'* (I had different ideas for myself, but destiny had other plans).

The misunderstandings between us usually began with something small, and often trivial, and then escalated and became like an impassable mountain. One day something like this happened. He was extremely angry with me over some small thing. It was past midnight, my nerves were so rattled that I also lost my cool and grew enraged. Our voices started rising and then I must have said something I perhaps should not have. He was beside himself with rage and stormed into his own room. I kept lying in bed sobbing. Then I fell asleep. When I woke up, I rushed to get the kids ready and dropped them off to school. I came home and asked Khanum, 'Has sahab got up? Did he have breakfast?'

'He hasn't come out of his room yet,' she replied.

I grew worried. Slowly I opened the door of his room and peeped in. He wasn't there. I asked around, all the servants said the same thing, 'Sahab has still not come out of his room.'

I sent one of them to my sister's place and found he wasn't there either. 'Maybe he's gone to the Botanical Gardens for a walk, it is after all, across the street,' I thought.

I spent the entire morning thinking he must have gone off somewhere, and that he would be back. In the afternoon I dialled Ishtiaq Bhai. He also gave the same reply – Abban had not gone to his place either. The brothers were not that informal with each other that I could assume he may have sauntered off to be with them. I grew extremely anxious. By evening, the entire house knew Abban sahab was not at home. Breathless from climbing the stairs hurriedly, my mother-in-law asked in a tremulous voice, 'Dulhan where is Abban?'

'I don't know Chachijaan.'

I was sitting there like a culprit in front of her. That old-fashioned helpless woman seated across from me, who had only ever shed tears in private, was crying uncontrollably. Her son was missing. The entire day had passed, there was no news of him. I didn't know what to say to console her. The two of us went to his room. A small suitcase was missing. We opened his cupboard and realised that a couple of suits, some casual wear kurta-pyjamas and one warm coat were not there either. We came to the conclusion that Abban had probably left Lucknow.

But where did he go? And to whom?

I telephoned my brother in Bhopal. He was also absolutely shocked.

'No, he's not come here,' he said. Ya Khuda what do I do now?

Begum Raza kept asking all sorts of questions and crying all the time. Like a criminal I sat there and repeated the same line over and over again. 'I don't know.' The news of Abban's disappearance spread like wildfire. I was bombarded with questions by his two brothers, their wives as well as some other relatives. All of them wanted to know what had happened.

My sister was livid with me.

'Why don't you tell us what happened?'

My silence enraged her; She started yelling.

I gave the same reply, 'I don't know.'

My mother came over. She didn't ask a single question, just sat with me and didn't say a word. My kids were very attached to her, she took them and went away to her house. No one seemed convinced with my answer. Everyone thought I was hiding something. But I wasn't. Abban and I used to fight and argue with one another almost every other day. The entire household knew when Abban was upset with me. He would go to his room and bang the door shut. Sometimes loudly, sometimes in a normal fashion. The servants had witnessed these scenes. Even my mother-in-law's relatives gossiped about us but because I never validated their assumptions with a remark, no one dared talk about it in front of me.

Despite the storm raging in and around me, I kept my focus on maintaining the daily routine. There was a barrage of questions from the children. I tried to make them understand whatever they possibly could in various ways and kept distracting them with homework and all sorts of games. But I was filled with dread. All sorts of irrational doubts kept creeping into my mind constantly. Dear God where could he be?

I remembered that day in Dehradun, when I was pregnant with my first child and was unwell. We had hardly been married a few months, Abban had come to see me at my father's house. We were sleeping in the veranda, lying, chatting with one another. I must have disagreed with him, opposed his views on something. He got so upset, he stormed out of the compound! When he did not come back after what seemed like eons, I walked out all alone to look for him in the dead of night, found him after crossing two dark lonely streets and got him back home.

If only I had feigned distress and created a huge uproar that night, perhaps he would have understood how irresponsible it was of him to walk out like this. But what can I do with my bold nature and this courage of mine? What do I do with this innate strength which forces me to tackle every situation? When faced with adversity I don't panic nervously with fear. That is exactly what I was doing this time as well.

All day long my mother-in-law sat on her prayer-mat and asked the Almighty for help. She cried, then came and sat with me. But never once, through words or even the slightest of hints, did she ever make me feel that I was to blame for what had happened. She remained as loving and affectionate towards me as she had always been. I am grateful to both my mother and mother-in-law for handling their grief, by themselves, in their own way. Despite being elderly women, they even managed to console me the best they could. Neither lady had received a formal education, they knew just a smattering of Urdu, had spent their entire life in purdah and for every requirement of theirs, they needed the help and support of a man. But they had tightly embraced the solid values of the age-old culture they had inherited. My mother-in-law maintained good relations with all her relatives, respected each of her daughters-in-law, most of whom, to begin with, were strangers to her. She dealt with their demands of wanting to live outside the joint family, their indifferent attitude and their brashness, (part and parcel of youth) by absorbing these differences into her all-encompassing love. Never once did I hear Chachijaan complain about any of her daughters-in-law. Even at this time her immense anxiety was only evident through her tears. She never uttered a single syllable, even once, that might cause me any pain. Genuinely, in her heart she did not blame me for what had happened because more than anyone in the house, she knew what I was going through.

The days passed; everyone began arriving at the conclusion that Abban must have committed suicide. I have no recollection how I handled the children. Neither do I have words to express with what difficulty I was wading through every second of the day. What did I eat? Was I sleeping? What was going on around me? But time is strange, no matter what happens, it passes. Two weeks went by. One morning the postman rang our bell. Khanum opened the door and came back with a telegram. It was from my brother in Bhopal. He had written, 'Abban is here with me. He reached yesterday.' Scared and nervous I immediately ran to show the message to Chachijaan. She was seated on her prayer mat. As I read it out to her she blessed me joyfully and then who knows how many times she prostrated herself again giving thanks to the Almighty.

During these two difficult overwhelming weeks, the one thought that kept bothering me again and again was, what should I do? If we don't find him, how will I face this catastrophe? Now that I heard he was, by God's grace, safe, I also said several prayers in gratitude but along with this I realised that this time round, the chasm between Abban and me could not be bridged.

Earlier during one of the low phases of our relationship, I had sent an application to BBC London for a job along with a recording of my voice on a disc. After some time, I received a letter addressed to me in which they accepted my application and asked me to join their network. That letter fell into Abban's hands. He wrote back to them, without my knowledge, that I was his wife and that I did not have his permission to work at the BBC. The chance of getting employed with the BBC was therefore gone forever. I still had my job at the radio station which paid Rs 150 a month. But what could one possibly do on such a meagre salary? Then I received a long detailed letter from my brother in which, along with giving me marital advice, he also informed me that Abban had decided to stay in Bhopal for the time being.

This was February 1947.

The first thing I did was send off an application to Delhi for the post of Radio Announcer along with a sample of my voice. If my boat had not been dragged into a painful vortex, the security of my kids would not have been jeopardized. They were happy and well-settled where they were, surrounded by the constant attention and affection they received from both their grandmothers, their two aunts and their uncles. The strain they might have felt because of our turbulent marital relationship would dissolve and get neutralised in the love and tenderness they received from their grandmothers. Even their maid Khanum, was extremely affectionate, capable and sensible. Her mere presence was enough to fill the kids with a sense of wellbeing and security. But what could I do about any of this now, the binding of the book had unravelled, the pages of my life had come undone. These three women, my only support, my allies, were merely silent spectators. They could do nothing. But their silence filled me with strength and determination.

Despite being shackled to the conventional thinking of an extremely orthodox society, both Chachijaan and Amma had managed to carve out a strong identity for themselves without letting ancient traditions dim their inner radiance. With their honesty and simplicity they remained pillars of strength for the entire family. So when these ladies heard me say 'I will not live in Kashana anymore' they accepted it as though it was the right decision to make.

Asad was studying in Colvin Taluqdar College but he was not happy there. Every other day he would come home and lament to his Dadi that the school was filled with spoilt rich kids who would show-off; that he was constantly getting into fights with them. Though with time his complains had begun to reduce, I knew I had to find a way to settle him before I left Kashana.

There was no one among the elders who I could consult. My sister had her own point of view. She felt I should go and stay with my brother in Bhopal. I was of the view that no one helps another for the rest of their lives. My brother was not a millionaire, even if he had been, he would not be able to take on the burdensome responsibility of looking after both me and my two children. My sister-in-law would not be able to indulge my whims and fancies for the rest of her days. In fact I was amazed how my own sister could even give such advice.

For day and days on end I kept thinking about what I should do. Then I came to the conclusion that Asad, who was 12, Mashallah, was an intelligent boy, good at studies and sports, I should put him in a decent boarding school. Amma and Chachijaan showered me with affection but these circumstances were beyond their control.

They had accepted my decision graciously. Their judicious silence reduced the burden of some of the most complex problems. I had decided I would leave Kashana. But where was I to go? How was I going to overcome such an enormous problem?

The greatest issue of course was, what to do with Asad and Saeed. Without resolving this I couldn't move forward. Saeed was studying at Girls La Martineré, which was a co-educational school till Grade IV. If my marriage had not fallen apart, we could have convinced Asad that Colvin College was not that bad. But now the situation was different. For several days I kept asking myself what I should do. Then I remembered, I knew Mrs Margaret Greyhurst, the principal of Girls La Martinére. I went to see her. She said, 'There is a boarding in Nainital called Sherwood. It's a good school. The principal is an Englishman by the name of Reverend Binns. I will give you a letter of recommendation, go and meet him.'

But how do I go all the way to Nainital? I had never travelled alone in my life! Perhaps I should write to the principal before going there? How on earth does one write such letters? These were the jobs men did. I felt so overwhelmed. I went back to see Mrs Greyhurst. She guided me, once again, in whatever way she could and helped me draft letters to the people she thought I should write to. After receiving a reply from Sherwood, I went to Nainital and met with the college principal. I really liked him. I found out about all the requirements, completed the formalities and had Asad admitted into Sherwood. When I came back to Lucknow I got his school uniform and other clothes organised as well.

When I told Amma and Chachijaan I had admitted Asad into a boarding school in Nainital, neither said a word. Nor did they raise any objection. Within the family it was just these two elderly souls whose acceptance and quiet support filled me with strength.

When I mentioned Sherwood to Asad, he was overjoyed and went through the school prospectus carefully. He was even more satisfied after reading the principal's letter and criticised Colvin College a little bit more. I was happy and relieved that my child had accepted such a huge change in his life and with an open heart. Otherwise, given the crisis I was facing and the leg-work I had already done, if Asad had not agreed to go, what could I have done?

By mid-March 1947 I went to Nainital with Asad and admitted him in Sherwood. Along with the principal, I met his teachers and matrons, walked around the dormitory with him, helped organise his personal items and settled him into boarding. When I was leaving, Asad walked with me till the school gate. I put my arms around him and said 'khudahafiz', goodbye. He didn't cry and neither did I. The only thing I remember saying is, 'Bete, I'll come tomorrow evening to see you.' Then slowly I began walking down the slope of the curved road outside the front gate of the school. I walked some twenty or twenty-five steps and turned around. Asad was standing by the gate looking in my direction. I walked a bit further, till I reached a bend from where the gate of the school was not visible anymore, took a few steps back and looked, my son was still standing in the exact same spot where I had left him. Till today, this image is etched deep in my mind. What must Asad have been going through? What must I have felt as I moved further and further away from my own child, holding on to my suppressed emotions? There are no words with which I can explain the pain I was experiencing. Those who have children will probably understand what a mother goes through for the sake of her child and what she must endure.

The next evening I went back to see Asad. The guard took me to a large heated hall where a slow fire was burning in the fireplace. Several children were sitting on the floor, busy doing something or the other. Some were playing ludo, others were battling it out at carom, while some lounged about reading books. Reverend Binns was seated comfortably behind a table some distance from the fireplace. The entire scene looked extremely peaceful. When Reverend Binns saw me, he got up, walked towards me and signalled for Asad to join us. Asad was reading a storybook. I thanked the principal, took Asad and went with him to his dormitory. I gave him the food I had brought, which is called 'tuck' in boarding slang. From Asad's conversation it seemed that he liked the school and would be able to settle well in his new environment.

When I was leaving, I was faced with the same scenario. Asad stood at the gate of the school till we were both well out of each other's sight. Even today if I shut my eyes I can vividly see my brave twelve-year-old son standing at the school gate, ready to face the realities of life with determination, to take on whatever hardship life throws in his direction. I felt crushed under the burden of these challenges that both my child and I had to face. But what could I do? I had done whatever I thought was right, with courage and conviction.

In my life, I have never taken any decision in anger or under pressure. I keep deliberating and when I realise I have to bite the proverbial bullet to solve things, I do so immediately. I don't shy away from hardships, instead I dig my heels firmly into the ground. This attitude has always filled me with strength and I have been able to face several life threatening situations. Getting Asad admitted to boarding and physically parting from him was an extremely arduous task. But I did it to the best of my abilities, silently and calmly.

When I came back to Lucknow, the house felt unbearably empty without Asad. But I kept convincing myself, 'This is what is best for my child. I have decided to leave this house. Once I go away and have no home to call my own, where will I keep him? And I still have the responsibility of another child.' A thousand thoughts did constant battle within me. I wanted to lose my mind. Go insane. But the habit I had, to keep focus on the need of the hour, helped me immensely. This is what kept me sane: I would get Saeed ready, drop him to school, tell Khanum what to cook, head downstairs to say adab to my mother-in-law and then sit there quietly with her for a while. We were both so emotionally drained, making small talk seemed utterly meaningless.

Meanwhile in Bhopal, my sister-in-law was about to have a baby. The previous year, Bhabhi lost her foetus in the ninth month of pregnancy and had barely survived the trauma. Since this was her second pregnancy in ten years of marriage, it had been decided, this time she would deliver in Bhopal instead of travelling to her maika, as was the custom. Bhabhi was full-term pregnant; Beevi decided she would go to Bhopal for the delivery. Bhabhi's parents had already reached Bhopal. The elderly couple were extremely orthodox. In fact Bhabhi's mother had not visited any city in her entire life except Lucknow. They lived in a small town called Biswan which is some sixteen miles from Mehmoodabad Estate. There were strict restrictions in their home; praying five times a day and keeping roza was mandatory. The women had to observe purdah at all times and were only allowed to leave Biswan when they visited Lucknow, which was once in five years.

This time for the sake of her daughter Bhabhi's mother had ventured further and reached Bhopal after a long and tiring overnight journey. Of course she wore a burqa. Apart from that, she still wore the obsolete twelve-yard farshi pyjama. It was extremely difficult to walk about in this cumbersome attire. The garment made it practically impossible for women to move about freely. This is of course the prime objective of any patriarchal society, to control women and make them completely dependent on a man.

Anyway, what happened is that Beevi could not make it to Bhopal. Instead, she sent her son-in-law, Kamman's husband, Dr Ammar Hasan. He was at the hospital at the time of delivery. After dropping Asad to Sherwood I came back to Lucknow around the 12th of March and by the 15th I was running a fever. It was a bad case of influenza. On the 20th we received a call from Dr Ammar that Bhabhi delivered a baby boy through caesarean section. As soon as she heard the news my mother-in-law came to see me and said affectionately, 'Congratulations, you have a nephew.' I remember I thanked her and said, 'Chachijaan, let bhabhi come out of hospital, then congratulate me.'

The next day my fever had gone. Although I was still a bit weak, I left for Bhopal by air on the morning of 22nd March. The flight landed around 9.30am. I got off, looked around but couldn't spot any familiar faces. I saw an English couple walking towards me. They introduced themselves and told me that Mehdi miyan's wife's condition was critical and that was why they were there to receive me. I went with them in their jeep and by 10.30am we were at the hospital. My brother was waiting outside. As he helped me out of the jeep he said, 'Your bhabhi passed away ten minutes ago.'

I froze in my tracks. Ya Allah what a catastrophe! Barely 33 years old, the only child of her aged parents, my bhabhi had just passed away leaving a three-day old baby behind! How were we to deal with this dreadful nightmare? My thoughts were racing, should we handle her parents, take care of the tiny little infant or start making arrangements for bhabhi's funeral? What should I do first... What? What? What?

I staggered forward. 'I must console her parents.' That was the first thought. I went to where they were. What did I say to them, what condition were they in, I can't really recall. All I remember is I kept doing whatever was expected at the time. I comforted her parents as much as I could, completed the last rituals for bhabhi's funeral and looked after the baby simultaneously. It was a nightmare of a day and it was just my brother and me.

Time moves on, leaving behind permanent scars that can never be erased. Death had taken bhabhi from us. 'Dust to dust, ashes to ashes,' We had to let her go. But what were we to do with her aged parents? What words could one use to console them? It felt as though the sky had fallen and the earth was exploding under me, but I knew I had to keep my feet steady.

Before dying bhabhi told Machchan Bhai, 'Give my baby to Saeeda.' On bhabhi's soyam, the third day after her funeral, Beevi arrived with my brother-in-law. It was heartbreaking to hear bhabhi's mother's gut wrenching wails. Consumed with grief, she fainted a couple of times. What could I say to comfort her, all I had were words and her anguish was way beyond those. Holding the baby in my arms, supporting bhabhi's mother, I sat like a statue.

Beevi helped me look after the baby. She loved both Machchan bhai and me immensely. But because of the twelve year difference there was a huge generation gap between us. She knew I loved her sincerely, but I was unable to make her understand that certain changes come about with time among young men and women. As a result we were not that close that I could put my head on her lap, let the tears flow and feel any better. I had to carry the burden of my grief by myself.

After twelve days I came back to Lucknow with bhabhi's parents and the newborn baby. Beevi and Allan bhaiyya had already come back a couple of days ago. Bhabhi's parents stayed with my mother for a few days and then went back to Biswan. I brought the child with me to Kashana-e-Raza and hired a governess by the name of Mrs Singh to look after him. Her fee was Rs 150 which in those days was a stupendous monthly salary.

My husband Abbas Raza was present in Bhopal while I was there, but we did not come face to face with one another. He did not even try to meet me. This renewed my faith in my decision that I should leave Kashana and go, as soon as possible. But where? That was in the hands of God. Meanwhile I got busy looking after the baby. We named him Ali. Saeed was Mashallah eight years old and as mischievous as ever, but he did not create any problems for me. His eyes twinkled impishly but his body language was that of a child with patience and wisdom.

In July 1947 I received a letter from All India Radio, Delhi informing me that my job application had been accepted. They wanted me to be in the capital by 10th August to take over the responsibility of reading news to the citizens of Hindustan. Mentally I was absolutely ready for this, but practically, the first issue I had to address was what to do with my brother's son. In whose care should I leave him? I discussed the matter with Amma and Kamman. Amma was silent but Kamman said, 'Don't worry Khalla, Nanna and I will handle Ali. You must go to Delhi.'

Ali, by the grace of God, was five months old now and was being looked after rather well by Mrs Singh. Feeling relieved after hearing Kamman's words, I went to inform Begum Raza that I would be leaving. She heard what I had to say and kept quiet. Then I told her, Kamman had agreed to take on the responsibility of looking after Ali and that I would be taking Saeed and Khanum with me. My mother-in-law was an extremely emotional lady, she began to cry. I kept trying to reassure her, as best I could and promised I would visit Lucknow regularly and would definitely come to meet her.

My decision to leave Lucknow must have severely hurt Amma as well. She may have even cried in private. After all she was my mother. She was extremely attached to my children and now we were all going to be separated from one another. Whatever Amma must have been going through emotionally, she never made it obvious to me. Instead, she began coming over to Kashana every day to help me sort and organise things. She helped me immensely with my packing. For some fifteen or twenty days, she came early in the morning and made sure I did the things I needed to, prior to my departure. During this entire time, she never expressed doubt or showed any emotional weakness. Neither did she turn to me even once and ask, 'But my child, where are you going?' My sister, however, strongly opposed my decision and went as far as to say, rather angrily, 'Why didn't you tell us earlier that you were not getting along with your husband? Now all of a sudden what has happened? And why do you need to go to Delhi? Go and stay with Machchan.'

For a couple of days I listened to all her criticism without uttering a word. Then one day I said, 'I tried till the very end to make my marriage work. I have two kids. I never wanted my children to have the psychological problems kids from broken homes do. Till I was trying to make things work, I never talked about my problems as I did not want people to gossip about us.... And secondly, you keep telling me to go stay with Machchan Bhai, that suggestion is not worth even a thought – it's absolutely impractical.'

I loved my brother a lot but I felt rather strongly, that if one loses the capability of standing on one's own feet, cracks appear in the best of relationships. When Machchan Bhai heard I was leaving for Delhi, he came immediately to Lucknow. He must also have been upset with my decision but he never tried to stop me. On 9th August before I left for the airport Amma tied an imamzamin[41] on my arm and said goodbye to me. She did not come till the porch to see me off. Just as I was about to get in the car Beevi said in a frustrated tone, 'I am telling you not to go... you never ever listen to me.' I kept quiet. My brother stepped forward opened the car door and helped Saeed, Khanum and me inside. His eyes were wet with tears.

---

[41] A cloth amulet in which money or coins are wrapped and tied to the arm of a traveller for safe passage.

9

Off the Beaten Track

———— ❦ ————

I arrived in Delhi during the most tumultuous time in our history, on the 10th of August in 1947. After 200 years of colonial rule India stood expectantly poised to celebrate its first Independence Day on 15th August 1947 after being irrevocably split into two autonomous dominions – Hindustan and Pakistan. Breaking through the chains of an extremely conventional and secure life, I had chosen to live the vulnerable existence of a single woman. Age was on my side; I was young and strong.

The pressing demands of circumstances and the voice of my own conscience had compelled me to find my courage. Overlooking all the gossip doing the rounds within the family, ignoring the criticism of society and forsaking the comfortable life of Lucknow, I broke bonds and ventured out, all alone, putting my life on the line. For a woman to walk out like this, alone – without any male support or approval, back in our days, leaving behind the safety and protection of home and family – was absolutely unheard of.

I will always remain grateful to both my mother and mother-in-law for handling an unprecedented situation like this with immense tolerance and patience. Despite the fact that both were uneducated, they did not create any emotional drama nor did they object to my decision. Instead they chose to maintain a dignified silence without crying on anyone's shoulder. And not once did they turn around and blame me for this unfortunate sequence of events. What large-hearted women they were.

When I arrived in Delhi on the morning of 10th August I was

received at the train station by Mahmoud, the son of an old family friend by the name of Iqbal Hussain. The three of us, Saeed, Khanum and I went with Mahmoud to his house which was located within the Hutments on Sikandra Road. Built during the Second World War, the entire complex was a gated community, with just one point of entry and exit. In 1947, at the time I came to stay here, there were close to 50 families living comfortably within this colony. Each spacious house was well-equipped with four large rooms, en-suite bathrooms, a kitchen etc.

I had been employed as an Urdu newsreader by All India Radio and had to report and take charge of my responsibilities the next day. I was at the office on the 11th where I met with AIR's Director of News and spent the entire day getting familiar with the premises and the layout of the building. I had to leave Saeed at the Hutments and even though Khanum was with him, he was constantly on my mind. After all, everything was new and unfamiliar to him. At the same time I was aware, that from now on, I would have to compromise with the demands of this phase of my life.

By half past five that evening I was back at Sikandra Road. Saeed came and sat quietly next to me. He did not utter a single word of complaint nor did he grumble; he was such an extraordinary child. I feel equally grateful to him, because if he had thrown a tantrum, become depressed or cried, then what could I have done?

That evening, Iqbal Hussain's brother Siraj Hussain came by. We knew each other and used to socialise quite a bit when he lived in Lucknow and practised law. We were sitting about chatting when Nuruddin Ahmed, one of Siraj's friends from Delhi, dropped by to meet him and immediately began asking everyone to accompany him to some club. When Siraj introduced us he insisted that I also go with them to the club. I excused myself.

Siraj said, 'Come along, we will introduce you to Noor's wife and daughter. Both of them are very interesting.' I apologised once again. Mentally I was so stressed out; I felt as though the burden of the entire world was on me. How could I get into the mood to have fun at a club?

The next day when I reported for work at the radio station, a weekly roster of my duties and timings had been prepared and was

handed over to me. On the 13th of August I was to reach office by
6am and read the 8 o'clock bulletin in Urdu. Mrs Vijayalaxmi Pandit,
sister of Independent India's first Prime Minister Pandit Jawaharlal
Nehru, had been a frequent visitor to Lucknow. She was Beevi's good
friend and because of that I met with her quite often. She treated me
like a younger sister. During one such meeting I mentioned I had
sent a written application to AIR Delhi for a job. Mrs Pandit was a
keen supporter of women's rights and immediately asked me to give
a copy of the application to her. 'I will try and see what I can do.'
She then sent the letter to a certain Dr Syed Hussain in Delhi with
instructions that 'the work should be done.' And so it was. How
could Syed Hussain not honour Vijayalaxmi Pandit's orders? That is
how I came to Delhi.

I was ready to deliver my very first news bulletin on air on the
13th of August 1947. Prior to this, no woman had been employed by
either the BBC (British Broadcasting Corporation) or AIR Delhi to
work as a news broadcaster. I was the first woman AIR considered
good enough to read radio news. Of course they had to train me
and I was taught how to first introduce myself on air with my
name and then start reading the bulletin. The quality of my voice
was appreciated. The feedback I got was that listeners were quite
impressed by the style in which I delivered the news. *The Statesman*
newspaper even published a few words of praise about me. I believe
some people said I must have planted this story. But that's pure
conjecture. When I didn't know anyone in Delhi at the time, how
could I get them to praise me?

That day when I got back from work around 5.30 in the evening
Saeed didn't leave my side for even a second. As I sat down to tea
with Iqbal sahab's family, I took the opportunity to inform my
hosts that I would start looking for a place of my own the following
day. Perhaps I could rent a small house or even two rooms as that
would be enough for the time being. Iqbal Bhai's wife was extremely
affectionate, she laughed and asked, 'What's your hurry, Apa?'

'You have four rooms here which are just about enough for
the needs of your family. Now the three of us have added to this
number,' I replied.

We were discussing the pros and cons of my moving out when

Siraj and Nuruddin Ahmed arrived. Once again they began insisting that all of us should go to Roshanara Club with them.

'Apa is going off to look for a house,' Begum Iqbal said.

'Okay, then let's help her look for one,' said Siraj.

I readily agreed. Saeed and I went and sat in Nuruddin sahab's car and off we went to look for a house in Delhi. On the way Nuruddin sahab gave some sound advice. 'You are a single woman,' he said, 'what will you do with an entire house? Why don't you try and get a room at the YWCA, the Young Women's Christian Association, for the time being?'

I was open to the suggestion so we drove straight to YWCA on Curzon Road. The secretary informed us that though they had rooms I would not be allowed to keep a child with me within the premises. She suggested that if I send in a request to the President of the Association, they might allow it as a special case. After our meeting was over, Nuruddin sahab again expressed a desire to take us all straight from Curzon Road to the Roshanara Club. Once again I excused myself. 'I'm on duty early morning at the radio station, please drop Saeed and me back to the Hutments.' They dropped us back and headed off to the club. After this I met him another two or three times at the house, each time he invited me to the club. Each time I refused.

Meanwhile after a considerable amount of struggle I managed to procure approval from the authorities at YWCA to keep Saeed at their Ashoka Road hostel. I decided to send Khanum back to Lucknow. Saeed seemed to have adjusted quite well to both my work-timings and his new surroundings at Iqbal sahab's place. I didn't think, for even a second, that he could be distressed or that he would not be able to settle in Delhi. Yes, what used to happen when I got back from work is that he would not leave my side. And he would be like this till his bedtime.

On the 15th of August India gained independence from British rule. What a proud moment it was for all of us! For the first time, we hoisted our own flag from the grand ramparts of the Red Fort in Delhi. Every minute of the impressive proceedings was broadcast on national radio. That day I left for work at the usual time in the morning but got back quite late. It was almost 8 at night by the time I reached the Hutments. I had prepared Saeed in advance that I would be at work through the day on the 15th and he reassured me, he would keep himself busy reading his books and would go outside to play with the other kids in the evening. Khanum was there, she had brought Saeed up from day one, he felt comfortable with her and they got along very well.

Iqbal Hussain worked for the Indian government at some post or the other in the Defence Department. He had already informed the Indian authorities that he was keen to join the Pakistani Defence services. At the time of Partition, a mutual agreement had been reached between the two newly formed countries that it would take approximately six months for Defence officials to transfer from one side of the border to the other to take up their responsibilities.

Hence, Iqbal Hussain sahab was scheduled to leave for Pakistan by March of 1948. Which is why my concern to find a place of my own, as soon as possible, was completely justified. When I was allotted a single room in the Ashoka Road YWCA, Begum Iqbal began insisting I stay with her till she was in Delhi. She knew the life I had been leading in Lucknow, the kind of socio-cultural environment I was used to; she was deeply concerned about how I would tackle the uncertain conditions that were slowly emerging within Delhi, that too with an eight-year old child.

I, on the other hand was absolutely oblivious of what the fallout of the formation of Pakistan could be and was unaware of the hardships one faced living in a big metropolitan city like Delhi. Lucknow was a sleepy old city, laid back, with an intoxicating air of complacency. Begum Iqbal had been in Delhi for decades and had her ear to the ground. She was aware of the impending catastrophe waiting to befall the subcontinent before it happened. She was worried for me and insisted I stay with her for the next six months. What an extremely kind-hearted woman she was. I had arrived at her doorstep without a home to call my own or any luggage as such and she had welcomed me sincerely with open arms. When I expressed reluctance at staying with her for such a long period of time, she went to the extent of saying, 'Fine, then you pay me what you would have given YWCA every month. But you must stay with me.' I had no choice but to agree.

Meanwhile, Hindus from Pakistan started crossing the newly formed border and arriving in India, as Muslims from this side gathered all their belongings to make the arduous journey westwards to Pakistan. When citizens of a country migrate *en masse*, leaving behind their homes and all that has ever been familiar to them, anarchy raises its ugly head. News of communal violence began filtering in. Muslims in Lahore were ransacking Hindu households and there was violence and bloodshed in the air. Trainloads of dead bodies began arriving from Lahore and the same fate awaited those who had left behind everything they ever owned to travel all the way to Pakistan. Plying recklessly between the two newly formed countries, trains became the new execution grounds. By the 25th or 26th of August incidents of communal violence rapidly intensified across various localities in Delhi. But till the 5th of September I continued going to office to read the news.

The 6th of September was perhaps a Saturday or a Sunday – I remember it was my day off. I was having a bath as I was in the habit of going for one as soon as I woke up. I must have barely been in the bathroom for two minutes when Begum Iqbal knocked loudly on the door. 'Apa, please come out fast... rioters are about to attack us!' I hurriedly threw on some clothes and came rushing out. Begum Iqbal told me that the Hindu residents of the Hutments (who were the majority) had alerted the two Muslim families living in the complex to leave at once. That if a large crowd attacked the complex, they would not be able to save us. Sitting unflappably in his chair smoking hookah in a style typically associated with people from Lucknow, Iqbal Hussain sahab looked unperturbed by the news he had just received. He puffed at the nozzle nonchalantly, as he simultaneously dialled some top government official in the hope of asking them to make immediate provisions for our safety. But the phone lines were not connecting.

Begum Iqbal looked extremely worried. She kept turning to me again and again and saying, 'Apa do something. He will keep smoking – we will all be dead!... He refuses to understand that the government and its administrative machinery have broken down... rioters have taken law and order in their own hands.' By now I was quite tense. To top it all the phone lines were behaving erratically.

At times they would connect and then suddenly go completely dead. Without saying a word I went to the neighbour's house and asked permission to use their telephone. I dialled Mohsin Ali sahab, a friend of my father's, who lived on Hailey Road. 'Mohsin Chacha the situation here is extremely dangerous, please tell me what I should do.' I called him Chacha or paternal uncle.

'Come over to my house immediately,' Mohsin Chacha said.

'But I am staying with Iqbal Hussain sahab. His family have been my hosts for a while now. I can't just leave them and come away,' I replied.

'How many people are there in total?'

'Counting servants... 16,' I replied.

'Bibi the agitators are targeting those houses where a large number of Muslims have congregated. That's why I will not be able to give shelter to so many people,' Mohsin Chacha said.

'Then leave it Mohsin Chacha... don't worry, I will try to find another solution,' I replied decisively. When I got back I saw Iqbal sahab still sitting by the telephone. He had managed to connect to the Defence Department and was asking them to send a police unit immediately for his protection. The answer he was getting from that end was, 'Yes, yes, we will dispatch them at once.' He turned to console his wife. 'I have made arrangements, a unit of eight or ten policemen will be here soon.' Then from across the wall of the Hutments we heard bloodcurdling screams.

'Beat them... catch them... don't let them get away!'

Suddenly the telephone rang. Begum Iqbal ran to answer it.

'Tell Saeeda beti to get everyone and come to my house immediately.' It was Mohsin Chahcha. I heaved a sigh of relief!

Every minute it was getting increasingly dangerous. Quickly, we took what we could lay our hands on, secured and locked the house and went and sat in Iqbal sahab's cars, (he had a Buick and an Austen) and raced top speed towards Hailey Road. By the time we reached it was 11 in the morning. We were just about getting out of our respective vehicles when Begum Iqbal quietly whispered to me in a rather worried tone, 'Apa I think I have forgotten the box which has all my jewellery in the cupboard.'

'Don't worry,' I said.

I turned to Mahmoud and said, 'Come on let's go back and get it.'

Before I knew it we were both zipping back towards Sikandra Road in the Buick along with Ghani the servant. When we reached there we found that Iqbal sahab's house had been completely robbed and looted. Doors were flung wide open, furniture, clothes, bicycle, books, everything was ruthlessly strewn about from one end of the house to the other. It seemed as though the rioters had descended on the place as soon as we exited and within that brief half hour, had caused as much destruction as they possibly could. There was after all no one to stop them. There was no sign of Iqbal sahab's police force.

Without wasting any time, I went to the room where Begum Iqbal said she had kept the jewellery box. It was still there! The houses within the Hutments had built-in cupboards with deep recessed shelves. Tucked inconspicuously right at the back, behind a heap of dirty clothes was the precious sandookcha, the chest filled with jewels. If one glanced at the shelf, it would look as though someone had left behind a bundle of old worn-out torn-up filthy clothes and probably that is why the jewellery remained safe where it was.

Mahmoud and I quickly retrieved the box. We tried to scan through and pick out a few of the other useful items lying trashed and scattered across the house and with Ghani's help, began stuffing them in the car. I told Mahmoud to take one load to Hailey Road and come back to get some more of the valuables. It was quite clear by now that we would never be returning to Sikandra Road again. There was an eerie silence all around. All of the other residents had closed their doors and were sitting inside absolutely petrified. As we collected our things, the sound of our footsteps reverberated through the ravaged house. But both Ghani and I were deeply absorbed in rummaging and collecting remains of the worldly belongings we saw scattered around us.

Suddenly a Sikh man came running inside and said, 'Mr Chibb's wife has sent me, she is saying you must come immediately to her house. Make your servant jump the wall now and run…! The rioters have somehow found out some Muslims have returned… they are coming back… they could be at the gate. You must come with me at once.' We made Ghani jump the wall; the Sikh manservant took the small suitcase I was holding. We walked hastily from No 13 Hutments towards No 15 taking the garden path which was strewn with coarse gravel. Even today, when I think of that day, I can hear the rough sound of our rushed footsteps echoing on the stony pathway. The silence was so deafening that the tiniest of sounds was amplified. No 15 was a short walk away. When I reached the entrance, a hand suddenly emerged from behind the front door, grabbed my arm and pulled me inside. That was Mrs Chibb. She quickly bolted the door shut, pulled the curtains together and said, 'Now please go and sit down quietly.'

I was so shocked, I sat down obediently. The phone rang, it was Mahmoud from Hailey Road. He was calling to inform Mrs Chibb that when he was exiting the gate, rioters had attacked his vehicle with sticks, but that he had managed to escape the crowd by accelerating the car and racing full speed out of there. He wanted to tell her to go get me from No 13. Mrs Chibb reassured him that she had already done this and that Ghani had been made to leap across the boundary wall and run to save his life. She barely put the receiver down when we heard loud terrifying chants. The rioters were back. Iqbal sahab's house was being looted for a second time.

After a while, the awful noises died down. By this time it was almost one o' clock in the afternoon. Mrs Chibb got some lunch for me. She spoke in a hushed voice and said, 'When Somnath comes back from work in the evening, we will drop you to Hailey Road.' She left and asked me to get some rest. But how could I do that? My heart was in Hailey Road. I had tried calling Mohsin Chacha's place earlier to find out how Saeed was doing, but I couldn't get through.

When I left Lucknow I could not have guessed even in my wildest dreams that someday, and so soon in the future, I would be facing such dangerous circumstances. I was worried sick about Saeed and just wanted to know when it would be evening and when I could be with Saeed and Khanum. Mr Chibb came home around 5.30. His wife narrated the entire story to him. Chibb sahab suggested we head out in the dark of night, and so we had to wait. Around 8 at night, Chibb sahab made me sit in the back seat of his car, asked his wife and daughter to sit on either side of me, made me cover my head with a dupatta so I might look a bit inconspicuous, and this is how I reached Hailey Road on that fateful night of 6th September 1947. To my utter dismay, I found out that Iqbal sahab had left Hailey Road and gone off to seek shelter in a refugee camp. And that along with his entire family and servants he had also taken Saeed and Khanum with him! Mohsin Chacha apologised profusely. 'I tried my best to tell Iqbal sahab, leave Saeed and Khanum with me. But he refused and insisted they were also his responsibility.'

Later I learnt that when I did not return from Sikandra Road, Mohsin Chacha grew extremely anxious. He kept saying that having so many Muslims congregate in one spot was inviting trouble. Iqbal sahab took offence at this, made some necessary arrangements and went off to stay at 'P' Block Refugee Camp. Everyone was simply looking out for themselves. People were petrified, their hearts were filled with terror and the thinking was that at least within a refugee camp one's life would be safe. Though no one was remotely aware of the hardships they might have to encounter there either. Nevertheless, my child and Khanum were now in a refugee camp and I was at Hailey road. And since it was quite late at night no one thought it practical to take me there. I was absolutely helpless and at their mercy. My mind felt numb with anxiety and constant worrying. I had to wait till morning.

At the time the famous tennis player Mahmoud Alam was also staying as a house guest at Mohsin Chahcha's, along with his wife Suraiya and their six month old baby girl. The silence around us was suddenly disrupted by the loud ringing of the telephone. Mohsin Chacha got up to take the call. After he put the phone down he turned to us and said, 'That was my friend Krishna Prasad. He called to say we should leave the lights of the house on through the night, rioters have alerted the Hindu community that a lit house would be taken as a sign of a Hindu home. They will attack all those houses which remain dark after midnight.'

I listened stoically to Mohsin Chacha. I was not scared or overwhelmed. I could only think about Saeed. Other than that, the only thought in my mind was that I must honour the need of the hour and do what's best in this given situation. Mohsin Chacha decided that aside from leaving all the lights on in the veranda and drawing room, he would also leave the doors of the house unlatched.

Around 11 at night a car drove up and stopped in the portico. An English couple got off and entered the drawing room. Old friends of Mohsin Chacha they had come out of empathy to stay the night with him at this time of crisis. They had got a sword and a gun with them. Their arrival filled us with hope, we were more in number now. I was still extremely anxious about my child and that concern was weighing heavy on my heart and mind. We sat in the drawing room like watchmen, intensely alert, when all at once two men ran in screaming hysterically.

'Save us, save us… please save us!'

One of them was completely beside himself with fear and kept repeating loudly, 'Convert me… go ahead make me a Hindu… but please… please don't kill me. Save me… save me…!' He was crying piteously. Mohsin Chacha tried to console the distraught man. When he showed no signs of calming down, Mohsin Chacha said firmly, 'Stop shouting. Keep quiet… No one is going to attack you here.'

The man calmed down but was still visibly petrified. Mohsin Chacha took him to another room and locked him in there. 'Now don't let me hear a squeak from you…. If you can, get some sleep.' The other man was made to sit with us in the drawing room. Two of Mohsin Chacha's servants had already been strategically positioned behind some bushes near the gate of the house with strict instructions to inform sahab if they saw a crowd approaching. Around two in the morning, these two guards came in. 'Sahab a lot of people seem to be heading our way… it looks as though the police is with them.' After a brief discussion the men decided that Mohsin Chacha, Mahmoud Alam and the Englishman would go outside the house without any weapon. The women would remain indoors and that if the need arose, they would not hesitate to use arms. And who pray were these 'women'? The English lady and I. Physically, she was tall and quite well-built. Between the two of us lay the two formidable weapons. My hand moved towards the gun and hers automatically fell on the sword.

The three-seater sofa in Mohsin Chacha's drawing room was positioned in such a way that its back faced the main entrance. Fixing the nozzle of the gun on the spine of the sofa, I positioned myself strategically behind it. She gripped the sword in her large hands and stood nearby, vigilant. The men had gone outside. We heard the sound of footsteps on the gravel getting louder and louder. We heard voices approaching; they seemed to be coming from the veranda but we couldn't really decipher what was being said. How could we? Our minds were frozen. I felt empty of all feeling.

A short while later, when Mohsin Chacha and Mahmoud Alam walked in they were met with the sight of two ladies, one holding a gun pointed in their direction, the other wielding a large sword. Both burst out laughing. Their minds had been so traumatised they couldn't control themselves. We looked at them, completely clueless. We had no idea what could have triggered this unrestrained outburst of mirth. In between spurts of laughter, Mohsin Chacha told us, the crowd of people at the gate was in fact a troop of policemen the government had sent for our protection. They were not rioters. At this, we also started to laugh and for a while the four of us were quite hysterical.

After that we all sat together in the drawing room and tried to make small talk, our ears alert to catch any untoward sound. By now I was beside myself with worry for Saeed. Somehow or the other, that awful night passed and day broke and it was finally the morning of 7th September. I immediately went and asked Mohsin Chacha to help me get to P Block at the Refugee Camp. The English couple said they would be happy to take me there, but that we should wait till a little later in the morning.

Around 10.30 we got into an armed jeep and reached P Block. A gigantic open area had been cordoned off and converted into a makeshift refugee camp with barbed wires. On one side there was a row of rooms lined one-after-the-other with a narrow veranda stretching in front of them. These rooms (which had initially been used as temporary offices during the Second World War) were however, inaccessible. Large locks hung silently from their locked doors. Meanwhile, the slender veranda was choked with as many people as could possibly fit in there. The remaining, thousands and thousands of displaced refugees seeking shelter from the ongoing mind-numbing violence had effortlessly spilled on to the open field. A large number of policemen had been stationed there for their protection. When I reached P Block along with the English couple, the police patrol was stopped to clear the way for us. It had barely been three weeks since British rule ended in India but the soldiers, deeply conditioned to follow protocol, were saluting the English couple as though they were still serving under the Raj. Since I was with them, I was also getting the same reception. If they could, they would have rolled out a red carpet for us.

All I wanted now was to find Saeed. Instead, what I saw in front of me was a massive throng, a sea of endless people, so many in number that due to the lack of space, their shoulders were grazing against each other's. I wondered, 'Where in this swarming crowd am I to find my eight-year-old boy and his old loving maid?' Once again the same English couple came to my rescue. They signalled to one policeman, turned and gesticulated to another, said a few words to each in their broken Hindi and in less than fifteen minutes the officers had located Iqbal Hussain sahab's family. Saeed and Khanum were with them! Without saying a word, Saeed walked up to me, came and stood by my side and held my finger tightly. He just stood like that – silent and calm as though nothing had happened. His palms felt warm. I reached out and hugged Khanum and reassured her that now I was there with them. What immense patience and self-control she had. Even she didn't utter a single syllable.

Begum Iqbal came up to me and said, 'Apa we have decided to leave for Pakistan as soon as possible. We don't feel safe here anymore. We have to be at the airport within half an hour. A plane is leaving for Karachi at noon. You also come with us. Tell us now so we can book a seat for you all on the plane.' I heard her words and felt as if I had turned to stone. 'Dear God from where do I find the strength to comprehend and assimilate what Begum Iqbal is saying?' I felt as though she was asking me to choose between life and death. I was completely against the idea of Partition and vehemently opposed the two-nation theory.[42]

---

[42] The two-nation theory is the ideology that holds that the primary identity and unifying denominator of Muslims in the Indian subcontinent is their religion, rather than their language or ethnicity, and therefore Indian Hindus and Muslims are two distinct nations, regardless of ethnic or other commonalities.

Indeed, I refused to even acknowledge the existence of Pakistan. But what should I to do now? There was so much unrest and bloodshed all around me, what decision should I make now?

Throughout my entire life I have never been able to forget that moment when destiny placed me at this life-threatening juncture. The truth and reality of my entire life flashed seamlessly before my eyes at blinding speed, like a movie reel... 'Iqbal sahab's family is leaving for Pakistan... Mohsin Chacha is here but he is himself dealing with all sorts of uncertain circumstances... I've stayed a night at his house... how will we spend this night?.... And where will I spend it? Today my son and his maid are also with me.... I have to save their lives no matter what I have to go through. Right now around us there is a high possibility of intense danger. Should I send Saeed and Khanum with Begum Iqbal to Pakistan?... But Khanum's children are here, in Hindustan. What will that poor lady do? And if my son goes to Pakistan what will happen with him there? Who will bring him up? After all the situation in Pakistan is the same, there is immense chaos there as well. At a time like this people on that side of the border are also only looking to protect themselves. What will this child of mine go through if he is separated from his parents and his family?'

Then suddenly like a bolt of lightning I got my answer. I knew exactly what I had to do. 'No Saeed, will not go anywhere. If he has to die, he will die right here with me in my arms. And I am responsible for Khanum's life as well and will be till the end of my days.' I turned to Begum Iqbal and said, 'Please don't worry about us. We will not go to Pakistan.' Socially, I no longer felt obligated to her or compelled to accompany her. Praying for their safe journey I said goodbye to them and came back to Mohsin Chacha's house. At the same time I thanked the English couple for their patience and support. If they had not been with me, finding my son in a refugee came would have been an extremely uphill task.

The same unpredictable fearful atmosphere was palpable at Mohsin Chacha's place. Mahmoud Alam was making calls on the telephone. Mohsin Chahcha was flipping through the pages of some book, he seemed preoccupied. The English lady had gone to the kitchen to prepare some tea. I heard Mahmoud Alam's voice telling someone at the other end of the line, 'Sibtey bhai please do something, we are in a very dangerous situation.' I was curious. I also had a relative by the name of Sibtey. I turned to Mahmoud and asked, 'Which Sibtey bhai are you speaking with?'

'The one from Rudauli,' he answered.

'My mother is from Rudauli and there can only be one Sibtey bhai there!'

I took the phone from Mahmoud and spoke directly with Sibtey bhai and began telling him our entire tragic story.

'Come to Rafi sahab's house,' Sibtey Bhai advised.

'But I am not alone, we are eleven people.'

'Well, get them all and come, I will inform Rafi bhai.' When I told Mohsin Chacha about my conversation, he agreed to go to Rafi Ahmed Kidwai's house.[43] Hurriedly, everyone began preparing to leave, taking just those personal items that were absolutely essential. I had hardly anything to pack. I felt as though I was part of a procession that had already been looted! When we ran out of the Hutments at Sikandra Road I had put three sets of clothes together along with two bedsheets. That is pretty much all I had with me now. Under the protection of the same English couple we left Hailey Road and reached Rafi Ahmed sahab's bungalow, at 6 King Edward Road. It was a massive house situated within an enormous compound.

Before Rafi sahab came here, this bungalow had been allotted to the Information & Broadcasting Minister Sir Sultan Ahmed. But at the time of Partition, he had to leave the house and the bungalow became the residence of the Agriculture minister, Rafi Ahmed sahab. Within the compound, towards the back of the house, there is a mosque, which is why this particular place was usually reserved for a Muslim government employee. The same house is now the residence of India's Vice-President and King Edward Road has been re-named, Maulana Azad Marg.

---

[43] Rafi Ahmed Kidwai was a politician, an activist, a freedom fighter and a committed socialist. After Independence, Kidwai became India's first Minister for Communications and after the first general elections in 1952 he was entrusted with the food and agriculture portfolio.

I am deviating and should explain why I have described Rafi sahab's house in such detail. You see when we reached 6 King Edward's Road, there was such a large crowd of people assembled within the compound that we had to more or less wade through this multitude of people to reach the actual house. All around us there was an endless sea of heads – women, men, children, political leaders, dhoti-clad politicians, sherwani-clad politicians – from government officials to leaders of the Muslim League and even Congress leaders wearing their conspicuous Gandhi topis. All of them had congregated at Rafi sahab's bungalow. The situation there reminded me of a couplet usually written in praise of God: *'Tere darbar mein pahonchey to sabhee ek huey'* (In Your court O Almighty, we all become one.) Rafi sahab's all-encompassing personality had drawn these people in; the doors of his house were wide open, welcoming each one. And on 7th September 1947, some of us also joined the crowd of people seeking shelter at 6 King Edward Road.

We were taken inside the house where, to the right of the lobby, there was a huge bedroom. As we entered, we realised there were quite a number of people already there. Each had staked claim to two or three yards of whatever available floor space they could find. When night fell, they would simply spread a sheet on the exact same spot, stretch out a bit and go off to sleep. They graciously accommodated us and we also got a bit of space to call our own. If one counted the people staying at that given point at Rafi sahab's, between the crowd outside and those staying inside, there must have been some 300–350 refugees.

When we finally managed to settle down, I took Saeed in my lap. He was burning with fever. Outside, in the city, all the markets were closed. Shops were either shut or were being forced open and vandalised. Fearful and nervous, people chose to stay within their own homes. The market at Connaught Place had been burgled and looted. Rioters and other anti-social elements were making sure terror, bloodshed and violence ruled. There was no law, no order. We heard fleeting bits of news that even the police had joined hands with the miscreants. Apparently, a successful businessman from Bombay by the name of Kareem Bhai had been dragged out of his car by rioters while on his way to the airport and chopped to pieces.

God knows by what means Rafi sahab's personal assistant Jai Narain, managed to get enough ration to feed the massive crowd of people seeking shelter from the riots. He got flour from someplace, pulses from another, a kilo or two of potatoes from here and there, then somehow or the other these were cooked and food was distributed evenly to everyone. Each person got something to eat, no matter how little. There was absolutely no question of eating to one's heart's content.

Saeed's high fever was probably the result of the tremendous fear he was feeling. He was trying to cope with the circumstances stoically by putting on a brave front. But the problem now was that we did not have access to proper food, a doctor or even any medicine. When night fell on that fateful day of 7th September, I managed to get a small wooden bench from somewhere, spread a thin sheet over it and made Saeed lie down. I sat beside him and slowly began to explain the situation to him.

'Beta you have fever. You see what is happening around us? It's difficult to get food, medicine or even go see a doctor. Should I send you back to Lucknow with Khanum in a plane?'

'Will you not come with me?' Saeed asked.

'If you want me to, I will. The only reason I was not coming is people may say to you, look your mother got scared and ran away from Delhi when things got tough. Plus you won't be alone, you have your Nanna, Khalajaan, Dadijaan, Phupijaan and your father; they will all be there with you. Even the doctor can come check you up and give medicines and then Inshallah you will get better fast.'

'When I get better will you call me back?'

'Zaroor, Of course! I will call you back, by then the circumstances here will also be better.' Saeed agreed to go back to Lucknow.

The next evening, I went to see Rafi sahab. I was quite nervous. When Rafi sahab spoke with a woman, he never looked her in the eye. In an extremely polite tone, I made my request, that I would like to send my son Saeed and his maid back to Lucknow.

'How will you send them?' he asked.

'This is what I have come to ask. How can I send them?' I replied.

'Will you be ready to send them tomorrow?'

'Ji, yes I will.'

'Then that's settled. Tomorrow Acharya Narendra Dev ji and his wife are going by air to Lucknow. Your child will be safe with them... You will send him right?'

'Ji hahn, I will have them ready tomorrow. I will send them.'

We had this conversation on the evening of 8th September 1947. On the morning of the 9th, I brought Saeed and Khanum out of the room and stood with them in Rafi sahab's porch. They had no luggage, just one set of clothes each which Khanum had wrapped firmly into a small tight bundle and tucked safely under her arm. Acharya Ji came in a jeep accompanied by an armed guard; he took Saeed in his lap, Khanum sat on the floor of the jeep in the back seat. Aside from Khudahafiz we did not utter a single word to one another. Then the jeep sped away.

My lips were sealed with prayers for their safe passage. By evening, my brain felt dead. Then I heard Jai Narain calling my name.

'There is a call for you.'

I ran into his office and grabbed the ear piece. It was my sister on the other side. 'Saeed and Khanum have reached safely. His fever seems to have abated. We have already called for the doctor... he has even prescribed some medicines... now don't worry.' Then she added in her matter of fact tone, 'Why don't you come back home?' I must have mumbled some excuse or the other, can't remember now what it was. Who could understand the pain I was going through?

For three straight days, from the 6th of September to the morning of the 9th, Khanum, Saeed and I faced exceptional challenges continuously. Saeed had not expressed even a tiny bit of anxiety or fear. At one time, my little eight-year-old son, who was new to Delhi, was even separated from me for an entire night! But the next day when he saw me, he simply smiled and without a single word of complaint, held my hand tight and stood close to me. Only when we touched did I realise he was running a fever. Before this day in September 1947, Saeed was an extremely playful and mischievous boy. The self-control and patience he internalised during that difficult time is hard to find even among adults. At the refugee camp, he had to sleep on the floor, he got only a handful of gram to eat and even lost a shoe! Despite such indescribably difficult circumstances, Saeed did not exhibit any anxiety or apprehension and this in itself gave me immense support.

From time to time I got updates from Lucknow about Saeed's health. He had recovered. Every time I spoke with him on the phone he insisted, 'Bibi call me back, I want to be with you.' I had made a promise, but the situation within Delhi was still no better than when he left. The decision to partition the country was causing unparalleled destruction and horror on both sides of the border, in Pakistan as well as India. How could I have called Saeed back to be with me at a difficult time like this?

When I arrived in Delhi barely a month back with Saeed and Khanum I could not have imagined, even in my wildest dreams, what would happen here, the kind of calamity that was waiting to unfold which I was now witnessing. I had managed to walk out of a conservative environment thanks to my bold courageous nature, but that world, at the end of the day, was extremely safe. I had absolutely no clue that Partition would turn into such a violent and ghastly event. After sending Saeed off to Lucknow, when I reported for duty on the 10th of September I was informed that for the time being, I should not come to work. Officials at the station said that they would let me know when they were able to put adequate security arrangements in place for their Muslim employees.

Aside from me, there were a few Muslim peons working at AIR along with an elderly yet evergreen gentleman who had been there for years. He was a jack-of-all trades with a brilliant personality. His knowledge was amazingly vast; he was fluent in Arabic, Persian, Urdu and Hindi, was extremely well-versed with the essays of prolific Urdu author and playwright Abdul Halim Sharar[44] and even knew the *Fasana-e-Ajaaib*[45] in Sanskrit. He was also familiar with the works of John Keats, Thomas Hardy, Lord Byron, Fyodor Dostoevsky.

The most coveted quality of a successful broadcaster is his ability to pick up a pen and jot a few crisp lines on any given topic when

---

[44] Author of *Guzishta Lucknow*, considered one of the best narratives on the genesis of the city and its inimitable culture. He lived from 1860 to 1926.

[45] Another well-known Urdu book written by a towering 19th century fiction writer Rajab Ali Beg 'Suroor' in 1843.

the need arises. Not everyone has the creative flair to do this. But this gentleman did. Within minutes he could write comedy scripts or serious literary stuff; he was also adept at scripting plays as well as writing up feature stories for broadcast which received immense acclaim. All in all he was a well-known, learned, accomplished radio personality whose name was Abu Baqr. God knows what a colourful life he had led that he chose Aawara, which means wanderer or nomad, as his pen name.

We called him Aawara sahab. Aawara sahab lived in a one bedroom house in Hauz Qazi. He would reach work sharp at eight and leave only by eight at night. He took lunch in the office canteen and we have no idea where he ate dinner. Basically, he had this strange mystical ascetic sufi kind of personality. He was a walking talking encyclopaedia. We would listen to him enraptured as no matter what the topic of discussion was, his knowledge was supreme.

Awara sahab belonged to a respectable family of Sitapur. His children held good jobs but he had decided to live in a one room apartment on his own terms. He never bad-mouthed anyone nor did he ever complain about people. He always entered the office smiling. If he had time, he would sit for a couple of minutes and make pleasant conversation, otherwise he would walk away saying, 'I have a lot of work to do today, we'll chat another time.' He called me Apa or elder sister. In those days I was Apa to any and every one I met – the universal older sister.

The start of September in 1947 proved to be tough on Awara sahab. In order to protect him from the ongoing communal violence, officials at the radio station had not allowed him to go home from the beginning of the month. Various patrons and some of his own friends got together and arranged clothes and food for him and brought everyday things he might need to the radio station. It was only by the end of September that we Muslim broadcasters got permission to return to work and even then we had to be dropped back to our houses in an armed Jeep, even during the day. On one such trip I met Awaara sahab again. In his usual cheerful manner he said, 'Apa these people in office made me into a clown! They got all sorts of strange clothes for me to wear, shalwar kameez, Lucknow's mardaana gharara (wide bottom pyjama) churidaar-pyjama and even a tehmat (a traditional Indian garment, similar to a sarong) any and everything! I was turned into a half-man, half-woman! And they fed me such delicious food. See Apa I spent such fun carefree days, I've put on weight!'

It's been a while since I got news of Awaara sahab. God knows how he is handling old age and the difficulties that come with it.

Even the few Muslim peons we had at the station were given full protection and looked after well. In fact the management did not let the Muslims employed at AIR step out of the building for close to fifteen or twenty days. One of the peons called Yousef kept squirrels as pets in the pockets of his shirt. We have no idea how he managed to tame them, but he did, as they never ran away! They would stick their heads out of his pocket, eat something and dive back down. A few years later Yousef proved to be very helpful to me.

Despite the fact that the country had been divided and was passing through a destructive phase, Hindus had not yet turned into fundamentalists. The general feeling amongst Indians was that the British had put us in this awful predicament and left. The hearts of people – from both communities – Hindu as well as Muslim, were free of hatred and enmity towards one another. Now, so many years after independence, the only way to save ourselves from witnessing the destructive results of the seeds of hatred we have sown, is to not let these feelings grow roots.

Saeeda Bano

(1913–2001)

Saeeda Bano (Bibi)

Saeeda Bano's father
Mir Majid Husain

The Raza Family. Standing, L to R: *Syed Masud Raza, Syed Abbas Raza, Syed Aley Raza, Syed Kazim Raza, Syed Hashim Raza.*
Seated, second row, L to R: *Hussaini Hussain Raza, Rana Raza Zaidi, Aqila Raza Naqvi, Justice Mohammed Raza, Begum Mohammed Raza, Kaneez Fatima Raza.*
Seated front row, L to R: *Syed Hasan Raza, Syed Qamar Raza Syed Sajjad Raza.*

27ᵗʰ Dec 1936 Lucknow

Bibi (centre right) amongst relatives and friends in the zanana, December 1936

From L to R: Saeed, Bibi, Asad, Sajjad Raza (nephew) and Abbas Raza.

TOP

*From L to R: Saeeda with Asad,
sister Begum Aliya Zaheer and
sister's husband Syed Ali Zaheer
who is seated inside the car.*

RIGHT

*Asad Raza standing behind his
younger brother Saeed Raza,
Sherwood, 1953*

Saeeda Bano's nephew Ali Mehdi
with his maternal grandmother
Begum Tajjamul Hussain.

Asad Raza with son Aamer
Saeeda Bano's grandson.

*From L to R: Asad, Salima, Aamer (Pipo),
Saeed, Naushaba, Huma (Chunmun)*

Shahana (Sherry) with Sonia Ma (centre)
and elder sister Shaheen (Shizzie)

Huma Raza with her mother
Salima Raza

Ayesha Raza with her elder sister, Huma.

Shahana Raza with her grandmother Saeeda Bano, 1996, New Delhi.

Nuruddin Ahmed with Dr S Radhakrishnan, First Vice President of India and later (1962–1967) President of India.

*Saeeda Bano in her later life,
1995, New Delhi.*

Kashana-e-Raza, Lucknow.
Begum Mohammed Raza's residence designed
by American architect Walter Burley Griffin

10

Delhi 1947

Amidst the general onrush of refugees at Rafi sahab's house it was difficult to differentiate between those who were seeking shelter from communal unrest and those who were determined to leave for Pakistan. Gradually the differences became apparent. Now we could easily tell the people who wanted to cross-over from the ones who loved Delhi too dearly to ever think of leaving. Regardless of intent, Rafi sahab helped each one. In fact, an endless number of arrangements were constantly being made to assist those who had decided to migrate by tackling innumerable protocols, so they could reach Karachi safely.

Rafi sahab's personal assistant was an exceedingly clever man by the name of Jai Narain. He was not only efficient but extremely organised as well. When close to 300 people descend at once and spread themselves out, inside the house as well as in its massive compound, ensuring there is enough for everyone to eat, that cleanliness is maintained, that there is some semblance of order, that a system is in place to handle such large numbers, was an arduous task. But Jai Narain was skilled at handling complicated jobs.

You could usually spot him standing in the veranda doing a myriad things at once – welcoming a fresh batch of refugees, helping another offload luggage while waving goodbye to those who were finally departing. He could be seen escorting Khadi-clad leaders (who had just arrived to meet Rafi sahab) to the drawing room while simultaneously consoling a distraught refugee who had lost probably everything he ever owned in the riots or whose family had been completely wiped out.

Everywhere you looked, there was a sense of urgency and calamity. And like a flash of lightning Jai Narain was sometimes here, sometimes there, helping resolve one complicated matter after the other. Rafi sahab himself loved challenges and Jai Narain more than measured-up on his pressure-gauge of expectations.

In those days, Dakota airplanes which could seat a maximum of 30 people, used to fly from Safdarjung Airport. Every single day, Jai Narain would take people, under police protection, right till the aircraft. This was his daily routine. This was pretty much the situation in Delhi when we received the gut wrenching news that some fundamentalists had brutally murdered Rafi sahab's younger brother, Shafi sahab. Shafi Ahmed Kidwai was posted as an administrator in Mussoorie. He was in charge of overseeing that the exodus of people to and from Pakistan went off smoothly in that area. Despite being warned continuously that his life was in grave danger he refused to leave the hill-town and was martyred in the course of doing his duty. Rafi sahab's family had great forbearance and patience. After laying her husband to rest in Mussoorie, Shafi sahab's widow, Begum Anis Kidwai, came to Delhi to stay at Rafi sahab's house. Though grieving deeply she showed remarkable restrain. She did not mourn publicly nor was there any display of tears. The members of their family handled their sorrow with grace and silence. They gave no indication of what they were going through during that difficult time.

Her daughter, Azadi, was already married and the other daughter Kishwar was a heart patient who had been advised to undergo an operation. In spite of these anxious concerns weighing on her mind, Begum Anis Kidwai could be seen sitting around the house calm and silent, holding her worries to herself. I would often go quietly and sit next to her. She wouldn't talk much, nor would I, but despite this in a strange way we became close to one another and personally this gave me a lot of solace.

Anis Baji passed away in 1982. Till the last years of her life we maintained our friendship. I still consider her a dear friend. Begum Anis Kidwai served as Member of Parliament for the Rajya Sabha from Delhi for two full terms. When her tenure ended, she left the official residence allotted to her as an MP and moved to a smaller house she had built for herself in some far off area. Later, she shifted out of there to some other locality, but no matter where she lived, I would land up to meet her. Seeing me at the door, she would get up smiling from her bed, 'Aah, so you've come,' she would say before reaching out affectionately to hold me in her embrace.

Though Begum Anis Kidwai was born and raised in an extremely conservative family where purdah was strictly observed, her father was an exceptionally broadminded parent. When he realised that his daughter was intelligent, he decided to get her tutored at home in Urdu and Farsi. An eager pupil, Anis Baji studied both languages assiduously. She even went on to teach the English language to herself. When the need arose, Begum Anis Kidwai could not only make fluent small talk in English but was also able to express her thoughts with clarity in this language. On a daily basis however she preferred using Urdu. The tone of her silvery voice was so endearingly dulcet it could coax flowers to bloom. Peerless at penning short biographies Anis Baji authored several books. She could sketch the character of the people she was writing about with such clarity that one could actually visualise them. I knew most of the people she wrote about. Each had a unique individuality and with the might of her pen Anis Baji has made them immortal.

She could see the unconventional path I had chosen for myself and was well aware of all the objections and criticisms that were doing the rounds about me. Yet not once did she make it obvious that she knew what was being said. Basically she was one-in-a million, a priceless human being, extremely lovable. I can only express what it felt like to spend time with her through these lines by Jigar Moradabadi: 'Mera paigham mohabbat hai, jahan tak pahonchey.' (My message is love, may its power reach as far as it can.)

Till the end of September 1947 an armed police vehicle escorted the car that picked me up from office and took me to the radio station. After eight hours of duty, I would be dropped home under police protection. The socio-political situation in Delhi had not yet normalised, though the violent flare-ups and deadly rioting had somewhat reduced. One would still hear horrifying stories of murder and violence taking place in some area or the other across the capital. This is why I was rostered to read news only during the day. Travelling by train to Lahore or coming from there to India was extremely dangerous. Coaches from both sides were arriving laden with dead bodies with hardly anyone, if at all, alive inside. This uneasy sequence of events continued till mid-October. Even going to the airport in Delhi was proving extremely dangerous. But man, by nature, is a resilient creature; come what may, the everyday hustle and bustle of life goes on.

Slowly and gradually the number of people staying at Rafi sahab's place began thinning out. By the end of September, Mohsin Chacha and his family had left for Pakistan. By mid-October there were just nine people sharing the larger bedrooms and about four living together in the smaller ones; though each room (whether large or small) had just one en-suite bath. Most of the squatters spread across the compound had either left for Pakistan or returned to their own homes. When we finally got some space for ourselves in the house, the ladies of Rafi sahab's family did not express any displeasure at having us around. They were used to living in a joint family, but certainly not accustomed to having strangers around! Whether their attitude was a result of Rafi sahab's generosity and large-heartedness or if they were themselves accommodating by nature, I don't quite know, but one never felt as though they disliked having such a diverse crowd of people around in their home. They dealt with these unusual circumstances with acceptance, patience and cheerfulness. Almost at all times of the day one would find people sitting in some corner of the house; there was a constant flurry of activity as people came and left. Cooking food for at least 40 to 50 people minimum, on a daily basis, was a given.

Now that the frequency of lawlessness had reduced across the city, tribes of politicians began arriving at Rafi sahab's house in large numbers. None of them had anticipated that the process of Partition would itself lead to such relentless bloodshed. They were stumped at the ghastly turn of events and would congregate regularly at Rafi sahab's house for meetings. Rafi sahab's drawing room was massive; if two women sat in the large chairs and slid back comfortably, they would go completely unnoticed. During those days the renowned scientist Salimuzzaman Siddiqui was also staying at Rafi sahab's along with his German wife Tilly and their son Rafiuzzaman. Salim sahab knew me from his Lucknow days.

He had married Tilly in Germany. No one in India had even the slightest knowledge of this.

During childhood Salim sahab's parents had arranged his engagement to his maternal aunt's daughter. Getting boys and girls affianced to their first or second cousins (from their maternal or paternal sides) when they were still under-age was a common practice among families in the 1900s. The actual wedding usually took place after the minors reached adulthood. Breaking an engagement was considered highly improper and meant shaming and insulting the family name.

Probably sometime around 1927 Salim sahab came to Lucknow and got married for a second time to his cousin. I remember attending the event along with his niece, Anwar. At the time I was studying in the 8th standard in Karamat Girls Muslim College. Now so many years later, I was meeting his first wife in Delhi. Tilly and I hit it off almost at once. As the crowd thinned out, the five of us, that is Salim sahab, his wife and child, Saeed and I began staying in one room. During the day we were all together but at night Salim sahab and Rafi would take their mattresses and go sleep on the drawing room floor.

Around mid-October in 1947 I got a call from Lucknow that Kamman had given birth to another baby girl. This was back in the days when my sister, my brother, their children, all of us in fact, were so close that no occasion – be it a birthday or a bismillah (when the child reads the Quran for the first time) was considered complete without us being there together. Amma was still alive and made sure we stayed connected with each other's lives. During Kamman's first delivery I was by her side the whole time. When I heard that Kamman was due anytime, I flew down to Lucknow immediately, stayed there ten odd days and came back to Delhi with Saeed. The situation within the city was still quite tense; things were not back to normal. But in keeping with my work schedule I would go to office in the morning and return by 5.30pm to Rafi sahab's house.

The havoc caused by Partition and the disintegrating effect that had on the social, political and cultural environment in Delhi was evident by the fact that everything seemed topsy-turvy and confusing. Suddenly one would see Mridula Sarabhai (Indian independence activist and politician) running into the house to meet Rafi sahab. Sometimes we would see Malviyaji consulting with him while Feroze Gandhi (Indian politician and journalist, husband of Indira Gandhi and the son-in-law to Jawaharlal Nehru) stood behind them. Even a fundamentalist like Begum Aizaz Rasul (Indian politician and the only Muslim woman to be a member of the Constituent Assembly of India) of the Muslim League could be seen trying to get Rafi sahab's attention. Rafi sahab would be standing there listening to all of them, mumbling, 'hmmm' or 'yes', trying to be as non-committal as possible with his monosyllabic responses.

Zakir Sahab (Zakir Husain, Third President of India) was a regular visitor. Shafiq-ur-Rahman Kidwai, an important person from Jamia Milia Islamia University, with his extremely intimidating beard could be seen strolling about in the wide veranda of the house. All these political heavyweights endlessly discussed the same thing – how to stop the ongoing bloodshed.

'Call Jinnah,[46] ask him to come to Delhi and offer an olive branch....'

'Perhaps Gandhiji should go to Karachi or Lahore and declare a fast unto death for the sake of peace.'

'Look, that's Khaliquzzamaan sahab[47] getting out of Jamal Mian[48] of Firangi Mahall's car....' Every minute at Rafi sahab's house passed eventfully. We were constantly wondering what would happen next.

Tilly and I usually occupied two chairs in an unlit corner of the enormous drawing room at Rafi sahab's place. Normally no one paid even the slightest attention to this corner. We sat there silently, making ourselves as inconspicuous as possible and witnessed some rather interesting scenes – the double-standards practised by politicians, the advice and opinions they shared, the anxiety they felt and the fear and shame these extremely important people were

---

[46] Muhammad Ali Jinnah leader of the All-India Muslim League and founder of Pakistan.

[47] Chaudhry Khaliquzzaman was a Pakistani politician and one of the top leaders of the All India Muslim League.

[48] Maulana Jamaluddin Abdul Wahab Firangi Mahall or Jamal Mian, was a scholar of traditional religious sciences who played a significant tole in the political and spiritual affairs of undivided India.

experiencing at the unexpected turn of events post Partition. They were not particularly bothered that anyone was listening to them or indeed about what anyone else was saying.

One day Khaleeq sahab and Jamal Miyan came over. Rafi sahab welcomed them into the drawing room warmly and then, with great seriousness and enthusiasm, began discussing ways and means to stop the ongoing communal unrest and the ceaseless bloodbath taking place on both sides of the border. We heard Rafi sahab say, 'Khaleeq you must go to Pakistan and bring Jinnah back to Delhi with you... then both Gandhi and Jinnah should appeal to the masses for peace ... they should put forth conditions that would be acceptable to people on both sides of the border.'

Khaleeq sahab agreed and left for Karachi along with Jamal Miyan right there and then, in front of us. His face was white with fear; he seemed extremely nervous. I thought, these are the same important persons who travelled across the country lecturing with great enthusiasm about the two-nation theory and the benefits of Partition, who made so many tall promises and here they are today, scared and completely ashen-faced.

There was a rumour doing the rounds, which was later even published in some book, that Khaleeq sahab apparently fled Delhi wearing a burqa. That is a complete fabrication. He left for Karachi from Rafi sahab's house in front of us. Yes, this much is correct that he looked absolutely petrified and never returned to Hindustan after that day. The lofty dreams of bringing back the proverbial olive branch drowned in the depth of fear and terror. Meanwhile, the horrific result of Partition on this side of the border had such a deep impact on Gandhiji that he decided to fast unto death. He announced that till the bloodshed did not stop, he would not break his vow. The entire country was in a state of shock. Then ultimately both the Muslims and Hindus came together to convince Gandhiji with utmost sincerity and honesty that communal riots would end.

As mentioned earlier I had brought Saeed back to Delhi with me. I was still living at Rafi sahab's and my office timings were the same, I would leave at 9am and return by 5.30 in the evening. All day Saeed would be at King Edward Road playing about mostly with Rafi sahab's nephew Khurshid. Sometimes the servants' children would also join in to play with them. Khurshid was probably a year older than Saeed.

One evening when I came back Saeed said to me, 'Bibi please give me two rupees?'

'What do you need the money for?'

'I don't want to tell you. You'll get angry.' That was the reply I got.

'Okay I won't be angry. Tell me why you need two rupees,' I said, more curious than ever.

'Bibi I winked at the washerman's daughter and now she is asking for two rupees and threatening me, that if I don't give her the money she will tell my mother.'

'But now you've told me… and see I am not even upset. But bete, how did you learn to wink at girls?' I asked.

'Wajju chacha was winking so I also did it. It's not difficult to wink.'

'Hmm… so anyway now you tell the washerman's daughter that you have told your mother the truth.'

Wajju miyan was a young lively lad with an extremely colourful personality. For years we teased him about this incident and each time he would put the blame on Saeed saying 'this boy is very naughty!'

This gentleman went on to hold several prominent positions. He was even posted as the Indian Ambassador to various countries where he handled difficult situations with tact and diplomacy. This was one of the harmless antics Saeed indulged in during our stay at Rafi sahab's. But one evening when I came back from office and went into the drawing room to get a cup of tea Dr Husain Zaheer called out to me. 'Your son nearly got himself killed today,' he said.

I looked up and saw Rafi sahab sitting at the head of the table with Khurshid and my son, standing on either side. Dr Husain Zaheer was sitting next to Saeed. I looked questioningly at Husain Zaheer. He laughed and narrated the following incident. 'A taxi came into the compound today and parked in the portico. Miyan Saeed went boldly, stood on its footboard, made a rude face at the Sikh driver teasingly, gesticulated with his hands mimicking the driver's long beard and asked, "want to eat some beef?" The man flew into a rage, took his kirpan (small sword carried by Sikhs) out and ran after

Saeed. Your son got saved thanks to the large number of policemen stationed here. One cop grabbed Saeed, another tackled the driver. Saeed was taken into the house. Somehow they managed to calm the Sikh down and sent him off.'

I only ever went into the dining area if it was necessary. At meal times all sorts of people congregated there. All of these people now heard what Saeed had done. Rafi sahab and Husain Zaheer seemed quite amused about the whole thing. Saeed sat cowering in his seat, seeking shelter in Rafi sahab's presence. In front of Rafi sahab I said nothing to him, took my cup of tea and came away to my room. Emotionally I was filled with fear and rage. The one thought that kept pulsing through my mind continuously was 'Saeed could have been killed today!'

A short while later Saeed walked meekly into the room. Without uttering a single word I began thrashing him. I beat him up, nice and hard, my hands were out of my control, I couldn't stop them. Saeed stood silently getting clobbered. When I got tired of hitting him, I pushed him on to a wooden bench, pulled him up again, made him sit-up straight and yelled, 'You get up from here and I'll break your legs!'

The two of us sat in our respective places, our heads bowed low.

I was pained at my own behaviour, I felt ashamed of myself. 'Why did I beat my child so mercilessly? Why didn't I have more control?' Prior to this I had never raised my hand on my children. Whenever they misbehaved I would simply explain to them what they had done wrong and usually they would understand. But this time the situation was different – it was a case of life and death.

Saeed looked extremely remorseful and frightened, he had understood to what extent this idiotic prank could have proved fatal. After a while I went and apologized to Saeed for hitting him. As it is, he was frightened after the Sikh driver chased him angrily, if instead of beating Saeed I had controlled myself and explained things to him, he would have understood. I was unable to do this. For a long time now I had been battling with such difficult circumstances that my nerves were completely frayed. I felt overwhelmed, as though Saeed's childish prank had brought me face to face with calamity. As I am writing this now I am unable to articulate what I was going through at that time and honestly I can't find the right words to describe the horrifying fear I felt.

Saeed was an innocent child; He was reasonable by nature. Whatever mischief he got into was not out of any malicious intent. I used to be away all day at the radio station and though he was physically safe at Rafi sahab's place, the environment itself was such that the child was pretty much left to his own devices through the day. He could roam about wherever he pleased within that massive compound. Close to 20-30 children lived there in those days. They all came from different socio-ethnic backgrounds and all of them were Saeed's friends. News of the destruction and havoc taking place across Delhi kept filtering in. As adults we could see that this was not only influencing their impressionable minds but that the unpleasant environment also affected their attitude. This is exactly what was happening with Saeed.

I sat for hours and spoke with him and drilled it into his head. I told him, 'The situation we are in right now is unusual. I need your help and support to tackle it. You are a clever boy, I know I can trust you.' And Saeed was, in essence, an extremely caring and loving child. He was simply a victim of his circumstances. After that frightful incident, he grew extra cautious himself. I also made it a point to tell him, every day before I left for office, how he should spend his time fruitfully. Even the other ladies in the house, especially Anis Baji, now kept an eye out for him.

Then as mentioned, by January 1948, I came to the YWCA. I had already been allotted a room and had permission to keep Saeed. I was trying my best to settle in, get into a routine, when once again the political situation in the country took a turn for the worse. Gandhiji was staying at Birla House. Every evening hundreds of his ardent followers would convene at this location to attend a prarthna sabha or a multi-faith prayer meeting in which the Father of the Nation gave impassioned speeches on peace, harmony and brotherhood. Quite a few men and women living at Rafi sahab's house attended these gatherings, without skipping a single day. One day I also decided to go.

A large crowd was gathered inside Birla House. On one side of the compound a podium had been erected for Gandhiji to sit and deliver his daily discourse. That day I saw Gandhiji in person. He walked in at a snail-slow even pace towards the podium, his skeletal body flanked on either side by his two grand-daughters for support. As he grew closer, the entire crowd stood up out of respect for him. His face looked radiant and luminous, as though a halo of light surrounded him. Slowly and gradually he reached where he was supposed to and sat down. After a rather long pause he addressed the gathering and said things that could be of comfort to the masses who were suffering and tried to reinforce the feeling of humanity among them.

I sat there listening intently to Gandhiji but what he was saying did not have any major impact on me. At first he came across as an extremely learned saintly character but when he started to speak, his words were steeped in sadness. I felt there was a sense of defeat, of failure in the soft tone of his voice. I am not sure if I felt like this because that was a fact or if I perceived it thus on account of my own state of mind.

Though Gandhiji was the personification of sincerity and love, man who is considered one of God's greatest creations, is rarely, if ever, won over by piety or virtuosity. Instead he falls prey to dishonesty, cunning and brute force. The result of this fact came to light on 30 January 1948 when a psychopath, who could not comprehend Gandhiji's message of non-violence and love, shot at him three-times, at point-blank range, in that very same prarthna sabha. That frail human being dropped dead, right there and then. We were all absolutely devastated. The entire nation went into severe shock. Suddenly we lost an exceptional man who knew what he was talking about. Since then, there hasn't been a leader in the world like Gandhiji and God knows if there ever will.

Within India, the socio-political situation seemed to be heading from bad to worse and we had cut off the very branch we were sitting on. On this sad occasion leaders from across the world expressed profound grief by sending condolence letters and conveyed deep shock and sympathy on hearing of Gandhiji's assassination. That evening I was scheduled to deliver the 6pm bulletin. Our newsroom was attached to Birla House and from here we used to do live recordings of Gandhiji's sermons. When we heard gunshots, Melville

De Mellow, one of our English newsreaders, immediately exclaimed, 'Someone has shot Gandhiji!' Within minutes we got the news that Gandhiji had succumbed to his injuries and died on the spot. I was sitting opposite the News Director at the time holding a stack of hard copies.

'I can't read the news,' I said.

'Well someone has to,' he replied.

I thought, 'He is right.' I picked up the papers and walked into the studio, I was crying profusely. A couple of minutes later the Director entered with another newsreader and said, 'He will read the news.'

Till today I feel grateful for this kindness.

When he heard the soul shattering news of Gandhiji's death my brother flew down immediately to Delhi. I made him stay at Rafi sahab's place as I had just moved to YWCA. After Gandhiji's murder, Muslims who chose to stay in India had grown even more scared. Concern for my wellbeing brought my brother all the way from Bhopal to the capital, where the situation was extremely uncertain. And now this calamity, that Gandhiji, who was a huge pillar of support for us, was no more. We watched his funeral procession sitting on top of cars and bid him a final adieu in our hearts.

His death had an extremely disturbing impact on the Muslim community. All of us were simply petrified. But now no one had the guts to start riots against Muslims. I managed to convince my brother to return home, though he was insistent I go back with him. His love for me brought him to see me on two occasions – in August 1947 and once again in January 1948 in the hope that perhaps I would go and stay with him in Bhopal. His sincere concern for my welfare gave me strength and solace. But how could I have gone and stayed with him? How could I put the burden of the decisions I had chosen to take in my life, on his shoulders? I had only ever lived under the guardianship of either my father or my husband. I was 34 years old. And I had no experience of my own, but instinctively I knew that aside from one's parents and one's husband, no third person can shoulder the responsibility of someone else's son, daughter or wife for the rest of their lives.

11

YWCA

'*Goshe mein qafas ke mujhey aaram bahut hai*'

(In this corner of my prison I am immensely at peace.)

When I lived in Lucknow, we often visited the YWCA to meet the secretary and request her to find us someone who could work for us as a house-help from among the residents living there. Here I was today seeking shelter in the very same place. The British had left India but the quality of cleanliness and orderliness associated with the western way could be seen in how things were maintained within the YWCA. High standards of sanitation and punctuality were followed which appealed to me and were a big boon in helping me adjust to living here.

During the time I was at Rafi sahab's, at the beginning of each month I would approach him and ask, 'if you give permission I can shift to the YWCA.'

He evaded the question, saying, 'At the moment it is not appropriate.' When I asked the same question in January 1948, he approved and by mid-January I was in the YWCA. My room rent at YWCA, inclusive of meals was Rs 150. I think they took an additional Rs 75 for Saeed's food. My salary was Rs 350 out of which Rs 225 went straight to the YWCA. God knows how we managed to live within the remaining Rs 125 but I count the YWCA as a huge blessing in my life, at least our meals were taken care of! Every other need could be reduced.

When any unbudgeted expenses cropped up, such as getting Asad from Nainital to Delhi, I would either sell my gold bangles or mortgage them with State Bank of India. In those days kids never travelled alone, it was absolutely unheard of. It was mandatory that they be accompanied by an adult, even if it was a servant. When Asad came to Delhi to see me, I had to make arrangements for a known watchman to escort him from boarding and then go back to drop him there as well. I would also have to arrange for a reliable servant to do the Lucknow-Delhi shunt with Asad.

As part of my dowry, my parents had given me a substantial amount of gold jewellery and I received quite a lot from my husband's side as well, innumerable bangles, several necklaces and a good amount of jadau-zevar, exquisite jewellery studded with diamonds and precious stones. Just the anklets they gave weighed 20 tolas. (One tola is approximately 12 grams) Similarly I received a lot of silverware. Back then, the price of gold was Rs 30 per tola. By the time I came to the YWCA, the price of both metals had escalated sharply. Before leaving for Delhi I had left my jadau-zevar in a locker at Punjab National Bank In Lucknow. I kept my silverware in the locker in Beevi's home for safe keeping. I brought only about a dozen saris and a few ghararas, which were robbed during the riots in Sikandra Road. I had to get new clothes stitched for myself which of course I couldn't afford on my meagre salary. The various gold and silver ornaments I had been given during my wedding took care of such unexpected expenses.

By the 14th of January I had settled down in YWCA. I spent the initial few days getting familiar with the place and it was perhaps on the third day that I learnt that the amount of sugar one was allotted was rationed. The weekly allowance was the amount that could fit in one cigarette box. Immediately I procured two empty cigarette boxes and sent Saeed to the dining room to get our weekly quota. Saeed came back with one box filled and said the bearer refused to fill the other. Even after Saeed told him why he needed two boxes, the man in-charge of dispensing the ration refused to oblige. I let the incident pass, thinking I would get it myself the next day. Breakfast at the YWCA usually started around 8.30. The next day, I reached on time and with my empty cigarette box in hand, went straight to the head steward and said, 'Yesterday, you did not give sugar for one person, please give it now.'

'Your son took two boxes,' he replied, rudely.

Ignoring his offensive tone I said, 'No, you gave him one box and...'

Interrupting me mid-sentence he said, 'NO... your son took both.'

That was it. I lost my cool, 'You really think we would lie for one measly box of sugar?' I scolded him severely. He tried to speak but by now I was in a rage. 'Quiet! Keep quiet,' I said furiously. He grew silent but seemed equally angry. I marched off to the office of the YWCA Secretary Mrs Jacob and informed her of what had just happened. 'Mrs Jacob I have given it off to your head waiter. He behaved rudely with me without any provocation; I am not used to people talking to me like that. I have blown him up. I have simply come here to inform you personally – before he comes complaining. I have given him a good piece of my mind. You don't need to do it as well.'

She started laughing and asked what happened. I narrated the sugar story and emphasised she shouldn't get too mad at him. 'But Mrs Jacob do explain to him that he needs to learn how to speak politely.' When this incident took place close to 150 women were in the dining area having breakfast. The same head waiter had been behaving arrogantly with others as well. Several of them were quite unhappy with his attitude. They were pleased I had blown him up; though personally I was regretting having lost my cool. The end result of this was that not only did he start behaving courteously with me from then on, but also spoke decently with others as well.

Another positive result of this incident was that as long as I stayed in YWCA, the waiters and the cook, including this head steward, looked after my children and me with affection and respect and even helped me during difficult times. I ended up teaching the chef how to prepare nargisi koftas (ground meat wrapped around a hard boiled egg and fried and then cooked in a rich gravy) and aloo–methi ki tarkari (potato made with fenugreek leaves) by reading recipes to them from cookbooks. My children loved these two dishes. Gradually I started adapting to my new surroundings. What helped immensely was that the YWCA was exceptionally clean, punctuality and discipline were maintained effectively and best of all, no one here was really bothered about the other.

By the grace of God Saeed was with me. When I got back from work I never felt lonely. On the whole, I lived quite comfortably at YWCA. Eating badly-prepared meat is difficult, but poorly cooked vegetables can be had easily with the help of pickles and chutneys. I mainly ate vegetables during my stay there. As such I had no complaint with YWCA, though there were some girls who grumbled constantly about things that were not right at the hostel.

The rent was extremely reasonable – my office was so close, I could walk back to the hostel in nine quick minutes and good old Mrs Jacob always treated me with kindness and respect. There was just one issue that bothered me; YWCA was filled with single women or those who had been abandoned or came from broken homes. Some were Indian Christians, others were Anglo-Indians and now thanks to Partition a couple of Hindu and Muslim women had also sought shelter there. Whatever their ethnicity, they had been compelled to stay there because of the adverse circumstances they had faced in their lives.

The lifestyle I chose to lead in Delhi was simple; I would head out to the radio station, read the news and return to the hostel. I was not in the habit of hanging about the office after work chit-chatting with people. Saeed was with me and we spent most of our time with each other. We would either play badminton in the evening or just go roam about in Connaught Place. But I was now starting to worry about Saeed's education.

At the time there was only one school in Delhi for a Muslim child – Jamia Millia Islamia. I started looking for ways and means of getting him admitted there. Travelling 12 miles to Okhla – the area where Jamia is located – I met with the Principal, introduced Saeed to him and after completing all the necessary admission formalities, went to the hostel, (for which one quite literally had to pass through a jungle-like area) and had him admitted. On Saturdays I would hire a tonga to go get Saeed back from Okhla to YWCA for the weekend.

Some days passed, then a friend of mine by the name of Arti told me that Saeed was not happy at Jamia; that once, he almost drowned in a canal and that at another time some teacher pulled his ear so ruthlessly that he ripped Saeed's skin off. The wound, Arti said, was still fresh. Saeed had not murmured a word of all this to me. He was very friendly with Arti and had confided in her. I knew I couldn't betray her trust so I thought of a plan. 'Beta', I said casually to him, 'last week I saw lice in your hair, let me wash it and see if they are still there.' Then I sat him down in front of me and pretended to search for lice. While doing this I gingerly checked the back of his ear. The wound was very much there.

'Saeed how did you get hurt here...?' I asked, pretending to be surprised.

'Master sahab pulled my ear very hard,' he replied by way of conversation.

I'm sure Saeed must have done something mischievous, but children cannot be punished so mercilessly that the skin breaks open. I was, to begin with, not entirely happy with the environment in Jamia. The overall administration of the school was slipshod, the place was filthy and the food, quite pathetic. But back then there was no other school for a Muslim child. Jamia was considered the only safe place.

Once again I grew worried about Saeed and didn't know what I should do. I went and met with the Principal and teachers at Jamia and somehow managed to keep Saeed there for an entire year. Then I took Rafi sahab's cousin, Ishtiaq Bhai's advice and decided to enrol him in Modern High School. Ishtiaq Bhai was appointed at some high post in the Ministry of Education; I faced no major hurdle in getting Saeed admitted.

The Principal was a certain Mr Kapoor and out of the 500 boys studying at Modern High that year, there was just one Muslim child, Saeed. I put him in boarding with the satisfaction that Modern is one of the finest schools in Delhi and felt content once again that I had solved the issue of where Saeed would eat and live in Delhi. Every Saturday I went to Modern and got him home for the weekend; home being YWCA.

A month passed, then Saeed's good old friend Arti once again came and told me that Saeed was getting into fights with the boys at Modern. The other children teased him because he was a Muslim. I grew tense.

Then one day by way of conversation I asked Saeed, 'Tell me about your boarding school… what is it like…? Do you like it?'

'Yes, basically everything is fine but the boys have made a song about me which I don't like.'

'What song Saeed?'

'They say… *Saeed to hai musalman, tere lambey lambey kaan, Saeed to hai pathaan, tu bechtaa hai paan.*'

(Saeed you are a Muslim, you have big, big ears; Saeed you are a Pathan, you sell paan.)

I laughed. 'Bete they tease you… but you are a Muslim, what's there to feel bad about?'

'Yes I am a Muslim but I am not a Pathan! I don't like it when they call me by that name!' I reasoned things out with him and convinced him that he shouldn't take things too seriously, that with time everything would sort itself out. By nature I knew Saeed was a peace-loving child.

A few more days passed. As usual Saeed did not complain to me but once again Arti mentioned that Saeed was now getting into regular fights with the other boys. This time I confronted him.

'I believe you get into fights in school?'

'Yes Bibi, I do. I have gotten used to the other children making fun of me, though I have made some good friends as well but there is one teacher who always calls me '*musalman bacchha*', a Muslim kid, in class. When he does that, all the boys start laughing loudly. So when I get out of class I fight with whoever I can.'

I tried reassuring him again. Temperamentally Saeed was a cheerful sort so it wasn't too difficult to explain things to him, but by now I was seriously worried. 'How long would this child be able to tackle such hostile circumstances? Especially when they are occurring on a daily basis…' I thought to myself. 'He may become a fundamentalist or a staunch Muslim.' My weakness for Saeed was preventing me from sending him away from me. But the question of his education was a major point of concern and I knew somewhere deep inside that I had to resolve this issue.

One time during his week-long winter break at Modern, Saeed came to stay with me at YWCA. He was playing about outside as usual when suddenly he came running inside and said, 'That gentleman who we met at Iqbal chacha's.... He has come.'

I couldn't understand who he was referring to.

'Ask him to sit in the lounge, I'll just be there,' I said.

When I went downstairs I found the gentleman was none other than Nuruddin Ahmed. He met me cordially and told me that during the 1947 riots he had to move out of his house and ultimately ended up taking his entire family to London. After settling his wife and kids there he had now returned to India without them. This was December 1949.

Nuruddin was attentive towards Saeed, sat about for a while and when he was getting up to leave, made the same old request, that I should go with him to Roshanara Club to celebrate the New Year. I excused myself saying I could not leave my child and that I wasn't really interested in socialising around Delhi.

For me the most distasteful aspect of living in Delhi was getting from one place to the other. In Lucknow I had my own car and wasn't dependent on anyone. But then the life I led there was vastly different from the one I was experiencing here. We socialised a lot more in Lucknow; I was never alone. My status in that society was also quite different. Here at YWCA I had fallen several social rungs below where I was economically in Lucknow. In Delhi, if I had to go anywhere, I went on foot. Office was luckily a short walk away. If I wanted to go further, say to Connaught Place, it was, at maximum a 15-20 minute walk.

The public mode of transport in Delhi, back in those days was either large taxis or tongas; there was nothing else. Both cost money. It was convenient to stick to walking. Besides, I couldn't even think of going anywhere aside from office since I had Saeed with me. We were together most of the time and we were happy.

Two days after his first visit, Nuruddin dropped by again. I offered him the Anglo-Indian tea we used to get at YWCA. He stayed for a while, talking with Saeed. Then he started coming over to see me at least two or three times a week. He would sit around, talk about his children or discuss the political situation in India. He was well-travelled, there was no dearth of topics for him to discuss.

His conversations were captivating and reflected the sincerity and honesty in his character. But at that time I was completely indifferent to him. I wasn't impressed by his personality nor did I start thinking I had finally found a friend in Delhi.

Yes what did happen is that gradually I arrived at the conclusion that he was a good human being, that he was probably lonely, missed his wife and kids, Saeed reminded him of his younger son and since the Muslim community had dispersed from India after Partition he kept dropping by to meet us.

After a few more visits I began to ask myself, 'Nuruddin is such a scholarly individual, experienced and worldly-wise, why does he come again and again to see me? I am not as educated, nor am I that beautiful that men simply see me and fall in love. The only thing I have is courage which is helping me hold on tightly to the reins of my life.'

But he continued to drop by. I began to trust that he was visiting me purely out of a need for friendship, not just to while away his time. He would talk about his family to me, praise his wife profusely and if some mention of his children came up, it appeared as though he loved them immensely. Gradually, he grew more confident in his visits. He would stay till late and aside from talking about a whole lot of things, would even discuss personal matters with me – such as the education of his children. He spoke candidly about his views regarding their upbringing. I listened quietly to him.

After giving a lot of consideration to the question of Saeed's education, I came to the conclusion that I should admit him in Sherwood. Asad was, after all, already there. Though he was five years older than Saeed, Asad was extremely loving and affectionate towards his younger brother. I started feeling the same overwhelming emotions I had felt when I sent Asad away to boarding. What saddened me even more was Saeed's intrinsic nature to make peace with any and every situation life threw at him.

When Asad left for Sherwood, he went into the confined surroundings of a boarding school from the happy environment of his own comfortable home. Saeed, on the other hand, had been living in Delhi for the past two years and had experienced some extremely unnerving and unpleasant situations. He had already changed two schools – each diametrically opposite to the other. He had also witnessed the uncommon lifestyle of living in a single working women's hostel, where hidden behind the seemingly disciplined life there was a strange layer of unconventionality. As soon as evening fell at YWCA, the 'boyfriends' would begin making their rounds. Saeed shared a great friendship with many of the women here. When he saw one of their male admirers driving in through the gate, Saeed would run to give them the news even before the watchman could, shouting excitedly, 'Your car is here, your car is here.'

In those days, my nephew Air Marshal Jaffar Zaheer, was a Flying Officer with the Indian Air Force and one of his lady friends, Barbara, was at the YWCA; as was his khalla, his mother's sister and his little cousin brother. What an amusingly interesting situation. Saeed was very fond of his cousin, Ajju bhai, the name by which Jaffar Zaheer was known. As a result, a couple of times my poor nephew had to face a lot of embarrassment. Like the day when Ajju's car entered the gate and Saeed came running to my room saying, 'Bibi, Ajju bhai has come to meet us.' He dashed off as fast as he had run in, went straight to Ajju, got him out of the car, held his finger, brought him to the lounge and even placed an order for tea and buns. As I walked down the stairs to the lounge, what do I see, Barbara entering from the other side. For a brief second there was an awkward silence. Then Ajju said, 'Khalla have you met Barbara?'

'Yes Ajju we know each other.'

'Khalla, I came to pick up Barbara,' Ajju said reluctantly.

'Yes, yes of course Ajju, it's absolutely fine, you both please carry on.'

I packed them off. Then Saeed and I sat and ate the buns and tea.

After this, I explained to him, 'Bete, from early evening you come, sit in the front veranda and start acting like a messenger for all the girls. This may not be the right thing to do. You saw what happened right now?'

To some extent Saeed had figured out the kind of life that the women led in this new habitat he was residing in. Though he didn't grasp the full depth of the reality. Being the mischievous restless soul he was, he had figured out how to keep himself entertained. Saeed was quite famous with the girls and since everyone appreciated how polite and well-mannered he was, they indulged him all the more. Someone got him chocolates, another bought him cakes, pastries were ordered for him. He became quite an expert at badminton and the girls often made him their partner. Miyan Saeed was on top of the world. Despite all of this, when I discussed the idea of sending him to Sherwood, he readily accepted.

Saeed's tonsils had been troubling him for a while and doctors had advised us to have them removed. This matter had to be resolved before he could be sent to boarding school. I went to meet a surgeon at Wellington Nursing home. He said he would arrange for a room and fix the operation on a particular date. Then I informed him honestly that I was a government employee working at All India Radio and that according to my salary, I was only eligible for a bed in the general ward, a private room would be out of my budget, but that I would not be able to stay in the general ward and neither would I keep my child there.

The doctor stared at my face. God knows what he saw but he said, 'Doesn't matter, I have a ward which has only four beds. I can reserve one for your child. You prepare to keep the child there for the night. I will operate the next morning. Can you pay for a private ward of this kind for three days?'

'Yes, this I can afford,' I replied.

That evening I reached the hospital with Saeed and sat with him till 11 at night. They had cordoned off each bed in the ward by putting curtains around the beds. It looked almost like a small private room.

Before 11pm Saeed started insisting that I head back to YWCA, 'Otherwise you won't get any food Bibi.'

I tried to convince him that I was used to getting back from the radio station by 11 at night and that my food was always kept for me in the hot case. Anyway, I said goodbye to Saeed, walked back to hostel and returned at 7 in the morning. Saeed accepted the pre-op formalities calmly and did not show any sign of nervousness. Once again he expressed concern that I might not have had my breakfast. I told him I was carrying biscuits, my toast and some fruit. He had to be on an empty stomach. Around 11am the nurse came with a wheelchair and took Saeed into the operation theatre. I walked

by his side. He seemed relaxed, and he chatted and laughed with
me. We reached the operation theatre, he got off the wheelchair, I
hugged and kissed him. He walked till the operation table with the
nurse. The in-between door was open. I saw him climb onto the
operation table, then the door closed. I went and sat outside the
operation room on a wooden bench. The corridor was empty and
absolutely silent. One or two nurses could be seen walking about
here and there. Fifteen minutes later one of them came out of the
OT and reassured me that everything was going well. She went
back in. Sitting there alone I realised how drastically my world had
changed. Two years back if any of my children even had a mild fever,
the entire family would have gathered around to be with me. Today
my son was undergoing a surgery and there was not a soul in the
hospital with me.

But this was the result of my own decision. If I had sent word
home, both his grandmothers, his aunt, his father would all have
been worried. They would have questioned me – why was I getting
the procedure done? They may even have objected. I would have
lost whatever semblance of confidence I had mustered to get the job
done. And what if one of them said they wanted to come be with me
during this time? Where would I have put them up? That is why, I
took God's name and decided to go it alone.

Another fifteen minutes passed. The nurse came and told me
the operation was over and that they would be bringing the patient
to his room in a little while. I had already stationed Yousef, the
office peon, there. Saeed was brought in sedated on a stretcher. The
nurses shifted him to the bed and warned me that when he regained
consciousness no one should speak with him. That he must remain
completely silent.

'He will only be allowed to talk tomorrow,' they said. By evening
Saeed was completely mindful and Yousef kept him entertained with
his squirrels. Thank God Saeed's condition continued to improve.
The next day he asked me rather seriously, 'Bibi were you looking
at me when I was climbing on to the operation table?... Were the
nurses watching?'

'Haan we were. Why what's the matter?'

'Nothing... I just wanted to know.'

When he asked me the exact same question again, a day later, I said, 'Why are you asking me this question again?'

Initially he refused to say anything. When I insisted he said, 'I just want to know if the nurses were also looking.'

'Maybe they were... but why are you so bothered?'

'Bibi, my knees were shaking with fear. I didn't want anyone to see that!'

'No one could have seen *that*!' I smiled and consoled him. 'The nurses were busy doing their own work and I was watching your face.'

That same evening he was discharged. I got him back to YWCA and sent prayers of gratitude to the Almighty for making such a difficult task, easy. These were the things that made me feel that 'rahmat-e-illahi' God's grace, has always been with me.

Now I had to start tackling matters connected with Saeed's admission to Sherwood. There was a lot of paperwork to wade through. I always get anxious handling such formalities as they are usually done in English and I have little confidence in my abilities in that language. The one thing I am most certain of, is myself. I decided not to stress with the nitty-gritties and shot off a request to the Principal regarding Saeed's admission. This was 1951.

One winter, while Asad was visiting me in Delhi during his vacations, as I walked into the YWCA after reading the afternoon news Harbans Lal, the waiter, came up to me and said, 'Saeed bhaiya has fever... I have been looking after him. I think it's chicken pox.'

I felt the ground slip from under my feet. I rushed into my room. Saeed was lying there in a semi-conscious state. I checked his fever, it was 105! I quickly lifted his shirt and saw bright red boils on his tummy. I thought it was small-pox, called a doctor, who told me it's probably measles or chickenpox. Immediately I went to see Mrs Jacobs.

'It's an infectious disease Saeeda, you will have to take the child to the Infectious Diseases Hospital.'

'Where is this hospital?'

'Near Kingsway camp some 12 miles from here.'

'Okay I will start making preparations to take him there.'

I can't recall exactly how many different stages of formalities and protocol I had to wade through that afternoon between one o'clock and five in the evening. After sorting all of them out, I borrowed Ajju's car and returned to YWCA just as the winter sun was setting in the twilight sky. I made Saeed lie on the back seat, Asad came and sat in the front with me.

Every year I made arrangements for Asad to stay in Delhi with one of our old friends, Ashfaq Bhai and his wife Mariam, who was an angel of a woman. She was extremely affectionate and my children lived in their house quite comfortably. But Ashfaq Husain had been transferred to the Indian Consulate in Washington. They were no longer in Delhi. Jamila, who had literally grown up in front of my eyes and was a great friend of my niece Kamman, lived in Karol Bagh with her second husband Brijbhushan. I wasn't too keen on Asad staying with her but she insisted, and I had no other arrangement in place at that time. Asad had barely been in Delhi five or six days and he used to walk down each morning from Karol Bagh to the YWCA to be with me. As I was about to get into the car, the phone rang. I was told it was for me. I stepped out, walked to the phone, and picked up the receiver. It was Jamila.

'Saeeda I have called to say I have guests coming over... I will not be able to keep Asad. Please keep him with you.'

Oh Lord, wasn't there enough chaos to start with?

I simply said, 'Fine, I will send Asad to take his stuff and come back here.' Tara Kagul, another friend was standing next to me. She had been looking after Saeed, applying cold compress on him through the morning, while I was busy running about making preparations to get him to hospital. When she saw my ashen face she asked, 'What's happened?' When I told her she said, 'You carry on, tell Asad after he gets his luggage he should come to me, I will arrange a place for him.' Tara and I had barely known each other for a year and a half while Jamila was a family friend, who had stayed at our place in Lucknow several times, our families had known each other for generations!

Anyway, I drove 12 miles to the hospital where a special room had been prepared for us. You couldn't really call it a room, it was more like a shed, closed in on all sides by four walls. It had an uncemented dirt-floor and the glass panes on the only two windows, were broken. Attached to this so called 'room' was a small shack which had a wooden commode. Near it was a solitary tap. Prior to leaving YWCA I had called my sister and asked her to send her servant Ali Husain's uncle, Nanhe, from Lucknow by the night train as I needed him urgently in Delhi.

I have no clue how my poor Asad reached from Kingsway Camp to Karol Bagh and then from there all the way back to YWCA. All I know is when he was leaving the hospital I also asked him to get Nanhe from the railway station and bring him straight to me. Asad was only 15 years old. He was just a kid. But the next morning, he reached the hospital with Nanhe in tow. He asked to stay with me but I convinced him to go back as I was worried for him. After all, this was an infectious diseases hospital. Though Tara Kagul had made arrangements for Asad to stay with some friends of hers, they were complete strangers to Asad. How would my child spend his time there? I didn't have the mental strength to even think of all of this. I had learnt to shut off several parts of my brain.

Before leaving for hospital I had gone to the radio station, met with the Director of News and informed him of the dire circumstances I was in. I also told him truthfully that I had used up all my leave for the year, if I needed to take days off now, it would be without pay and that I couldn't afford to do this. I asked permission that instead of reading news twice a day, if he could allow me to do the night bulletin. At least this way, I could still come to work. He gladly agreed.

For twelve straight days I stayed at the hospital. Each time I drove down alone, in Ajju's car, at 11 at night, crossing through Darya Ganj, the Railway Station, Kashmiri Gate and the University area to reach the hospital in the dead of night, I would give a thousand prayers of thanks to the Almighty. During this time, on the 26th of January, we celebrated Republic Day. There was heavy traffic right up till Darya Ganj. Four rows of cars were stuck on the road as everyone had stepped out to see the fireworks on this special occasion. Those twelve days were a trial by fire for me. Sometimes I wonder how on earth I managed. And all on my own. What comes to me by way of an answer is that God's blessings were with me – my car did not get a puncture the entire time. Even now when I think about those days, my head bows in thankfulness to Him.

When there is constant shortage of money, one must learn to switch one's mind off, suppress a thousand desires and simply keep cutting costs. When I think of all I went through in my life as a result of this perpetual lack of funds, it makes my heart bleed. By admitting Asad in boarding I managed to solve a major issue for myself but I failed to understand that a child has other needs as well; that emotionally he is still connected with his parents. He not only needs their love but also requires them to express their feelings towards him. Asad could not have got the love and attention one expects from parents from his teachers in Sherwood. Each week, I wrote long letters to him, but could I not have made a quick trip to see him? And yet, it wasn't possible as I never had the money. Every year they celebrated their annual Founder's Day and this was followed by the mid-term break. Most other parents visited Sherwood to see their children. I couldn't. All I could do was call my children to Delhi during their winter vacations and even that was difficult. The kids first went to Lucknow, then came to be with me in Delhi for some fifteen or twenty days. I couldn't afford to keep them for longer and these few days were only possible thanks to favours from kind friends. I was staying at a working women's hostel, where was I to keep my two boys? No one can truly understand what I went through to have them over. Sometimes they stayed with Ashfaq Bhai, one or two times at Jamila Brijbhushan's. Wherever they were made to stay the situation was most inconvenient for them. They would have breakfast then come to be with me at YWCA and after they'd had lunch, evening tea and dinner they would go all the way back to where they were staying. Two times, my friend Tara Kagul, made arrangements to put them up at her friend's place – someone I was not even acquainted with! My situation reminded me of this couplet by Asgar Gondvi: *'Chala jaata hoon hasta khelta, mauj-e-hawaadis se.'* (Laughing away playfully I pass merrily through waves of misfortune.)

When the relationship between a husband and a wife comes undone, children get badly impacted. How was it possible for Asad or Saeed to understand the problems I was facing in my life? The only thing they could comprehend perhaps, and feel, was everything they were being deprived of. Yet, despite the unpleasant circumstances they had to deal with, they always came to meet me cheerfully. Never once did either one ever complain that they were not fortunate enough to enjoy the simple joys they saw other children experiencing. Thirteen or fourteen is a difficult age in a child's life. Saeed was five years younger than Asad, emotionally he did not go through what Asad must have endured. As Asad grew older he crossed into his 'teenage' years – an extremely delicate phase in a child's life, when children become over sensitive and touchy, when they desperately need the guidance and mentoring of their parents for the protection and proper development of their self-respect and ego. How was I to get the strength and ability to deal with these stages of his life?

When a woman leaves the safe, tried and tested path of marriage and moves off the beaten track to lead her own life, she is, to begin with, severely condemned for her decision. I kept busy trying to preserve whatever bits of courage and inner resources I had, as I knew I must earn a living and support myself. As a result, I remained completely clueless of all the hardships my children were enduring at this time.

Asad's first year in Sherwood did not go off too well; he was not happy there. Principal Reverend AE Binns had been transferred and the new principal could not relate to Asad's personality. I asked Kamman and my brother-in-law Tasavur (Aqila's husband) who visited Nainital each summer, to meet with Reverend RC Llewelyn and explain to him that he needs to give closer attention to Asad in order to understand him. That the child, by God's grace, is intelligent. It really depends on the wisdom of the teachers and the principal to be able to tap the talent and abilities of a child so the latter gets motivated to study and can channel his expertise in the right direction. Thank God both the principal and staff of the school took my concern into consideration. Their changed behaviour had a positive impact on Asad. The effect of this was visible in his report card. On the sports field Asad's name always topped the medals list. Hockey, football, tennis, athletics, Mashallah, he excelled in all these games and brought home several prizes every year.

One year I finally managed to attend Sherwood's annual Founder's Day. Asad played a conspicuous role in all the sports events, and was ranked first in several of them. I have a photograph of this day.

He is holding a banner-like flag on one side and another child is holding it at the other end. Basically, Asad had made peace with his circumstances and adjusted well to boarding life. By 1951, I gathered all the courage I could and admitted Saeed into Sherwood. Saeed was an expert at hiding his feelings. Thankfully his older brother was going to be there with him. After staying with me in Delhi for two years Saeed had a good enough idea of the kind of life I was leading and knew instinctively that the comfort he was used to in his own home in Lucknow was not to be had here. Despite seeming happy within the given situation in Delhi, he immediately agreed to go to Sherwood. Once he reached boarding, he quickly acclimatized to that environment. I was satisfied knowing Asad was there – he was by now in Senior school.

12

The Forbidden Path

After Saeed left for Sherwood I felt incredibly lonely but there was not much I could do about this. Nuruddin was still visiting me, in fact he used to come every evening and each time insist I go with him to Roshanara Club. Slowly and gradually I began to be impressed by his sincerity. We would talk freely and candidly with each other about our respective children. If anyone was going to London I would shop around and make gift parcels to send on his behalf to his wife and children. I even sent them mangoes! In this fashion, quite unintentionally, the overpowering feeling of mutual understanding and friendship we shared grew stronger. I even went to the Club with him. And to the cinema. Not once did he declare any love for me, nor did it cross my mind for even a split second that we may be straying onto a forbidden path.

Several months passed, one day he asked me to have dinner with him. I agreed. He ordered food and had it brought up to his room; he was staying at the Marina hotel. After eating we were sitting about casually chatting about this and that, when all at once he got up, came and sat at my feet and said, 'Please don't get offended... but I love you.'

Ya Allah, the days were going so well! Where did this problem crop up from? And what do I do now? Our lives are totally different... our paths can never cross. Rapid thoughts were flitting across my mind like a movie reel. When he tried to embrace me, I started crying. He moved away and sat down.

Then he said, 'See I know you quite well and can understand

what's going through your mind... If there is place in your heart for me then we can continue our friendship, otherwise stop meeting me.' 'Yes we will stop seeing each other.' I replied in-between sobs. He dropped me back to YWCA. A week passed. He did not call, nor did I try to get in touch with him.

There was a natural ease and skilful cleverness in the manner in which Noor met with me, I could see nothing but sincerity in it. Now that we were apart and an entire week had passed, I realised to what extent he had made a place for himself in my heart. Every single moment of that time I missed him terribly. I felt lonely, as though my life were empty and meaningless.

Another constant refrain in my mind was, 'Whatever happened is for the best... it is better not to meet Noor. He loves his wife and children. And on no account can I neglect my children. I not only had to see to it that both were being brought-up correctly but I also had to give them a mother's love and care. Their education and wellbeing was my responsibility. If I allowed myself to get swept away by the strong current of this love, what effect would it have on my kids? Dear God, what was I to do?

Though I came across as an independent woman living life on her own terms, and without a man, I was well aware of my limitations. I also knew that I was trying my best to fulfil my responsibilities. Yes I had separated from my husband but that was after giving that decision a lot of thought. We had both arrived at the point in our marriage when staying together would have been calamitous.

On the measly salary of 350 odd rupees, I made the colossal decision to move to Delhi and live alone. The fact that I had immense courage and still do, is pure coincidence. Perhaps this was the gift of growing up in a city like Bhopal or perhaps I inherited this determination from my father who, thanks to his prudence, managed to have a rational, sane mind. He could tackle life's adversities with bold tenacity, despite the harsh treatment he received from his step-mother.

There is no arrogance in what I am writing. I have carried the heavy burden of life on the strength of my voice. I have a fiery temper but I also know when to control it. I'm a bit too frank, but I'm not in the habit of saying bitter things, criticising or even hurting anyone deliberately.

I am always grateful to the Almighty that people were eager to hear me read news on radio and appreciated my work. But I never gave this public acceptance undue importance. Hundreds of letters would pour in from various parts of the world in praise of my voice. Several gentlemen even expressed a desire to marry me! Though some of the listeners went as far as to curse me, asking that now that Pakistan had been formed why was a traitor like me still living in the enemy state? From this side of the border, some my own countrymen would write in saying, 'Get out of our country, go to Pakistan.'

After a while, this continuous barrage of reproach ended, but hordes of letters continued to arrive regularly. I didn't give them too much weightage nor did they get to my head. I met and mingled with everyone but I did not know how to tell witty jokes or interesting anecdotes, sing or even make delightful gossip at a social gathering.

The Delhi Gymkhana Club opened its membership to women. Several girls from the hostel applied. They tried to persuade me to do so as well. But I was hesitant, first because it meant my expenses would escalate and second, I still did not have my own transport. I disliked the idea of being picked up and dropped by others. The YWCA was centrally located, bang on Ashoka Road. From here I could walk to office and even to Connaught Place. Both places took care of my immediate and recreational needs. I didn't think it necessary to join a club. Basically, having a good time, going to a club, socialising with people, these things did not even strike me.

The rhythm of my life was quite regular: my time was split routinely between reading news in the morning, afternoon or evening. Depending on the time slot, I would reach office and do my bit. In between, till Saeed was in Delhi, I was busy with him. After he left, there was of course absolutely no dearth of people in the hostel, one could always find someone or the other to spend time with. By the 1950s Nuruddin had started visiting me frequently. Whenever I was free in the evenings, he would drop by. But as I've just said, we had now decided not to meet any more. This agreement lasted about a week. Suddenly one day I saw his car come into the hostel gate. My heart jumped with joy. He came, he sat, he went off; I forgot all my resolves. Then as before, he began coming over to see me. This time round, the one thought that bothered me constantly was that I should not be meeting Noor. A couple of times I even put a lock on my door and went and sat in someone else's room. He came, the watchman came upstairs to inform me, saw the lock and told him, 'Sahab she has gone out.'

Noor usually came around five in the evening; I went to the radio station two hours later. When I walked out at 7pm I saw his car parked outside the gate. He was sitting inside. He gave me a reproachful glance. I repeated the same dialogue again. 'I really don't know what to do... please forget that we ever met.' Nuruddin was silent; I couldn't get myself to say anything else. The next day, I left my room at 4pm and went to sit in someone else's; Noor came around five, the guard saw the door locked, went and informed him that I wasn't in. I did this exact same thing for the next two days as well.

On the evening of the fourth day, as I left for work at 7pm I saw his car parked outside the gate. This time there was no escape. He got out, walked towards me, looked at me accusingly and said, 'Come, let me drop you to the radio station.'

To avoid this kind of encounter one time I decided to leave YWCA before 5 and went and sat with a friend in her house and left for AIR directly from there. I tried this for a couple of days. Then Noor started coming to see me at 11 in the morning. By then my defences had grown weak, I did not put up any further resistance. When he came to see me, I was there, present, ready to meet him. The two of us would sit quietly with each other for hours, seeking refuge in innumerable cups of tea and coffee. Noor had a tremendous personality. He was a man of integrity, extremely outspoken, sincere, exceedingly intelligent and attractive.

In the early days I felt nothing towards him. I was so preoccupied with the kids and my own problems that when Noor dropped by, I was often slightly annoyed and wondered why he had come. But when he kept at it and his visits became a regular feature for a full year and a half, slowly and steadily I started liking the idea of him coming to see me.

Now that our feelings for each other had changed into something much more meaningful, another thought started tormenting me intensely – that my existence must be very painful for Noor's wife.

But these thoughts remained vague and suppressed. He would come, sit, talk reassuringly about our relationship. When he grew a bit more familiar with me, he even discussed his past affairs! Gradually I learnt that the man with such a tremendous personality had not been idle. He was always having affairs with some European lady or the other. But they were all casual attractions. This time he had become fascinated by an Indian woman. God help!

Two years back when Nuruddin came to India after leaving his family in London, he had decided to go back in the summer of 1951, when the courts closed for two months. Nuruddin Ahmed sahab was a barrister and a renowned criminal lawyer of the Supreme Court. When he left for London in June 1951, he took me to the airport to see him off.

During his absence, I once again began hatching plans. I decided that first and foremost I would not write to him, and when he returned I would simply disappear. Perhaps go to Bhopal and be with my brother. And then, we'd take it from there.

His letters continued to arrive in the mail. I did not reply to a single one. One day, without any prior information, sometime in the middle of July, his friend Dr Sharma dropped by to see me. He showed me one of the letters Noor had written, 'Send me news of Saeeda immediately. It is a matter of life and death.' I was ecstatic with joy! With my heart beating irrepressibly, I said, 'Please write and tell him, I am well.' Dr Sharma insisted I write to him myself, which I did and he replied, quoting this line from a poem by the famous Urdu poet Mirza Ghalib. '*Betaabi se har ek taar-e-bistar, khar-e-bistar hai*' (This pining for you has turned every thread in my bed to sharp thorns.)

I sat holding his letter close to my heart. Many years back I had watched a film called *Baijoo Bawra* in which the lead actress, Meena Kumari, sings a famous song whose lines resonated with what I was feeling at this time:

> '*Jo main aisa jaanti preet kiye dukh huey,
> nagar dindhora peet tee, preet na karyo koy.*'

If I had known being in love would cause such intense pain
I would have traversed the city screaming out loud, 'don't ever fall in love'.

This was my plight; but what could I do? It was clear that he could not be mine, nor I, his. Before Noor returned to Delhi, I went off to Bhopal. I left a letter for him at his hotel, saying, 'I am taking long leave of absence from work and going to stay with my brother. For God's sake end this relationship. You love your children and your wife dearly, by the grace of God, may this always be the case. Don't make me a sinner.'

Earlier, whenever I spoke with him on this topic, his reply was simply classic. 'My wife loves me a lot. For my sake she will tolerate you as well.' Then he added, 'I have done things this like before,' and topped it by claiming that those affairs were fleeting relationships which usually ended within a year or two, 'But somehow it's not the same with you!'

'Good God, what kind of logic is this? If my case is different, then that is even more disturbing! Your wife may fall ill because of us... I will be filled with remorse and guilt... our kids will be in a state of utter confusion... we have the rest of our lives left... how will we survive this?'

I couldn't get leave for more than 15 days at a stretch. After that time ended I was back in Delhi. Nuruddin constantly called the YWCA, and when he heard I had returned, he came over to see me. This time we did not need any words. He stayed as long as he possibly could. What did we speak about? I have no recollection. Discussions, arguments, logic, guilt and that unrelenting pressure on our conscience – all this was over now. He had won; I had lost. Whatever happened from this moment on in my life was written in my destiny. I could not have changed it.

I believe my voice sounded quite appealing on air. There was a request from the Ministry of Defence that the Republic Day commentary on 26th January should be broadcast in Saeeda Bano's voice. This was most probably in 1952. At the Republic Day venue the broadcaster's booth was located directly behind the VIP seating area. Whenever I got time off from doing the commentary I would go sit there. My brother-in-law Syed Ali Zaheer was close to Feroze Gandhi and that year my niece had come all the way from Lucknow to watch the Republic Day parade. She was staying with me. Earlier we had decided that Saeed would take a taxi in the morning around

6 o'clock and come straight to YWCA. Asad would reach there from St Stephens college and then my niece, Asad and Saeed would come with Feroze Gandhi to watch the grand parade and sit in the VIP enclosure.

Since I had to deliver the broadcast I was on duty from 6am and so I got busy with work. In the midst of all that was happening, when I found a bit of time, I saw my niece and Feroze Gandhi sitting in the front row; I assumed Asad and Saeed were there with them. When the parade finished, I walked quickly towards the front row where Feroze and other important dignitaries were seated. That's when both Feroze and my niece told me that Asad and Saeed had not reached YWCA. 'We waited till 9 o'clock and then left.'

We were in the midst of our discussions when Pandit Jawaharlal Nehru saw us. He came over to where we were and asked, 'What are all of you doing? Have you had breakfast? You guys have to get here so early in the morning, you must be famished. Come over to Teen Murti House... I will give you brown bread to eat... homemade brown bread.'

Who could refuse the Prime Minister of India? We reached Teen Murti House (Former residence of the first Prime Minister of India) and were made to sit in the front veranda on the top floor. Spread out in front of us were the verdant Mughal Gardens and sitting next to us, Nehruji himself. He was busy giving precise orders to the waiter to bring brown bread, cheese and God knows what. Though we were in seventh heaven my mind was preoccupied. I was worried sick and kept wondering where Asad and Saeed could be. Panditji buttered the warmly toasted brown-bread himself, then he sprinkled it lightly with salt added a dash of pepper and asked, 'Have you ever eaten bread like this?'

'No I haven't,' I replied, thanking him politely as I took the slice.

He then made another toast for me, which I ate as well. But by now I was extremely anxious. Here was the Prime Minister of our country, being hospitable and there I was worried sick with thoughts of where my children could be. Panditji saw the concern on my face and asked, 'What is the matter? What is bothering you?'

'My son is lost.'

'How old is your son?'

'Eleven.'

'Eleven year old children do not get lost… he will come. Have your tea, it is getting cold.'

In my heart I so wished Asad and Saeed could have been with me. They would proudly remember this moment, when they ate toasted brown bread prepared by the Prime Minister of India, who made the effort of sprinkling salt and pepper on it himself before handing it around to us. These thoughts were racing through my mind as we finished breakfast. Then we took permission to leave. As we were walking out, Panditji said, 'An 11-year old cannot get lost. You'll find him.'

I did a courteous adab and thanked him for his reassurance. As we reached YWCA I saw Asad and Saeed sitting there waiting for me. When I asked them where they had been, Saeed said, 'I stood at the gate trying to stop a taxi from 5.30 in the morning, but none of them stopped. Then after some time, I began to walk.' Asad said, 'I took the bus from college but it reached late. We climbed up the tree to see the parade.' I felt extremely vexed but I didn't tell the kids that I had gone to Teen Murti house.

During the days when I was staying at YWCA, I received a letter from Akhtari who, by now, had transformed herself socially into Begum Akhtar. Addressing me affectionately as 'My Dear Bittan,' she wrote, 'you have committed an extremely dishonourable act by leaving Abban Bhai.'

She then went on to fill two whole pages on this subject. Akhtari ended her letter dramatically with the opening lines of a couplet by Haider Ali Aatish,

sunn to sahee jahan mein hai tera fasana kya,
kehtee hai tujhko khalq-e-khuda ghaybana kya

Do pay heed to the stories doing the rounds
to what society says about you behind your back

I didn't reply to her letter. But a few of the other lines of the same poem kept echoing in my mind.

'tabl-o-alam hi paas hai apne, naa mulk-o-maal,
Hum se khilaaf hoke karegaa zamaana kya.'

All I have is this drum and flag, I've conquered no country amassed no
wealth,
What will the world gain turning against me?

I was amused and thought, 'how strange is life… do such things
really happen? Just yesterday Akhtari was seeking my help to get
married and lead a respectable life and here she is today, going so far
as to think she can put me in the place she was by accusing me of
being dishonourable.' But I felt no ill-will towards her. She continued
to socialise with Abban. I was content knowing that at least he has
some means of keeping himself busy. Otherwise his temperament
was such that he did not want to meet anyone nor did he consider
anyone a friend.

Several years after this episode, Akhtar phoned me and said she
would be visiting Delhi and wanted to see me. She even came over
and met me, quite affectionately. She did this whenever she was in
town. I never brought up the topic of her letter. When a woman
chooses to lead an unconventional life, it is not possible that she will
find people who will understand her or sympathise with her.

My mother was in Lucknow and I would often get this strong
urge to go meet her. A second class railway ticket in those days cost
Rs 20 and for a third class compartment the price was six rupees.
Since I didn't have the means to travel second class I bought the
cheaper one and went to her at least once a month, even if it was
only for a day. I'd call my sister from the station and she would send
a car to pick me up. And then, out of the blue I'd appear at Amma's
side with an excited adab and startle her. 'What,' she'd say joyfully,
'how come you're here?

'I had a day off so I came over.'

In that one day I would soak up as much of Amma's unconditional
love as I possibly could. I got enormous emotional strength merely
from being with her. And after reviving my tired flagging spirits I
would return to Delhi by the evening train. Those were the days
when people in our social circle did not have so much as even a clue
that there could be any other means of travelling than by car. For

long distances we journeyed in second class compartments, which back then were far superior to today's first class. Tickets could be purchased on the spot at the station. In fact all the daily necessities of life were easily available without spending a lot of money.

On 12th January 1954, my mother passed away; I remember it was a Tuesday. I reached Lucknow on the morning of the 2nd to be with her as she had been complaining of excruciating pain in her stomach for the past few days. Dr Hameed (a well-known doctor who had served as the Viceroy's Honorary doctor in Lucknow) had checked her out and his diagnosis was that she had stomach cancer.

Beevi immediately telephoned me at YWCA; I was in office. That night when I returned I learnt I had received several calls from Lucknow through the day. I dialled Beevi back at once. All she said was, 'Come as soon as you can – Amma is not well.'

Almost instantly I knew that it must be some devastating disease. I took the morning flight to Lucknow. Amma was in extreme pain. Despite that when she saw me she said, 'Ohh… how come you're here?'

'You know I keep landing up without warning… here I am.'

Amma grew quiet. She was in agony, sweating profusely. I could only look after my mother for a few short days. During this time, it was difficult to see how restless the debilitating pain was making her. Amma was physically so weak and frail, we couldn't even think of putting her through an operation. All I kept thinking was 'Ya Allah, how will my mother tolerate this pain?'

The night of Tuesday the 12th of January proved extremely tough on her. Both Beevi and I were constantly by her side, every single minute of the time. At one point, due to the agonising pain she expressed a desire to sit up. Supporting her on either side with our bodies, Beevi and I raised her to a sitting position. We heard her murmur softly, 'Dear God may everyone be blessed with daughters like mine.' I held back my tears. Those words she whispered feebly that night have stayed with me throughout my life, compensation for all the hardships and tragedies I have gone through. After completing her funeral formalities I returned to Delhi. The one pillar of strength I had in my life was now gone forever. Though my brother and sister were still there, I had thus far never taken any help from them. Nuruddin continued to be with me like he used to. He understood the grief of losing a mother and was very supportive during this time. Once again I gradually started taking control of my life. Amma was no longer there with me, but the immeasurable strength she had given me was definitely still there.

In 1952 Asad got admission to Delhi University's prestigious St Stephens College and from July of the following year he started living in Delhi. Asad was an enterprising lad. The story of how he got admission into Stephens is quite interesting. In his Senior Cambridge exams (Grade 12) Asad got top grades in all subjects except Mathematics; he scored 33 per cent in Maths and that too with difficulty. His aggregate therefore dropped. However because he was excellent in sports, and had won many prizes for his school, and he was the Sports Captain (he gave outstanding performances in hockey, football and tennis) and had also represented his team to Pakistan, the Principal of St Stephens was profoundly impressed and gave him admission.

By June 1954 I managed to rent a house on Feroz Shah Road from a Member of Parliament on condition I keep one room vacant for the MP to stay in when the Indian Parliament was in session. I gladly agreed as I still had access to one large bedroom, a drawing and dining area, the front yard, kitchen and a servant's quarter. After having lived in a working woman's hostel, this felt like a palace. Now began the search for a decent maidservant who would help me run the house. While asking around a certain Janaki sahab at AIR said, 'why don't you take my maid Sonia?'

What else could one ask for; I simply lucked out!

I had seen Sonia at his place and was well-aware of her work. Janaki was quite a cruiser, wore his heart on his sleeve but had decided to settle down and had just recently married Hope Philips. Because Sonia knew of all his past affairs, Hope used to be perpetually annoyed with her. So Sonia was packed-off to my place in a proper diplomatic manner. Janaki was a Christian so the only food items Sonia knew how to prepare were Jal Farezi (A type of Indian Chinese preparation made with marinated meat, fish or vegetables in oil and spices in a dry, thick sauce) Bhuna Gosht (pan-fried mutton with spices) Aloo ka jhol (potato curry) and pretty much nothing else. I read out many recipes from the cookbook *Asmati Dastarkhan* and taught her how to prepare a variety of dishes. On the whole, Sonia was a good cook and on a day-to-day basis the meals she prepared were quite enjoyable and satisfying.

But what a character she was! Sonia was a middle-aged woman born into a low-caste family of sweepers but she always called herself a Brahmin. She had several excellent qualities; she was extremely loyal, one-hundred percent honest when it came to money matters, extremely loving, never shirked any work (would even go buy groceries herself) had an abrupt-manner of speaking and was a master at telling white lies. When it came to her appearance, Sonia was dark-skinned with features that were nothing to write home about, but she carried herself with a great dignity and her face had immense character. Despite working with me for almost 27 years, she left with the same skill-set with which she had arrived; neither did she learn to do things in the house the way I liked them done, nor did she feel bad about getting scolded by me.

Sonia was a Hindu; the country had been Partitioned, several people incited her saying she shouldn't be working in a Muslim's house but her reply would always be, *'hamara dharam hum jaanein, tum kaun batane wale?'* 'I know my religion… who are you to teach it to me?'

She kept the kitchen awfully filthy. One day I said to her, 'you are almost as dirty as a Muslim cook.' In a voice dripping with innocence she promptly replied, 'no… not even that much.' When it came to eating, Sonia had absolutely no will-power. She would happily polish off sweets, kababs, savoury snacks, whatever she could lay her hands on. I would simply look the other way. I maintained this method of dealing with all of my servants throughout my life. Sonia was with me when both my sons got married and celebrated this occasion with immense joy and love. Then she got equally involved in raising their kids. My grandkids adored Sonia. When they grew older I would often hear her telling them, 'ohh I am only staying here because of you kids… otherwise Begum sahab… uff God save us from her!'

If I overheard her uttering this sentence and asked, 'Soniaaa… what are you saying…?' She would quickly reply, 'nothing Begum sahab… I am only telling the children a story.'

Now if I would have made a big hullabaloo, insisted that 'no…
I heard you… you were saying something else,' she would begin
to cry hysterically, the kids would be angry with me and the issue
would escalate

Sonia had two children, a son and a daughter. The girl had been
married off and the boy had fallen into bad company and become
a hoodlum. One day we got terrible news that he'd been murdered.
He was barely 24 years old. It was painful to see Sonia's condition.
I decided to take her to her house for the funeral in my car. As we
approached the area where she lived, she insisted, in-between tears,
that I leave, that she would manage to go by herself into the by-lanes
of the inner-city locality. When they saw a car approaching, quite
a few ladies from her mohalla (neighbourhood) came out of their
houses and began gathering around Sonia. They held and escorted
the distraught mother up to her house; I came back home.

The next day I sent my cook to Sonia's house to find out how she
was doing. He came back and said she was completely distraught, that
her tears would not stop. Then after a brief pause he added, 'Begum
sahab did you know she is a "bhangi" (one of the untouchable castes
of Hinduism) a sweeper. In fact the entire locality where she stays
is filled with lower caste people.' I immediately scolded him. 'Bade
miyan you believe any rubbish you hear… And even if she is a sweeper
how does that affect us…? And what are you trying to imply?'

'Nothing Begum sahab, I just thought I should tell you…
otherwise personally… for me, everyone is equal.'

'It's all right Bade miyan, if Sonia calls herself a Brahmin for us
she will always be a Brahmin. Have you understood? Don't let there
be any difference in the way you treat her from now.'

'Very well Begum sahab, that's how it shall be.'

Till he stayed in my employment Bade Miyan kept his word.
During this difficult time in Sonia's life, he went every other day to
her place to find out how she was doing.

When I shifted to the MP's house on Feroz Shah Road Asad
often came from college and stayed with me for a day or two at a
stretch. Nuruddin had also started spending more time at my place.
By now Asad was around 19 years old. Sonia was there to cook for
us, so I was relaxed on that front. But I grew extremely anxious with

the situation I was in and kept wondering, 'how should I tell Asad about my feelings for Nuruddin? He comes every day perhaps Asad has already heard something from here and there. After all who can stop people from gossiping?'

Thoughts like these kept bothering me for several days and then suddenly I felt I should simply tell Asad about the nature of my relationship with Nuruddin. Now I may have decided to tell him the truth but the dilemma was, how do I go about doing this? What words should I use to explain a situation like this to my teenage son? And what exactly was I trying to make him understand? I gathered all the courage I could find and sat down to talk with Asad. I can't recall verbatim what we discussed but I clearly remember towards the end of our conversation I said, 'Bete, if you can understand your mother's emotions and can think of staying here... of accepting this situation in your heart, then leave boarding, come stay with me. If not, then whatever decision you make – I am fine with it.'

I remain grateful to my son for the rest of my days for the simple reply he gave. He said, 'Bibi you don't need to say anything more.' A couple of days later, Asad left St Stephens boarding school and came to stay with me at 114 Kaka Nagar.

Nuruddin used to come home every afternoon, have lunch, proceed to Court and then return in the evenings. This was his routine. He usually had dinner in his own house. Sometimes I would go to the Roshanara Club with him. By this time, his older son had come back from London and was staying at 10 Alipur Road with him.

How Nuruddin and I were managing to carry on with our intimate relationship, despite having to live apart, only the two of us knew. In order to be with each other, every single day we arduously journeyed over *pul-e-sirat*, the metaphorical bridge that passes over Hell, which is supposed to be thinner than hair and sharper than a sword. Every day I would tell him, 'your bond with your family is increasing, they are about to come back from London... I have my own responsibilities towards my children... how will we manage all these commitments?'

'My wife loves me a lot... she will either accept you or leave me and go back to London.'

I was never satisfied with this answer and always found this reply rather strange. But whenever I brought up the topic, he would give me the same argument, several times, over and over again in great detail. Then he would proceed to present various logical explanations to support his argument and promise that 'As soon as Billy comes, I will tell her what the current scenario is. I am sure we will be able to work out an amicable solution.' Sitting there listening to him I would forget all my counter-arguments. Fascinated at how his mind worked I would keep staring at him. What else could I have done? I was a victim of my fate.

In January he left from old Delhi railway station for Bombay to go and get his family. I was given orders to be at the New Delhi station, since the train stopped there for ten full minutes. And I was there. He got off, came and talked to me for a few minutes and gave me many reassurances. Then the train pulled away. I came back home. Four days later he was back in Delhi. He immediately telephoned me to say he would be coming over in the evening. He came for a while. I did not ask any questions. We spoke about some other things; then he left. The one thing he used to do regularly, every single day, was telephone me before 7am. He called the next morning and then again before he went to bed. As was his routine, he came over the following afternoon, ate lunch, rested a bit and left for the Supreme Court.

After this, things changed. The next day he did not come over to the house; neither did he call me that night. Four or five days passed like this. The morning calls continued, but at night – sometimes he called, sometimes he did not. Though he continued coming over to see me in the afternoon. On the sixth day I asked, 'Have you spoken with Billy about us?'

'No… not yet,' he replied, adding 'but I will tell her… in a day or so.' I kept quiet.

Men are so unrealistically optimistic. And God knows why, for their sake, in order to believe them we women also pretend to remain in the blind-spot, though our instinct keeps sending us repeated warnings and asking us why we are being so damn foolish.

Billy had found out about our relationship when she was in London. When she reached Delhi, the wives of Nuruddin's friends filled her in with all the little details the first chance they got. On the sixth day, before Nuruddin could say anything Billy confronted him angrily saying she knew everything. An intense fight broke out between them. Instead of using this opportunity to get his wife to arrive at a mutual solution to this convoluted problem, Nuruddin began defending himself!

Now when he came over to be with me, he was visibly restless. But nevertheless he came – every single day. The morning calls also continued, though the evening ones grew erratic. After three to four days, when I asked him how things were, he admitted things were grim. 'Before I could say anything, Nikko's wife and Fakhruddin's sisters had already told Billy about us, adding more spice than necessary... the situation at home is very tense and unpleasant... everyone is against me.'

'If you had decided to tell her, you should have done so yourself, straight away.' I replied

Then once again for the umpteenth time he gave the same reply, 'It doesn't matter, Billy is so angry with me she will not stay. She will leave me and go away.' I didn't believe him for even a split-second but what could I have done? Anyway he continued coming over like he used to, though I could sense that he was now caught in a deep dilemma. My instinct was telling me Billy would not go back. Why would she give up the life of comfort she was leading here in India along with the advantages that came with being the wife of the illustrious criminal lawyer Nuruddin Ahmed to go and lead a nameless existence toiling away in London? As far as the question of Nuruddin's infidelity went, well she was used to this by now. Nuruddin was always having affairs. At one time he was involved with a German lady, then with an English woman and had even had a brief romantic fling with a Sindhi woman. The problem he was probably facing now, in his relationship with me was that he had never met someone like me. From his point of view, I was an extremely unconventional and extraordinary Muslim woman.

If one analysed him then Nuruddin was an absolute traditionalist, famous across Delhi for his rare intelligence and distinguished personality. God knows in what moment of youthful weakness he ended up marrying a Jewish woman while he was in London. When they came back to India, Nuruddin's maternal grandmother, who one hears was extremely authoritarian, converted his English bride into a Muslim and named her Bilqees, which became Billy or maybe that was her name to begin with which is why they chose Bilqees. Anyways, his granny compelled Billy to start wearing Indian clothes and proved successful in domesticating her and turning her into a typical Indian housewife.

Billy must have definitely loved Nuruddin madly, otherwise no English woman would have agreed to adapt themselves, this wholeheartedly, to another culture in such a cheerful accepting manner. They went on to have four children, two boys and two girls. The eldest daughter passed away with typhoid fever when she was barely 14-15 years old. Both Billy and Noor shared the burden of this grief; common sorrow strengthens marital bonds.

Perhaps Nuruddin saw himself as being irresistible to women or then perhaps I came across to him as an educated progressive-minded, independent Muslim woman, one who matched up to his expectations of what a woman should be. Though Nuruddin was a staunch traditionalist, when it came to himself, the rules were different; everything was permissible. Even though he was extremely honourable, trustworthy and liked by everyone, at heart he was really an old fashioned gentleman. He had his flings and flirtations yet he kept a tight grip on his deep-rooted desire to keep his family together. After meeting me he was faced with a strange dilemma and found himself stuck at the proverbial fork in the road.

If one marries a woman from another culture, she can definitely love her husband intensely but she cannot provide that familiarity and oneness which a man feels when they marry a woman belonging to the same ethnicity, who speaks the same language. Which is why sooner or later, in cross-cultural marriages, a certain emptiness creeps in. This vacuum was perceptible in Nuruddin's life. After staying in Delhi for five years without his wife, he probably saw in me flickers of all those qualities he had secretly been yearning for in a woman and had till then not even acknowledged to himself.

In 1955 when Billy returned to India, Nuruddin was faced with a difficult predicament. He would come over to my place during the day like he had been doing and would have lunch with me. I was also spending time with him in the way we were used to. But our hearts were heavy with guilt. One day he suddenly dropped by in the evening and asked me to go somewhere with him. Ever since Billy had returned, I had completely stopped going out with him in public. That day when I refused he said, 'Just come till Lodhi Garden bridge. I need to talk to you.'

Lodhi Garden was a stone's throw from my house; I agreed. We drove off. When we reached the bridge he stopped his car. For a couple of minutes we sat there silently. Then he began talking about all sorts of things... about Billy... about himself... I don't quite remember everything now but what I remember most vividly, is the last sentence he uttered. 'Billy is threatening me a lot I will have to break up with you.'

I stared dumbfounded at him. He was crying. 'Dear God, must one live to see this as well?' I thought to myself. And is this the same man who quoted Ghalib to me while we were apart, that '*Detuubi se har ek taar-e-bistar, khar-e-bistar hai*' (This pining for you has turned every thread in my bed to sharp thorns.) The man who had me believe he could not live without me, who kept repeating, 'Billy is so devoted to me she will accept you.' Once when he was in London and I had not replied to his letters for two full months, he sent his friend to find out how I was doing saying 'Find out how Saeeda is and write back immediately – it is a matter of life and death!' And that same man is telling me today to bury the deep love we have shared for the past five years with one another?

I heard him out and decided not to create a scene though I was crying uncontrollably. I don't recall how we said goodbye to each other but I took the next day off from work and went to Nangal to be with my nephew. I stayed there 15 days. Each day felt like what Ghalib has written so perceptively in one of his poems: '*qayamat ka bhi hoga koi din aur?*' (Can anything be worse than the day you left me?)

It felt like the end of the world to me. But I knew I had to come back and face reality, and that is exactly what I did. The emptiness in my house felt unbearable; I would wander about all day restlessly thinking 'O God, how will I wade through the rest of this long arduous life without him?' In my head I compromised with various situations I believed were quite practical. If he could come and meet me for only half an hour every day – I would accept that. If he couldn't come, but agreed to speak with me on the phone, that too would be enough. After all what else was there for me to do? I had tried desperately to make sure that our love did not turn into a painful episode. Right from the beginning I had told him not to start something we would not be able to handle later. And when he insisted that everything would work out fine, I thought how naïve he was. But I never disbelieved him. How could I? After all he would speak with me for hours on this subject.

On my part, I tried my best to make him understand that there is no wife in this entire world who would willingly share her husband's love with another woman. Of course it's different if the woman has no choice or if it's part of her religion or culture. But Billy was British. And while women in the West accepted their husbands' infidelity they would not tolerate another woman becoming a permanent part of their husband's life while they were still married to him. And here she was, having to face a strange predicament – Nuruddin was looking to strengthen his relationship with another woman and expected his wife and kids to accept this convoluted situation in a mature manner. How could this even be possible? But Nuruddin kept repeating, 'Billy will agree.'

But that is not what happened.

After getting back from Nangal I spent the entire day feeling extremely uneasy and restless. Around dusk the doorbell rang. I opened the door and saw Noor standing there. Good God now what do I do? He moved me to one side, walked in, shut the front door behind him. Taking my hand in his, he led me to the sofa. We sat down. He didn't speak a single word nor did I. I have no idea how long the two of us sat like this, it must have grown dark outside because I heard Sonia's voice saying, 'Begum sahab should I serve dinner?'

I looked up at the clock, it was 8.30 at night. Noor immediately said, 'No, I will not have dinner. Khudahafiz. I will come tomorrow.' And once again his wish was my command.

True to his words he was there the next morning. Then he started coming over the way he used to. He would have lunch with me and leave. If he had a case in the Supreme Court he would leave early, otherwise he would spend the extra time at my place. I didn't taunt him and say, 'Oh, but you wanted to break ties with me.' The only thing that changed was that he no longer dropped by in the evenings like he used to. Gradually he opened up and told me that there was a lot of tension in his house. Putting my own intense feelings for him aside I said, 'Then don't come to see me.' This time he didn't give the same old lines. He simply remained silent. And several months passed like this.

In August my sister came over from Lucknow to stay with me. By now I was earning Rs 525 a month. Asad was in St Stephens. He had left boarding and was living with me. Saeed was studying in La Martiniére Boys, Lucknow. Financially we were always in a bit of a tight spot, though somehow or the other we managed. I didn't have the means to buy furniture and decorate the entire house all at one go. I had thought of doing up my place bit-by-bit by either buying a few pieces at a time or getting them made. As soon as Beevi arrived she began objecting. 'What is this Saeeda, why can't you buy inexpensive pieces and do up the entire house?'

I was getting a set of two cane stools and one settee, which was almost like a sofa, for twenty rupees. Beevi insisted I should buy them and then look into getting them re-upholstered. I didn't want to settle for just about anything, after all I had the good fortune of living in a proper house after ages. Anyway, at different times, on three separate occasions Beevi pressured me to buy the cane sofa-set and when I sought refuge in silence, she turned to me and said, '*rassi jal gayee bal nahee gaya.*' It's a Hindi idiom which simply means 'even after suffering so much, you have ego issues?' Perhaps she was right. I was like a charred piece of burnt rope.

I had taken on the gamble of life, without any support, on a meagre salary of a little over 500 rupees a month. I had no other money to my name, nor did I have anything tucked away in some bank, neither was there anybody who I could fall back on. Even my mother had passed away; she was perhaps the only person I could have asked for help. The truth hurts terribly. When I heard Beevi's caustic remark, tears welled up in my eyes but I did not utter a single word in reply. Seeing how her words had hurt me, Beevi grew silent.

As sisters we often had such tiffs. She loved me a lot but she also quarrelled with me. I believe the reason for this was that by nature my sister was the mature serious kind. I, on the other hand, was exactly the opposite. Till I was fifteen years old, she completely dominated over me. As a child I wore what she chose and was totally under her influence. But by the time I turned sixteen my own personality started to come to the forefront; I began developing traits Beevi did not approve of. Beevi was barely seventeen when she was married off. At seventeen, I was playing hockey in IT college, winning Inter-College Tennis championships and participating in various outdoor games. To top it all I was lively, mischievous, free-spirited; at this age, my sister had already given birth to her first child.

After growing up in a place like Bhopal where women led a privileged existence, Beevi was married into the suffocatingly patriarchal Lucknawi society, where she fell easy prey to the fierce taunts of an extremely ill-tempered mother-in-law. Despite this she tried to manoeuvre the ups and downs that are part and parcel of married life, in a cheerful and virtuous manner. The self-control and forbearance with which she handled the constant pressure she was exposed to, eventually took its toll on her. Beevi would often get excruciatingly painful migraines which kept her in bed several days at a stretch, unable to so much as even move. If I happened to meet her, she would take out her entire frustration on me.

After the birth of her first daughter, my brother-in-law went off to London to study law. For those two years Beevi came to stay with us in Bhopal. I was seventeen and became extremely close to my little niece Sakina, whom we call Kamman. I still love her immensely. Later on, Beevi had three more kids. Each one is tremendously dear to me. When Beevi fell ill or was overwhelmed with any situation, I took on the responsibility of looking after her and nursing her back to health. But because I was much younger than she was, the relationship we shared remained that of an adult and a mere child. We didn't have the kind of bond that develops between siblings who are closer in age. My brother was also six years older than me and both Beevi and he often tried to boss me around. I was very obstinate. I wouldn't back-chat nor was I rude but I wouldn't listen to them either. Since the atmosphere at home was filled with love and affection, I soon forgot the anger I felt towards my two siblings.

I was called several names at home, happy-go-lucky, arrogant, peevish, weepy, angry... and God knows what else but I was also seen as an affectionate and loving child. And thanks to the love and acceptance I got from both Amma and Miyan, my shortcomings kept morphing into positive traits. My father had four step-brothers who I believe were always against him. But Miyan got good jobs for all of them in Bhopal and helped them throughout his life. I have heard my mother taunt Miyan and say, 'Those people keep bad-mouthing you and you just keep forgiving them.' His reply was always the same. 'So should I also become like them?'

According to the standards of those times my sister Aliya Zaheer was an educated girl. She spoke fluent English and knew all the rules of social etiquette – a skill which in reality is simply a result of the trust a person has in their own accomplishments and abilities. In terms of worldly possessions, Beevi did not lack for anything. She was after all the daughter in law of Sir Wazir Hasan and Lady Wazir Hasan[49] the wife of Syed Ali Zaheer[50] a renowned barrister and politician from Lucknow and the mother of four healthy beautiful competent children.

Beevi had made a name for herself by working on several social welfare programmes and she was eventually appointed Chairperson of the Central Social Welfare Board. Despite this, she lacked the innate confidence and the emotional resilience that allows a person to accept everyday disappointments cheerfully and which helps them to stay happy and keep those around them satisfied. As she grew older Beevi began to show signs of a strange duality in her personality. Her mother-in-law and her sisters-in-law could be extremely cruel and critical, completely oblivious to the fact that they had hurt someone's feelings. This was their basic personality; there are people

---

[49] An Indian jurist who became the first Indian Chief Justice of the Awadh Chief Court (1930–1934). He was also President of the All-India Muslim League. His wife Sakinatul Fatima was known as Lady Wazir Hasan. Famous for her bluntness and fiery spirit she discarded purdah in 1931 when Gandhi launched the Civil Disobedience Movement.

[50] Indian politician and minister in Prime Minister Jawaharlal Nehru's cabinet.

like that in this world. My sister, however, was brought up by principled parents, in an atmosphere of love, affection and empathy. When she said angry bitter things to hurt anyone she would become extremely restless. Afterwards when she had calmed down and her inner goodness surfaced, she would go through a strange sort of mental disturbance. This split in her personality began to manifest itself in Beevi's day-to-day life. She met guests cheerfully but turned moody and irritable with her husband, children, servants and close relatives. Because she was much older than most of us, we tolerated her behaviour. But the person worst hit by this constant unrelenting irascibility was Beevi herself. As a result she forgot how to stay happy and then slowly and gradually Beevi started to forget who she was. In the last few years of her life she could not recognise anyone at all.

During the initial days of her battle with Alzheimer's, Beevi would sit by herself, a deck of cards in hand, playing Patience as the last traces of her inconsistent memory flickered to make their final escape. After a while she stopped doing this and could be seen sitting alone, silently. She hardly ate and grew progressively weak till she couldn't even get out of bed. Then one day, long after her memory was all gone, her soul broke free. Beevi passed away in her sleep.

When Beevi visited Delhi she mostly stayed with me at my place. In those days, there was a broker, who got after my life to buy a 500 square yard four bed house in Chankayapuri which was being sold for Rs 50,000. Forget Rs 50,000 I didn't have even 5,000 to my name! I mentioned this to Beevi and said, 'Give me 50,000 rupees from Amma's money. I will mortgage the house in your name and if I am not able to pay you back, the house is yours.' Beevi's reply was that Amma's money was all tied up in shares and could not be touched. I found her answer quite distasteful but kept quiet. This topic ended here. I didn't get the house. There was absolutely no question I would be able to arrange that kind of money by myself. Two or three months after this incident, Beevi told me she had bought two plots of land in my name in Bhopal, that each plot was 1500 square yards. I heard her out but didn't comment. In my head I was thinking because she had refused to loan me the money to buy land in Delhi, she has compensated by buying land for me in Bhopal. Another few months passed. Once again Beevi was visiting

Delhi and staying with me. Usually when she came, I was busy in office. Since Beevi was the Chairperson of the Social Welfare Board she was involved in several social projects which kept her extremely occupied as well. One day, however, it so happened that we both had some free time. While we were sitting and chatting, she mentioned the land she had bought for me in Bhopal and said, 'You don't have any money. Can I give one plot to Kamman and keep the other for myself?'

I was shocked and wondered what on earth had happened to this sister of mine who claimed to love me so much? Controlling my irritation, I asked her, 'Then why did you buy land in my name in Bhopal?' That was when I found out that Nawab sahab Bhopal told my brother that he wanted to give every Bhopali approximately 1500 square yards of two plots each for just one rupee per square yard. To begin with Beevi could have bought two plots in her own name, as she was also a Bhopali, but because her husband was a well-known barrister in Lucknow and was a minister in the central government, he did not want his name associated with Bhopal. This is why they could only buy the two plots in my name. And this is what they did.

After hearing these details, I said only one thing to my sister, 'You are older than me, I can't talk back to you, but I do want to say this, I will pay 3,000 rupees to you and the plots will remain in my name.' We never had any conversation regarding land ever again. After about a year, I took fifteen days off, went to Bhopal during my vacation and asked my brother for the papers of the land. He gave them to me. I complained to him and asked him quite boldly, 'Why didn't the two of you think of my wellbeing?' I didn't consider Nawab sahab Bhopal's offer of giving us land as anything short of a miracle. And here I was without the faintest inkling that I might be able to actually buy land or even a house for myself without anyone's help. That day, God's benevolence made this possibility a reality for me.

After living in Kaka Nagar I moved to Cornwallis Road. In September 1955, while I was still in Kaka Nagar, Nuruddin was asked to accompany a delegation to China. It was a month long tour during which he had to travel across several cities gathering information about their living conditions etc. His flight was at 2am. The night he was leaving there was a heavy downpour. I did not have a telephone line in my house. My niece, Hammi, was working at the radio station for some French programme. She used to leave for AIR at around nine at night and return by two in the morning. A car would pick her up and drop her back. Fed up with the incessant rain, I went to the radio station and kept calling the airport to find out if it was safe for the plane to take off in such poor weather. The world was a simple place back then, far from what it is now where kindness has completely vanished. The duty officer at the airport enquiry desk spoke politely and reassured me in every way possible that it was safe for the plane to fly. When I called back one final time at about 2am he told me the plane had taken off safely.

After a month Nuruddin returned from China and came straight to my house from the airport. He gave me whatever gifts he had brought for me, sat for a while, then left for his own place. The next day when he came over to see me, he seemed a bit withdrawn and quiet. I was used to all his moods and didn't think of asking what the reason was. After a short pause he asked, 'Why were you phoning Billy? And why did you tell her that I come to your place every day? And what was the reason for telling her how much time I spend with you…? And yesterday you even told her I came straight to your house from the airport?'

Shocked at his outburst my only reply was, 'I'm not going to say anything in my defence, except that I have never telephoned Billy in my life.'

'Then who has been giving her all these details?'

'I don't know…'

'Maybe Jamila Brijbhushan did? She has met me at your place before,' Noor asked, trying to guess.

'Ya… maybe… but she wouldn't have news of us meeting every day.'

He knew me well enough to know I don't lie. Nevertheless he was puzzled about who knew so much about us and was keeping Billy informed. Not that he stopped coming over but now when he did, he looked extremely tense and whatever peace we had for a couple of hours, ended. My apartment in Kaka Nagar was on the first floor.

One day, it so happened that Noor walked towards my bedroom window and was standing lost in thought when he looked out and saw a white imported car parked downstairs.

'Whose car is that?' He turned and asked, 'Who lives downstairs?'

'The station director Mr Mathur.'

'But... this car belongs to Bahadur, Mathur's wife's brother,' Nuruddin said.

'I don't know any of this Nooram...'

'Hmmm, so this is the story... you see, Bahadur's wife is an Englishwoman and she has been spying on us.'

Well, now at least we knew that it was Bahadur's wife and daughter who were giving Billy minute by minute updates about us. But what was the solution? How were we to deal with this problem?

In the days I am writing about, the world was a decent place. Power and position had not corrupted the minds of top government officials. Mr Ranganathan, an ICS (Indian Civil Services) officer, was Secretary of the Housing Ministry. I made a call to his Personal Assistant and asked for an appointment to meet with him. Within three of four days the PA called back to tell me my meeting had been fixed. I met Mr Ranganathan and told him I have an old maid who is finding it difficult to climb stairs to the first floor. I requested him to move me to a ground-floor house. He heard me out, was most sympathetic and issued immediate orders that whichever ground floor flat gets vacated next should be allotted to Mrs Raza.

A few days later, while chasing up on this matter I got to know that 13 Cornwallis Road had been allotted to a person who was extremely superstitious; that gentleman did not want to live there simply because according to numerology the number 13 has an ominous connotation. I responded to this piece of good news by writing to the authorities to please consider transferring that house in my name as I had no such false beliefs!

In March 1956 I moved to 13 Cornwallis Road. I recall quite clearly that the government departments back then functioned so efficiently that my telephone line was installed from 114 Kaka Nagar to 13 Cornwallis road that very same day. The same year Asad completed his Bachelor's degree. The question now was how to find him a job. I didn't want to take anyone's help in this matter and my own network was quite limited. Though a lot of people in Delhi knew me as they had heard me read news on radio, but I never really socialised much with anyone. My mornings, afternoons and nights were spent juggling my shifts at the radio and my spare time was spent romancing!

Asad decided to sit for the Indian Administrative Services exam. I was a bit concerned as he was not the studious kind but had managed thanks to his intelligence. When I heard his decision I was a bit hesitant as the IAS exam requires sustained hard work. But then I agreed. Asad enthusiastically began studying for the Civil Services. When the exam date drew closer he invited two of his friends to come and stay at our place, saying if all of them were together they would study harder. None of this was going to make a major difference to me (I was at work most of the time) but the story was different for Sonia who had to cook more food and also had to fulfil their constant demands for tea and coffee through the day.

One day, out of the blue, Asad got an interview call from Air India. He left his friends, went off to Bombay and was immediately given an appointment letter and asked to join their Bombay office within a week. He came back to Delhi, gathered his stuff and left for Bombay immediately. His two friends, Sushil and Ibrahim stayed on at our place. They sat in our drawing room studying away, drinking innumerable cups of coffee all night. Every morning, Sonia muttered something or the other and argued with me about the extra work she was handling. I tried to console and keep her happy the best I could. Sonia had this amazing quality. She could easily forget her troubles and get busy with work.

Two months after Asad left for Bombay I was turning out weeds in the garden when what do I see, Asad entering the house! I was elated. When I asked him how come he was back, he said his training was over and now he would be posted in Delhi as a sales officer. The news made me very happy. We already had a house, we could stay together and my loneliness would also be over. Until this time the relationship I shared with Asad was extremely good; if guests came to stay at our place and we ran out of space he would come and sleep in my bedroom. We welcomed many a New Year together playing cards with each other. I had no social life as such. Asad was content with his group of friends. I was either at office or would spend the day at home. When Nuruddin came over I would spend time with him, otherwise I would keep busy reading or writing. Sometimes, a few of my friends would also drop by; that was the extent of my social life. By this time I had bought myself a car. It was a convertible Sunbeam and cost me Rs 3,500. Asad's small group of friends was expanding and he would often ask for my car and go off to meet them in the evening. I never objected. This was probably around 1958. Little by little, Asad began coming home late. I used to read the morning news and according to my schedule, I had to be in office by 7. This meant I had to get up by 6 in the morning. When Asad came late, my sleep would get disturbed and I would find it difficult to wake up early. Initially Asad was apologetic about this but after a while he began disliking the fact that I was telling him off. Over time this unpleasantness became a sore point between us.

Around this time Asad got married to a young lady by the name of Salima. Despite my limited means, I made all arrangements for his marriage with great affection and eagerness and we even managed to do all the ceremonies with considerable pomp. I had the wedding invitations printed from Begum Mohammed Raza's side as she had not yet left for Pakistan. We sent invitations to Nehruji and Mrs Pandit as well. In fact we went personally to deliver Nehruji's card. What golden days those were when a commoner like me could have access to the Prime Minister. Nowadays all the Ministers of our country roam about in bullet-proof vests and have armed bodyguards stationed constantly outside their homes.

When Asad and I went to deliver Nehru's card, he greeted us warmly and personally welcomed us into his office. Asad was completely floored by his easy style of conversation. I also came back rather satisfied. Mrs Pandit sent a gift for the couple and Nehru sent a letter of felicitation along with an apology that he would not be able to attend as he had an important engagement.

All of us – members of my family and I – welcomed Salima to our house. But slowly and steadily Asad became quite rebellious towards me. He would often tell me, 'Salima has a happy family.' Asad was young, how could I explain to him that there was no way I could recreate, the same joyful well-settled atmosphere in my home that he saw in Salima's? How could I expect him to understand that I slog from morning to night, that despite my meagre salary I am shouldering the responsibility of my kids, and more, that I was involved in a futile relationship with a man? We had no lively parties at my place, we never went out for movies or dinners or even so much as a picnic.

Like a soldier, my life continued to move ahead in a predictable fashion. All sorts of exciting exhibitions would come and go, I wouldn't so much as wander, even by mistake, in their direction. In 25 or 30 years I must have gone to the cinema no more than on two occasions. We were always so short of money that I am sure Asad must have also felt the pinch several times. For example, I remember he was to go to Lahore as the captain of his sports team and I started telling him off about having too many expenses. Ideally I should have been happy for him, expressed some sort of encouragement at that time, but I couldn't do this. This upset Asad; we exchanged some unpleasant remarks. It was only later that I realised how wrong I had been. It's so difficult to explain what the constant shortage of money actually does to a person; it changes them for the worse. Asad went to Lahore and came back victorious. But on this special occasion I failed to create the atmosphere of joy and jubilation that I ideally should have.

Despite my own shortcomings I had full confidence that Asad would be able to understand my situation and for a long time he did. About a week after their wedding, both Asad and Salima came to me and said they wanted to take up a house in Patel Nagar and live on their own. I agreed, but only my God is witness to what I felt emotionally at their decision. I could not sleep the entire night. Asad, however, showed some consideration for my feelings and added, 'Bibi if we are unable to manage by ourselves... we will come back here.'

I didn't say anything; after all I had already given my consent.

For three full days I was extremely restless. Then I said to Asad, 'Bete, I want to say a few important things to you. Firstly, a relationship between two people grows when they live with one another. If Salima and I stay together we will get the opportunity to understand each other. This is how tolerance, love and affection develops between people. Secondly you have just started working; your income is not that much. I have a two bedroom house. Circumstances dictate that you should not bother about a house, a servant, rent and the burden of running a home for the time being. When you have the means, you can have a place of your own. Thirdly, your in-laws are communists, they will somehow manage to go all the way to Patel Nagar in West Delhi, but I am a victim of my environment and habits. I will not be able to reach that side of town. Lastly, if Salima does not know what it's like to live with me, then when I get old and a time comes when I may have to move in with you, I will not feel comfortable doing this.' Asad heard me out patiently and after a week he came to me and said, 'Bibi we have changed our minds we will stay here with you.' I heaved a sigh of relief. After this we stayed together for about six years. Yes, we had a few misunderstandings but nothing that could not be sorted.

On the 9th of February in 1960, Asad and Salima had a beautiful baby girl. I was beside myself with joy. Mashallah I had two lovely sons, but it had always been my deepest desire to have a little girl. Now that Asad had a daughter it felt as though my wish had come true.

'I will bring up this child,' I told Salima.

'Zaroor for sure Bibi, she is your daughter as well.'

My mother liked the name Chunmun. I suggested this as the baby's nickname, everyone agreed. The formal name chosen for her was Huma Fatima. Every day was now Eid for me and every night, shabb-e-raat (a night of worship and salvation) Sonia and I were completely engrossed in taking care of baby Chunmun. For the initial seven or eight months, the mother stayed with the baby. Then in December 1960 Asad and Salima went to London for two weeks and I brought Chunmun into my bedroom.

The only one problem with Salima's trip to London was that the Indian government was handing out a measly 25 pounds, in total, as stipend towards expenses for the trip. One could not get even two meals a day in that country for that amount. The two of us put our heads together and came up with the idea that we should buy a lot of saris, which she could sell in London to get some extra money. We were sure the goods would sell as we knew lots of people in London.

We began making rounds to Chandni Chowk (one of the oldest and busiest markets in Old Delhi) and were thoroughly enjoying ourselves buying saris. I also ended up getting one for myself. It was a South Indian sari for Rs 150 which was either made in Madras or Bangalore. At that time this seemed very expensive and I regretted having spent so much money on myself. I still have this sari with me; it is now worth almost Rs 2,000 or perhaps even more.

13

The Rhythm of Life

———— ❧ ————

Time moved on, my routine stayed the same. Nuruddin's entire family, including all his children, had moved back to Delhi. But he would still come to my place, as he had been doing, every single day. He would have lunch with me, rest a bit, then leave. If for any reason he couldn't make it during the day, he would definitely drop by at night, even if it were just for 15 minutes. I had cheerfully accepted the way things were going between us. His wife did not acknowledge my existence, nor did she go back to London, as he had predicted. Though Nuruddin tried several times to reassure me that she would.

During this time, on 14th August 1961, Asad and Salima were blessed with a baby boy. We named him Aamer Mumtaz Raza. His pet name was Pipo. Sonia got busy raising both the kids. She loved them immensely. We also employed another maid to help with the housework.

As the children became older, they grew delightful. Chunmun often eyed one of Nooram's rings. In order to indulge her he would take it off and give it to her to play with. Excitedly she would put it on her tiny little finger, walk about dangling it babbling, 'thee my ling… thee my ling,' in her small childish voice. Pipo was also pampered but temperamentally both kids were quite different; Pipo was serious and quiet, while Chunmun was always laughing and playing about. She was a chubby little thing, constantly somersaulting and tumbling all over the place. If we enrolled them in a beauty competition for toddlers, both would have won first prize.

Like other children they were also obstinate at times. They cried and threw tantrums but on the whole they were cheerful kids. As soon as Nuruddin came home, he would get busy with them. Usually he entered the house carrying bags of fresh fruit. Then he'd start playing with Pipo and Chunnu. After lunch when he would go to lie down, both children would run and nestle on either side of him then doze off. After a while Noor would leave for office or go back to his own house. In the course of time he became exceedingly fond of my grandchildren. It gave me immense pleasure to see Noor happy and relaxed. He was facing a lot of tension as there was no joy left in their home. My existence was a perpetual thorn in Billy's married life.

One day Noor came home looking extremely sad and disheartened. We sat about silently for a long while then he said, 'Someone from my office called me today, he is a clerk. I know him... he told me he had seen an official announcement on the office board about Ameena's marriage to Ahuja. You must be aware of this?'

'Yes I am,' I replied.

Noor held his head in his hands and sat there looking deeply distressed. Then he turned to me and asked, 'What should I do?'

'Now that you know what is going on, tell Billy that you are aware of the notice on the board,' I replied. I don't know what happened after this. I did not ask and Noor did not mention anything. What did happen though was that one fine day Ameena left for Moscow. She stayed with the Indian Ambassador for a month, and then she married in Moscow. Whatever I heard about her after the wedding was from Nooram. But I don't know the details. On the basis of the fact that Ameena has the right to meet with her mother, Noor allowed her to come to his house. What I heard was that she stayed with him but her husband stayed at the Meridien hotel. I often told Noor that if he had accepted the fact that she had married a Hindu without his permission, he must also forgive her husband. He adored his children and undeniably loved his wife, but in the heat of the moment, many hurtful things were said, which could not be taken back.

Both my grandchildren were growing up. In 1963 we admitted Chunmun to a kindergarten close by. Sonia would walk her down every morning and then go back around 11 o'clock to pick her up. Chunnu took no time in making friends and mingling with the other kids. One day when Sonia went to get her she came back saying Chunmun was not in school. It was 12 in the afternoon; Noor was home. Salima and I immediately got in the car and drove down to the school and began asking around if anyone had seen Chunnu. There was a children's park across the road, we rushed there to look for her. Salima was extremely tense, I was trying to remain calm, then we saw Noor's car racing down the road. He told us Chunnu had reached home. We all heaved a huge sigh of relief. When we asked Chunnu where she had been, she said innocently, 'I came home with the washerwoman's daughter.' She was barely four. 'You must never do this again,' I said. Then I sat her down and explained why we were so worried, that sometimes children get kidnapped and so on. She never did anything like this again.

In April 1965 Asad got transferred to Bahrain as Assistant Manager of Air India. While I was delighted to hear this, the news made me sad. I was thrilled Asad was doing well and getting promoted. Salima would finally get a chance to set-up her own home – something every daughter-in-law desires, but this meant the kids would be going away. I was extremely attached to them and loved both intensely. They were equally happy staying with me. Noor also disliked the idea of the children leaving because for as long as he would be at my place they were stuck to him. We spent some wonderful days when we stayed together for which I am extremely grateful to Salima. In my experience grandkids are usually more attached to their maternal grandparents. They form a strong bond with the paternal ones if the daughter-in-law allows it. I have often told my friends that I am indebted to my daughter-in-law for letting her children become close to me. Now our friends and family members started inviting Asad for farewell parties. One day I suggested, 'Why don't we also have a party for all your friends at our place Asad? How many would you like to call?'

'Ji… some 35?' he replied.

Our two-bed house at Cornwallis Road had a large lawn and a spacious back yard. We decided to host the party in the front lawn. In those days I had a trained cook as well as a boy named Abdul to help with the extra work; he was equally adept at his work. I didn't have to worry about anything. When the big day came, we placed chairs around the lawn and methodically arranged the tables in such a way that the vegetarian food would be separate from the non-vegetarian. One after the other guests started arriving in small groups. Along with juice, alcohol was also being served. Finally it was time for dinner. Salima and I were discussing which one of us should go to the kitchen to supervise this process when Asad came and said, 'Bibi I have just invited another 15 people.'

I felt a bit apprehensive. We could fall short of food, but I said nothing to Asad and went straight to the cook and asked him what we should do. 'Don't worry. It's okay,' he said confidently. In any case there was nothing I could have done at that moment, so I put my faith in God and served dinner. And we did not fall short of food! Later, a few women, all of whom were pure vegetarians, came up to me and said the raita, yogurt with vegetables, was extremely tasty. I thanked them politely but had no idea what they were talking about. But then, when I examined the food, I realised that what they were relishing and helping themselves to again and again was not yogurt but a continental chicken dish called Chicken Fricasse! If we served it the way it had been prepared, we would have fallen short of food. So the ingenious cook simply added milk to the creamy white gravy and increased its quantity. It now looked like a runny yogurt. I sought refuge in silence and kept my mouth tightly shut throughout dinner! A few days later Asad left for Bahrain. Shortly afterwards he called Salima and the kids to be with him. The house became depressingly silent. But I had to learn to endure this as well as I had everything else.

In the same month I retired from reading Urdu news and was appointed as Producer for AIR's Urdu Majlis. The nature of my job was completely different now. To add to this there was a huge change in my personal life. Nuruddin had become Mayor of Delhi city and it was extremely difficult for him to come over to my house as easily as he used to. The Government of India had allotted him an official car. He did not want to come to see me in this. So what he would do is get off somewhere and then take a taxi to Cornwallis Road. This meant he had no fixed timings anymore and could drop by pretty much whenever he found a window of opportunity, in the evening, morning or sometimes even 11 at night! Yet not a single day passed when he did not come to be with me or telephone me early in the morning, there wasn't a day that he skipped calling me at night only to say shabba khair (good night). How he managed to do this, I have no idea. Whatever time and attention he could give was more than enough for me. But oh! The mental anguish he must have endured. His nerves must constantly have been on edge. I knew what he was going through. To begin with he had high blood pressure. On top of that, he continuously had to face one intensely stressful situation after the other – the pressure of being Mayor of Delhi, tackling complicated criminal cases in Court, shouldering innumerable problems at home and to make matters worse, there was my presence in his life.

I often fought with him and demanded, 'How long can we go on like this?' Our heated face-offs turned bitter, we would reach a point of brutal honesty. He would get furious and walk out of the house. I would sit there holding my head in my hands. A couple of hours later what do I see? Noor walking in. He would come sit next to me and say, 'I desperately need some peace... if you also keep getting upset with me where will I go?' And I would think to myself, 'I wish he didn't have to say this to me.' We were both living out what was already written in our destiny. Whenever he walked off in a rage, I reproached myself severely for what I had said. When he came back, my anger and my principles simply vanished. I was ready once again to carry my cross and walk on.

Back in 1953 I told Asad, 'Bete, I do not want you to hear rumours about me from here and there. Nuruddin is a very special part of my life. If you can accept this, please stay with me, otherwise you can stay in the boarding at St Stephen's College.' Today when I think of what I had said to my young son, my head spins. After all, that age is such a difficult and tricky one for a boy. Now imagine a mother trying to explain to her teenage son that she is feeling emotionally helpless for a man! I am not claiming to be a person with outstanding morals, but several times it has happened to me that my honest and frank nature has enabled me to overcome the most difficult situations in life.

Allan Bhaiyya and Beevi met Nuruddin in 1950. I introduced them to Noor, without bothering to think what they might think of us or our relationship. I am sure I had quite a reputation in society! People must have spoken ill of me and associated me with all sorts of terrible things. But my children, my relatives and friends trusted me and allowed me to lead my life with dignity, the way I had chosen to live it. They never made me feel ashamed of myself. Not only did they treat me with respect but also maintained a dignified and courteous relationship with Nuruddin. Nuruddin came and went like he was used to. I had compromised with all the complexities of our relationship. But each day brought with it unrelenting hardships. I was reminded of the story *The Legend of Farhad and Shirin* in which the fictitious character Farhad has to overcome the arduous task of carving out a canal through impenetrable mountains and then divert a tiny rivulet of water through it, just to win the love of Shirin.

In April 1965 India and Pakistan declared war on each other. Later in that same year Salima and the kids came to Delhi to visit me. Within a short span of time we saw trenches being dug around houses. Loud sirens blared through the night warning us of impending air strikes. Glass doors and windows were being covered with thick black paper and in order to further minimise outdoor light, the upper portion of all car headlights had to be painted black. All sorts of restrictions were now being imposed on us. We couldn't come or go as we liked nor could we drive around freely in the city. I used to leave for work at around 2 or 3 in the afternoon and get back only at night. I grew worried about Salima and the kids. Rumours were already doing the rounds that the intensity of war was going to escalate. I started stopping them from going about in the town.

One day, in the dead of night the air raid siren resounded noisily through the city. Chunmun woke up with a start. She was sleeping with me. Within seconds Ali, Salima and Pipo came running in wondering what we should do. I suggested we hide under the beds to stay safe. The kids giggled at the suggestion. Ali who was, Mashallah, extremely tall, could not fit all the way in. His legs stuck out awkwardly. 'Fold them in,' I said to Ali. After getting Sonia to squeeze herself under one of the other beds, I finally got in myself. The kids were hysterical with laughter. When the second siren went off, we crawled out. This was the auditory signal that danger was over. Chunnu and Pipo were extremely amused at this experience.

I told them that during World War II women of the Auxiliary Unit had advised people residing within war zones to take shelter under beds or within trenches, so that if a bomb detonated anywhere nearby, they'd be protected from the shards of splintered glass from shattered windows or debris from crumbling buildings.

It began to dawn on us that the severity of war was intensifying and things were becoming unpleasant. I told both my servants that if they were anxious and afraid, they should return to their villages. Assuring me that they were not, they dramatically proclaimed, 'How can we leave you and go? Where a drop of your perspiration falls, we will shed our blood.' The very next day, they rushed off to their own homes, having suddenly received news of their father's illness! I suggested to Sonia if she was worried she should also go and be with her relatives in Aligarh. By way of a reply she uttered a single guttural sound '*Oohn*' and with an irritated look went about doing her work.

I wanted to send Ali, Salima and the kids to Lucknow as soon as possible. But how was I to do this? There were rumours that Muslims were being attacked in trains. I was deeply engrossed in such thoughts when Salima's father, Dr ZA Ahmed called.

'So, what are you doing?' he asked. 'This war is not showing any signs of ending. You should send the kids to Lucknow. I am leaving today – why don't you send them tomorrow?'

'You are absolutely right,' I said excitedly. 'I can only send them with you, after all there is no question of Salima travelling alone with the kids to Lucknow. As a Member of Parliament you will also be able to get train tickets easily.' Unlike today, trains back then, departed from Old Delhi railway station. Later I came to know that when everyone got to the railway station, it was pitch dark. Even the porters had vanished. These people had to carry their own luggage to the train. In my desperation I even asked Ali to go with Salima and the kids to Lucknow. He was about sixteen years old. He did not agree. Anyway now only Ali, Sonia and I were left in Delhi. We were not scared or anything but of course we knew we had to be careful to stay safe.

As was his habit, Nuruddin dropped in sometime or the other during the day to be with me. One day I got a call from his secretary. 'Sahab has had a heart attack,' he said. 'He is in Wellington Nursing Home... he has asked you to be there by 8.30 in the night.' How do I express what I felt at that time? I was anxious and restless and wanted desperately to fly off and be by his side immediately. But the wretched shackles on my feet were holding me back. Through the day I kept telling myself, 'Sit down quietly, you can't mention a word of this to anyone nor can you rush to be with him. There is no possibility of even finding out how he is doing. You have the entire day to wade through like this, just focus on your work, finish it, do the evening broadcast.'

That is exactly what I did. How I managed, how absolutely miserable I felt, there are no words to describe that. Evening finally came and at 8.30 I reached the nursing home. Munshiji was waiting for me. He immediately took me to Nuruddin's room. I forced myself to appear calm, I did not want Noor to see how worried I was. I held his hand and sat on the bed for a while. Then I drew up a chair next to his bed and sat there. He kept talking to me, telling me how he was feeling, what had happened, how it all happened and that the doctors had advised complete rest. They had even asked him not to speak. He was to remain in hospital for 15 days. I listened patiently to him. Then, true to his nature, Nuruddin began giving me the usual orders. Around 9am, he said, Munshiji would call every day and tell me how he was feeling, and then from 3 to 5pm I was to go to the hospital to be with him, and then I was to return later, after work, and be with him in hospital from 8.30 to 10pm. Damn my courage, my patience and my perseverance! I did all this and did it with all my heart. This is what I was meant to do. This was my destiny. We were in the thick of war with Pakistan. Forget the night, even during the day our movements were being controlled. Despite this I would drive in the dead of night, headlights half-blackened, from office to hospital, hospital to home, every single day. Several people told me not to do this. They even tried scaring me, threatening me, I simply heard them out and kept quiet. For ten full days I continued doing this. By the grace of God, Nuruddin's health continued to improve. Early in the morning on the eleventh day, a taxi came and stopped outside my gate. And what do I see, Noor walking cheerfully into the house in his kurta pyjama. I screamed, 'What have you done?'

'What have I done?' He replied, smiling. 'I was asked to take a walk... I strolled across to see you... now I can go back.' For five days he did this. Meanwhile I followed all the instructions he had issued. By then, thanks to the Almighty, he regained enough strength and was given permission to go back home.

One day prior to being discharged he said to me, 'I have been advised to take regular walks. Every morning around 7.30 I will go till the banks of the Yamuna to take a walk, you come and join me there. On the first day I will meet you at 8.30am in the park near Buddha Temple, after this we will meet in some park or the other close to my house. We will fix up where to meet beforehand.'

As I write this today I realise how childish all this was. But at the time, just to catch a glimpse of him or meet him, even if only for a few minutes, was a question of life and death. Our rendezvous continued for about 20 days. I barely got to spend half an hour with him before I had to head back, as the distance to the places where we fixed to meet was usually eight miles from my place; going and coming made it 16 miles. When this phase ended, he somehow managed to call and say shabba khair every single night. These were the games people played in their youth! We had crossed this stage of our lives many moons ago. But as and when we could, both of us indulged wholeheartedly in such romantic escapades, well into our twilight years, almost till Noor and I were in our sixties and seventies, like fellow travellers at the end of night. Obstacles often have a way of creating possibilities. Some days later doctors gave Noor permission to drive and our lives got back to normal again. By this time, Saeed had, Mashallah, finished his Bachelor of Commerce degree and got a job as a sales officer with the Indian Oil Corporation. His first posting was in Tezpur, West Bengal. Once again the grace of God was with us.

In August 1965 Kamman came down from Srinagar to Delhi to organise her daughter Sabiha's wedding. 'Khalla, I want to finish with this responsibility within fifteen days,' she said. We put our heads together and managed to complete all the arrangements within this short span of time. The wedding went off rather well.

The reception dinner was held at India International Centre and was attended by Mrs Indira Gandhi and Lal Bahadur Shastri (Second Prime Minister of India from 1964 to 1966) I have a photograph of this occasion which has the bride and groom, their respective parents, Mrs Gandhi and Shastriji in it. In the background you can see my Chunnu running about joyfully. She was barely four or five years old.

The one thing that sticks out in my memory about this event is that almost throughout my sister continued to criticise every arrangement we made. She objected to everything; nothing we organised was to her liking. We sought refuge in humour and made light of things by saying, 'She sure is playing the role of a typical mother-in-law!'

The renowned *qawwal* Mubarak Hussain of Bareilly and his troupe performed on one of the days. The show did not go off as well as we expected because of all the commotion at the wedding. All of us were quite disappointed. In his days, Mubarak Hussain was considered the absolute best. The tuneful *na'at's* (poetry in praise of the Prophet Muhammad PBUH) he sang in his melodious voice were often composed by Nawab Sahab Rampur, Raza Ali Khan. Those beautiful musical compositions now lie buried with the singer.

By September 1965, the Indo-Pak war was over. Salima and the kids had returned from Lucknow and left for Bahrain. But the political situation between the two countries was far from good. This breakdown in diplomatic ties had led to a sort of cold war. Kewal Singh, the Indian High Commissioner to Pakistan, had just returned from Islamabad to Delhi. During his tenure there, he had not only witnessed the war but also gained first-hand knowledge of the socio-political conditions within Pakistan. He was, of course, equally well-versed with the ideological environment in his own country. After consulting with radio officials at AIR he put forward a proposal: since there was no possibility of starting a political dialogue between India and Pakistan, why not try and reach the people of Pakistan through the airwaves, with the use of our voices? He suggested launching a nine-hour programme, specifically for this purpose as he believed this would help us express our friendliness towards Pakistan and show them the similarities between our two cultures. He proposed filling the programme with radio plays, literary discourses, ghazals, songs and classical music, aside from holding discussions on how seasonal festivities are celebrated with equal fervour on both sides of the border. In his opinion if we could reach through to the people across the border via radio, we would be able to create a special place for ourselves in their hearts. On the 30th of April 1966 Iqbal Malik, External Services Director at the time, called and handed me the responsibility of starting this programme. Salamatullah was chosen as the Technical Assistant for the show and Farrukh Jaffar was appointed Announcer. We were given orders to start airing the show by the 15th of May.

Iqbal Malik was a highly competent professional who had mastered the art of making radio programmes both entertaining and consistent. I was known for my sincerity and perseverance, which is perhaps why I was asked to compile and edit the programme. To produce a nine hour radio show replete with all sorts of elements from recreation to literature, religious values as well as world news – basically every possible kind of information – was a mammoth task. We were given 15 days to do this. Iqbal Malik was an excellent leader. With his intelligence and professional expertise he was able to create a novel and exciting format for the programme. Translating his ideas into action to produce an entertaining and informative show was my job. Since I never shied away from hard work, in no time at all, I was able to grasp what the order for the programme should be.

Salamatullah worked tirelessly and Farrukh Jaffar was an extremely conscientious woman. On the 15th of May at 7am All India Radio's first transmission of its Urdu programme successfully addressed the people of Pakistan through the air waves. I was the announcer for all three programmes broadcast that day, which meant, from 7am straight till midnight, my voice continued to reach out to the Pakistani public. A day earlier, on May 14th, Iqbal Malik had advised me to make some changes to the programme. I did this. Some ten minutes prior to the first transmission, Iqbal Malik came into the studio. Though we were all extremely excited, we appeared calm and relaxed. Iqbal sahab asked to see the changes he had recommended.

'Yes, I did them the way you suggested,' I replied

'No, I did not ask you to do it like this...' He said angrily and began shouting at me in the studio. There were five minutes left for me to go live on air. My temper began to rise. He was by now roaring like thunder. Exercising all the self-control I could, I said firmly, 'See, I have to go on air in five minutes... please leave the studio right now.'

Iqbal sahab left. After exercising a lot of patience and self-restraint, I was able to control my blazing temper. For the next two hours I presented the morning transmission, which was being heard by several listeners including the Ex-High commissioner, Mr Kewal Singh, the Director General of AIR, a large section of the Indian population and the whole of Pakistan. Several days prior to its launch, details about the Urdu programme had been advertised on radio and published in the newspapers. People had started talking about it. And it started on such a heated note! I wonder if the listeners could tell the announcer was extremely hot tempered!

The second transmission went on air from two in the afternoon to five in the evening and the last one, from eight at night to midnight. All three broadcasts were in my voice. I have been told, that back in those days, my voice sounded heavenly on radio. Allah knows best. We had already prepared a three month schedule for the show. The programme for the second day was ready. Now Farrukh Jaffar had to take up the responsibility of being the announcer. I was however present from morning till midnight and the entire broadcast happened under my supervision. On the third day, Iqbal Malik called me to his office. I was his employee I had to go. He asked me to sit down. I sat.

'I am sorry for that day Mrs Raza,' Iqbal sahab said.

I was quiet.

'Let us forget it,' Iqbal sahab said.

'Yes... let us forget it,' I replied.

He asked if I would like to have some tea, I excused myself politely and came away. Iqbal sahab was not a bad boss. His technical suggestions always enhanced the show and polished it to perfection. But when he lost his cool he would completely forget where he was and lose all sense of the moment and the occasion. With time I had become aware of this habit of his. Anyway after this incident we had no major difference of opinion though I always remained cautious around him.

For three months consecutively, Farrukh Jaffar, Salamatullah and I were the only people keeping the Urdu service running at AIR. Since it was just the three of us in the department, quite often we would reach office early and go back to our respective homes only by nine at night. In the meantime, the authorities began to search for other Urdu speakers with relevant radio experience. From the Urdu Majlis they hired Salam Machhli Shahri and Kishwar Zaidi, an announcer from Kanpur called Mujib Siddiqui, another newcomer by the name of Iqbal Warsi. After testing the quality of their voices, these people were selected to work at the Urdu Service. They also hired Mrs Madhavi Muttoo as Music Producer, Anwar Khan for drama and a few others for office work. Each of them was given an appropriate designation within the Urdu service.

I was handed the responsibility of producing a programme for women and children. I found this quite annoying since I had been working on almost all radio formats. But then it's a man's world and I was not some highly accomplished woman who was well established. Though I had managed to carve out a special niche for myself as a newsreader, I had become bored with the monotony of reading news, every single day. That is why I had expressed a desire to produce other programmes.

When the Urdu service was launched it gave me the opportunity to showcase my abilities, and to demonstrate that I could handle any genre of programming within radio – though technically I was not an expert at any. Along with working on the Women and Children's show, I had to analyse the news, broadcast a short five minute bulletin and was also given the responsibility of producing another five minute show called 'Dekhi-Suni.' All the announcers were working under me. These things were more than enough to keep me busy. The only difference now was that I did not have to work from 9am to 9pm.

From the third week of May fan mail began arriving at the office. Within days 500-600 letters turned to 1000 and 2000! Most of these came all the way from Pakistan. It was my job to reply to them and read some of them during the broadcasts. I did this till the very end of my employment. The three to four years I spent at the Urdu service were not entirely devoid of problems or complications, but they were, all in all, extremely interesting. Coming in contact with different people was exciting. One had to get a group of 15 musicians together at short notice just to record a five minute song and if one person did not turn-up on time, we would have to cancel the entire recording! Producing a radio drama is a Herculean task. It involves stringing together various elements – literary discussions, humour, drama, songs, practically any and every bit of information you can lay your hands on. To distil elements of a nine hour show into a one hour women and children's programme, was like fitting an ocean into a tiny little bottle. One had to make sure the programme was entertaining enough for kids, that it imparted knowledge in a light hearted manner, had amusing elements of drama and song in it and all this had to be squeezed into thirty minutes. But I didn't complain. It kept me busy and that is what I was most grateful for.

Sometime in 1966, a friend's daughter by the name of Nazneen got me acquainted with a certain Syed Nazir Hussain from Patna. After we had met with each other a couple of times, he said quite informally, 'I have heard about your son Saeed, that Mashallah he is a very nice boy. I am concerned about finding a decent match for my daughter Naushaba.'

'Ji yes, Saeed is a good child.' I agreed.

'Are you also looking for a bride for him?' he asked.

'Yes I am.'

'Then you must meet with my elder girl. I am quite sure you will like her. At the moment they are in Karachi.'

'Sure, when your family comes to Delhi you must introduce us,' I replied.

When Nazir sahab came back to Delhi again, I met his daughters. I liked his elder child, but Saeed was in Tezpur, it was not easy to get him to come home. When Nazir sahab spoke again with me on this topic, I praised his daughter and told him frankly that I liked her.

'Then send a proposal,' Nazir sahab said.

'How can I do that?' I replied. 'Let the boy and girl see each other first, let them agree to marry, only after that can I send a proposal. Let's say for arguments sake I send one and Saeed does not agree to this match, then it will be so embarrassing for me.'

'No, no I am quite broad-minded, I will not feel bad,' Nazir sahab said.

'You may not, but I most certainly will not like it. I have already written to Saeed. I am trying to call him over, let him come, then we will fix something.'

Saeed was extremely lazy at writing letters. When he did not respond, I sent a telegram. It read, 'Feeling very low, come immediately.' Almost instantly Saeed took leave and landed up in Delhi. After he arrived, I arranged a party for the youngsters. There was Saeed, a couple of his friends, Sabiha, Fawzia, (Kamman's daughters) Kamman, Nazir sahab's three daughters and some other people. I ordered a variety of snacks and handing over the role of host to Kamman, made some excuse about work and went off to a friend's place. We did these get-togethers another three or four times at Nazir sahab's place and mine. Saeed had taken leave for a week and wanted to spend some days with his father in Lucknow as well. So I told him the truth and asked him candidly, 'Tell me, do you like the girl or not?'

'I like the girl, but I don't want to marry right now... my salary is not much.'

'How much do you earn?'

'About 1000 rupees.'

The cost of living back in 1966 was not such that one could not live on 1000 rupees a month. My own salary was similar and I was living quite comfortably. 'See Saeed, if you like the girl, remember she will not sit around and wait for you. But I don't want to force you – you decide for yourself. You are going to Lucknow, discuss this with your father and send me a letter.'

Three days later Saeed called from Lucknow and said, 'Bibi I am ready to get married, you can take the proposal to Nazir sahab.' I was extremely delighted with Saeed's decision. The girl's name was Naushaba. She was dressed in simple, plain looking clothes and seemed like a rather reserved, serious kind of child. The first day when I had invited all the youngsters to my place for tea, I also sat around with them for a short while. Before leaving I had a cup of tea. When I finished and reached across to put the cup down on the table, Naushaba immediately asked, 'Would you like some more?'

'No thank you,' I replied.

That one sentence won me over. 'What a considerate child,' I thought to myself, 'she doesn't even know me but is so aware of everyone's needs.' After this, I began to like everything about Naushaba. But three of my friends and Nuruddin were not happy with this alliance. The collective opinion of my friends was that she was not dressed properly, and she wasn't well-educated. They thought I could have chosen a better bride for Saeed. Nuruddin said some rather awful things about Nazir sahab and added, 'You should have at least asked me.' My reply was, 'I have never discussed my kids with you, why would I do it now?' Anyway, whatever fate had in store, happened. Till today I feel responsible for what transpired in their relationship.

At the beginning of January 1966 Nazir sahab insisted we have the engagement ceremony. I was a bit hesitant as there had been a death in the family; my brother-in-law Tasavur Husain Naqvi (Aqila's husband) had passed away due to a heart attack in December. In 1966 I took a matrimonial proposal for Nazir Hussain's daughter along with some Indian sweets and fruit to Nazneen's house. Zakia, Raffat and Hammi were with me. After scouring the market for an appropriate ring, I had one custom-made. It was a princess cut Burmese ruby ring with two concentric circles of deep red gems with a solitary diamond embedded on top. The marriage date was fixed for October.

We informed Asad and Salima about the wedding. Salima came down some days earlier to help me with the preparations. Asad flew in a week prior to the wedding. When just a few days were left for the big day Asad came to me and said, 'Bibi I want to have a party for some of Saeed's and my friends before the wedding.'

'Of course, please do,' I replied.

As mentioned we had a huge lawn in the front as well as at the back of the house at Cornwallis Road. The party was held in the back yard. A lot of boys and girls were invited. I sat about with them for a while and then left. Along with food, drinks were also being served. Around two in the morning I heard a strange loud noise, as though someone was crying hysterically in the drawing room. As I got out of bed to see what was going on, I met Salima in the veranda.

'Bibi, go to sleep,' she said. 'These people are making such a racket… laughing and doing all sorts of strange mimicry. Don't bother going outside. I'll shut the drawing room door.' Salima sounded convincing so I went back to bed. Several months after the wedding I found out that the noise I heard that night was actually Asad. He kept hugging Saeed and crying, 'My kid brother will be married tomorrow.' When their friends saw him, an older brother, crying thus, they were hysterical with laughter. Anyhow, this incident was soon forgotten.

The next day we took Saeed's marriage procession to the girl's house. Our guests were given a warm and cordial welcome. The arrangements were well-planned. A special throne-like seat had been decorated for the groom. The nikah took place. Then dinner was served, it was formal, elaborate and extremely tasty. After the rukhsati we brought the bride back to our place. Salima's room was given to the newlyweds. We arranged Naushaba's trousseau in my room along with the assortment of fresh fruit as well as dry fruit and sweets which had been sent with her and Sonia slept in there. The drawing room was converted into a bedroom for Asad and his friends. Sleeping arrangements for Salima, Kamman, my two grandkids and Tasneem were made in a large tent, which had been pitched in the back yard. Sakina Begum of Rampur had lent us the tent along with her servant Khurshid to help out at this time. During the day there had not been a single cloud in the sky; it never rained in October. By about 1am just as we settled down and dozed off a slight drizzle started. Kamman woke up. 'Khalla, I think it is raining.' I was extremely sleepy and a bit apprehensive. I thought the drizzle would probably stop after a few minutes. We woke the kids, Salima and Tasneem and asked them to go crash in the drawing room. 'Kamman and I will stay here. We will call you when it stops,' I said. They left and within ten minutes a heavy downpour started. The cloth roof of the tent began dripping. The servants Abdul and Khurshid came running out to help us take all the bedclothes inside. We entered the house completely drenched. Kamman and I had to change our clothes. The two servants were also soaking wet from head to toe and were given Asad's clothes to wear. We also went and sat in the drawing room with the others. By this time it was raining cats and dogs outside. Khurshid stuck his head out from the side of the kitchen door and asked, 'Should I make some tea?'

'Yes, yes… absolutely,' we all replied gleefully.

Lo and behold, we were now having tea at that unearthly hour of the morning. We went and helped ourselves to some of the delicious savoury snacks that had come from the bride's house, which are a speciality of Bihar. The kids woke up and began eating with us. We sat there, eating, sipping hot tea and chatting joyfully till morning. After the wedding Saeed and Naushaba went off to Allahabad. Asad, Salima and the children headed back to Kuwait. Asad was now posted there as Assistant Manager, Air India.

In January 1967 we received a telegram from Pakistan. My elder brother-in-law Aley Raza's son Qamar had suddenly passed away. Dear God, death had snuffed out the light of my bhabhijaan's life – her darling son was no more! What must she be going through? I felt dreadful and couldn't shake off the sadness for days. But there was nothing I could do. Damn this Partition, it had literally split our country apart! Though we felt emotionally numb there was nothing we could do but sit in Delhi and nurse our grief. Sending a condolence message via telegram seemed so meaningless. After all this was family. Qamar whom I loved and played with as a child, my bhabhijaan's first born, was no longer in this world! His marriage had been arranged with my second brother-in-law Kazim Raza's adopted daughter Talat. Qamar had such a charming personality. He was carefree, playful and jolly. Bhabhijaan adored him. Now that child, who was dearer-than-life itself, had gone, leaving his parents to face the harshest test of their lives!

The wound from this severe blow was still raw when, on the 21st of December, that same year, Masud Raza also passed away. He had apparently gone to attend a New Year party, had a massive heart attack and died right there and then. That is how 1968 began. Masud Raza, my youngest brother-in-law, was a civil servant working at some high post in Pakistan. In October of the same year he had come to India on an official visit and had stayed at Sherwani Lodge. Masud had spoken with Saeed and it was decided that he would come one evening to have dinner with us. The day he was heading back to Pakistan, Masud came to our place in the evening. His flight was at midnight. He left from our house around eleven that night. Thankfully Saeed had the opportunity to meet with Masud during that trip. On the 21ˢᵗ of December we heard the devastating news that Masud had passed away.

In July 1968 Mrs Violet Alva sent me as a representative to attend the Working Women's Conference in London. The event was scheduled for 10ᵗʰ August. During those days, Chunmun had come to Delhi for her summer vacations and she was with me. Leaving her in Sonia's loving care and under Naushaba's watchful eye I went off to London. At the time Naushaba's father, Nazir Hussain, was posted in London as a Public Relations Officer. When Salima got to know I was going to London and staying with Nazir sahab, she counted out seven shillings and put them in my handbag. 'If for any reason no one comes to get you from the airport, the bus fare from the airport is exactly seven shillings. You don't even have to count it. It will save you the effort of trying to figure out which coin is a pound and which is a shilling.'

Since I was travelling by KLM, my flight was routed via Amsterdam. Asad had not only arranged for my ticket but also got Ajit Singh (Manager for Air India in Amsterdam) to book a room for me at the Krasnapolsky Hotel. Though I had been to Bahrain in 1967, this was the first time I was travelling further west all by myself. I faced no problems during the journey. After all I was the mother of Air India's Assistant Manager. Throughout the journey, the staff took good care of me and treated me extremely well. I stayed in Amsterdam for three or four days. Saeed's friend, Ian Carter's sister Mariam Dagroat came to the airport to receive me. Since we had never met one another before, she had an announcement made at the airport informing me how I would be able to recognise them at the Arrivals.

Mariam took me on a grand tour of Amsterdam where I saw how the Dutch cultivate their world famous tulips using a special technique. I visited the greenhouses or 'hot homes' where large-scale preparations were in place to keep flowers fresh for a longer time before they are sold off. Mariam took me to see the historic city of Delft. It is known the world over for its unique blue and white hand-painted pottery and its canals, on either side of which are large houses and attractive buildings. In one touristy area, three windmills were positioned so accurately behind one another they gave the illusion of being just one.

After visiting Amsterdam when I finally reached London, I found that Nazir Hussain, who was now related to me, was not at the airport to receive me. The seven shillings Salima gave came to my rescue. Thanks to them I managed to reach Victoria Terminal and from there phoned Nazir sahab. He said he had had to go to the doctor.

'I have pain in my hand, but I am coming to Victoria Terminal now.'

He arrived an hour later and immediately said, 'Come let's take a bus.'

'No Nazir sahab we will take a taxi. I will pay for it,' I replied.

He then pointed lamely towards his hand and mumbled something about pain. I pretended not to hear him. He had to carry my suitcase. I finally reached Nazir Hussain's house in Sutlam.

From the very next day I made enquiries and decided to paddle my own canoe. Meetings for the Working Women's Conference were being held at Grosvenor House in Park Lane. We had to be there in the morning and stay at the venue the entire time. I would reach Nazir sahab's house only in the evening, it was a short ten-minute walk from the train station. I stayed there 15 days; every kind of comfort was made available to me. Nazir sahab was most hospitable and polite. Then I went and stayed with my friend Ms James for a week. Three weeks are not enough to see London city, still she took me around and showed me as much as she could. On two occasions I did a broadcast for the BBC about India and even gave an interview.

From London I went to Kuwait, spent a week with Asad, before heading off to visit Syria where I stayed with the Indian ambassador, Virasat Kidwai. His wife, Begum Bilqees Kidwai, was an extremely sweet lady; she liked me a lot. She took me to see some of the famous tourist spots in Syria including Masjid-e-Nabvi (PBUH) where Hazrat Imam Hussain's (AS) revered head had been placed and where Hazrat Sakina (Hazrat Imam Hussain AS's four-year-old daughter) stayed when she was imprisoned.

After visiting some other historic landmarks I went to Hazrat Zainab's (daughter of Hazrat Ali A.S and granddaughter of Prophet Mohammed PBUH) tomb which is located within the Sayyidah Zaynab Mosque in Damascus. From the minute I entered I felt extremely at peace there. A strange sense of serenity and silence pervaded the air. Though architecturally the monument itself is rather simple, almost bare, its ambience is captivating. It radiated such an intense feeling of calm and wellbeing that I had the overwhelming compulsion to spend the entire time in this holy place. I have heard Hazrat Zaynab was a remarkable woman with tremendous self-control and fortitude. That, despite the calamity that befell her, she maintained composure and resilience. Can it be that her personality has left an indelible mark on the atmosphere surrounding her grave? It certainly felt like that.

Within a year of his marriage Saeed was transferred from Allahabad to Delhi. I was delighted. After all it is the presence of children that makes a house a home. Ali was also with me. Boys are usually busy doing something or the other by themselves. The initial days went off well, then Naushaba began sleeping till late in the day. Saeed and I would have breakfast around nine o clock and leave for work. She would wake up after this. We usually met only at lunch time, after which I would leave for work and return at night. Nuruddin always had lunch with us. He would rest a bit and then also leave for work. For some time this was the routine and rhythm of our lives. After a few days I learnt Naushaba was pregnant. Naturally all our attention was now focussed on her well-being – that she should eat right, get enough rest and stay happy. I wrote to her mother to give the good news. She wrote back saying, 'Send her to Muzaffarpur for the delivery.' Saeed said, 'Bibi Muzaffarpur is a small town, they will not have the kind of medical facilities we have. The child should be delivered in Delhi.'

Early morning on the 20th of December in 1967 Naushaba told us she had started labour. We had already booked a room at Wellington Nursing Home and made all necessary arrangements. I asked my neighbour Pushpa Verma to come with us to the hospital. Dr Verma was our neighbour at Cornwallis Road. Pushpa was his wife. She was a loving lady and a good person. She immediately agreed to go with me. By around 9am we reached the nursing home. Naushaba was in pain though the cramps were mild but of course she was very restless. I sat with her, holding her hand. Pushpa was also there, a source of great comfort for me. During the day, we took turns having lunch. By 2.30 in the afternoon Naushaba's contractions intensified and she was taken to the delivery room.

Saeed was strolling about anxiously in the hospital veranda. Pushpa and I were outside the delivery room. Around 3 o'clock a nurse came and gave us the good news that by God's grace Naushaba had given birth to a baby girl. The nurse then walked up to Saeed and said, 'Don't worry, your sister is well, she had a daughter.' Saeed, Mashallah, always looked ten years younger than his actual age. The nurse thought Saeed was Naushaba's brother!

After three days we brought mother and child back home. Both of them were doing well. Good old Sonia took charge. She was an experienced hand as she had already brought up my older grandchildren. She eagerly took on the responsibility of raising this baby as well. Saeed and Naushaba chose Shaheen as the name for their baby. Mashallah, the child had the most adorable face. At night, when she cried, Saeed, Naushaba and I took turns strolling and calming her down. I had kept Chunnu's cot, which Pipo had also used when he was a baby. This now became Shaheen's crib. Chunmun gave Shaheen an interesting nickname which we all liked – she started calling her Shizzie. We had decent, well trained experienced servants and did not have to face much anxiety handling a new-born baby. Yes, this much was true that Naushaba turned out to be a bit lazy – she would sleep anytime she felt like and she constantly complained of headaches. The young lady was actually rather moody. The cure for this in our house was Bi Sonia – she would simply step in and take care of the baby.

Saeed is an extremely peaceful person. Perhaps that is why we never sensed that there was any apparent tension between him and his wife. Naushaba usually woke up by 11 in the morning. No one in the house objected to this. I was in any case never home and the servants, like I said, were efficient and good at their work. I didn't know things were not going well in Saeed and Naushaba's marriage. I failed to see the signs. Outwardly everything seemed fine. After all when a girl from another family comes to live in your home, there are bound to be differences in their way of living and yours and it takes time for these to harmonise. On the face of it, our days were going along smoothly. Another year passed.

In December 1968, Bea (Begum Bhopal)[51] mentioned that on the 24th she would be leaving for Calcutta for her son Mansoor Ali Khan Pataudi's wedding. He was marrying popular screen actress Sharmila Tagore. Bea and I had known each other for a long time. She wanted me to accompany her to Calcutta. When I mentioned this to Nuruddin, he got a bit annoyed and said, 'If you want to try and please her and be a mere part of the entourage, go.' He did not want me to go. But men hardly ever say what they are feeling directly. They want you to try and guess what is on their mind.

Despite not being of the same social status as Begum Bhopal, I would have liked to comply with her wishes and would have gone, simply because she wanted me to. After all, my father was a Minister in her grandmother Nawab Sultan Jahan Begum's court. I was conditioned to observe social etiquette and respect her status. For me she was first and foremost a princess, then she became the Begum of Pataudi and was finally given the nominal title Begum Bhopal. If I had gone for the wedding, I would definitely have had to respect the social hierarchy between us. I don't call maintaining royal protocol flattery. Just because Begum Bhopal no longer had any political authority, if I started meeting with her as an equal, it would be highly insolent of me. Anyway, I am meandering. To cut a long story short, I did not go for the wedding.

The wedding was on 28 December. On the same morning, around seven o' clock, Saeed and I were having tea in my room when the phone rang. Saeed answered it. After listening briefly to what the person on the other side was saying, the words, 'Oh, no' escaped his lips. I looked at his face and knew immediately that his father had passed away. Without saying a single word I wrapped my arms around my son. He was trying to stop his tears. He got up

---

[51] Sajida Sultan was the second daughter of Nawab Hamidullah Khan, the last ruling Nawab of Bhopal and mother of famous cricketer Nawab Mansoor Ali Khan of Pataudi who captained the Indian cricket team from 1962 to 1970.

quietly and went to be with his wife. Straightaway I began making arrangements for air tickets so both Saeed and Naushaba could leave for Lucknow at once. Asad was in London. I booked an overseas trunk call to Nazir Hussain after explaining the urgency of the matter to the operator. Within 45 minutes we got through to Nazir sahab. I asked him to contact Asad at once to let him know what had happened. Asad was staying with Salima's aunt, Zohra. Within two hours Asad called back saying he would be arriving the next day.

Naushaba and Saeed left for Lucknow by the two o'clock flight along with their baby. Before they even took off from Delhi, I called and informed Akhtar and Ishtiaq bhai to make arrangements to have them picked up from the airport. I also asked them to go to Kashana-e-Raza. Both were of immense help to us during this difficult time.

By noon the next day Asad reached Delhi from London. Kamman, his close friend Virendra Bhardwaj and I were there at the airport to receive him. He was going to take the 2 o'clock connecting flight to Lucknow. I went with him to Palam Airport. I had decided to accompany Asad to Lucknow. For 24 hours I had been in a dilemma, struggling with the idea of whether I should go to Lucknow or not. Then the thought flashed through my mind that at a time like this people attend funerals to share in the sorrow of their friends and these here were my own two sons who had just lost their father.

Along with Asad, Kamman, Virendra, I also reached Lucknow. On the way to Kashana, I got off at Ali Zaheer sahab's house. Around six in the evening both my sons came to Ali Zaheer sahab's house and took me to Kashana with them. I met Naushaba, she was trying to handle as much as she possibly could while looking after a one-year-old child. Food had not been cooked in the house. Akhtar had thoughtfully made arrangements for some milk, fruit etc., for the baby. It was a strange and sad time. Despite all of us being in the house, Kashana felt deserted and silent. Asad and Saeed were busy making arrangements for the funeral. They wanted to take their father's body to Neotani. Abbas Raza was to be buried next to his father's grave. The spot had been reserved for Begum Raza but destiny had taken her to Pakistan.

The funeral procession left for Neotani by nine at night. Both my boys returned to Lucknow at three in the morning after bidding their father a final farewell. I laid out the dastrakhaan and served them food at this late hour. Kamman, Virendra, Akhtar and Ishtiaq bhai were with us. Their presence was comforting for me, otherwise it would have been difficult to see my children in this state; they were devastated with grief.

Hajra Begum, Salima's mother, had been staying in Kashana for some time. She had dinner with Abbas Raza the night he passed away. After the meal they said good night and retired to their respective rooms. The next morning, when Abbas Raza did not come out of his room for a long time, Hajra Begum grew anxious. When she learnt from the servants that he was still sleeping, she went into his room. Shocked at what she saw, she immediately called the doctor. Abbas Raza had slipped into eternal sleep. After the doctor confirmed this, they informed us. A couple of days later Asad and Saeed returned to Delhi after taking care of all the formalities in Lucknow. Asad was posted in Kuwait, he went back and life resumed its normal rhythm.

Then came 1969. And what a strange year that was! Our days were passing along smoothly. Nuruddin's wife Billy went to visit their daughter Ameena in Washington and had just returned to Delhi at the beginning of November. She'd travelled on the same plane as Mrs Violet Alva.[52] Every single day Nuruddin would call me from his house around 7 to say good morning. That was the norm. On the morning of 20 November his secretary called.

'Memsahab passed away last night,' he said.

'Who...?' I cried abruptly.

'Memsahab!' He repeated.

I put the receiver down. 'Good God what a tragedy. I held my head in my hands and sat, unmoving. What must Nuruddin be feeling, I wondered. I could not even reach out and be with him at this time, the restrictions imposed on me thanks to our relationship did not allow me to pick up the phone and speak with him. I got up and like I did every single day, changed and went to work. I felt as though I was in a trance. I have no idea how the day passed. Akhtar's

---

[52] Indian lawyer, politician and Deputy Chairperson of the Rajya Sabha and member of the Indian National Congress.

ghazals were being recorded at the radio station. I remember someone coming to me and saying, 'Begum Akhtar is looking for you.' I even met with her. But it all happened mechanically and the entire time I didn't know where I was or what was happening. Around half past five in the evening I came home.

I had barely rested for a few minutes when Nuruddin walked in. He looked at me with heavy, sad eyes. For a long time we sat together silently without exchanging a single word. Then he told me that around midnight Billy started coughing. The bouts got worse and refused to stop and eventually she died like that, in Nuruddin's arms. 'What a lucky wife.' I thought to myself.

The next day, I read in the newspaper that Mrs Violet Alva had also passed away. She had apparently had a heart attack. What a strange coincidence. Both women had flown back together from Washington and both died on the 20th of November. During their lifetime though Billy and Mrs Alva lived in two absolutely different worlds, they were destined to leave it on the very same day.

Nuruddin came home the next day around 11 in the morning. I was back from work at 1pm. We had lunch together. When he came to the room, I realised Nuruddin's eyes were moist. I couldn't control my tears either. We both cried together. Then I said to him, 'Why don't you rest for a while, I am going to office.'

When I got back, Noor was still there, he hadn't gone back to his house. He stayed at my place till late and we had dinner together.

Now he began to come to my place in the afternoon. He would have lunch, go to the Supreme Court and then to Alipur road. He would come back to Cornwallis road by 7, have dinner with me and go back home late at night. As the days passed, this became his new routine.

The thought that started bothering me now was that when Noor's wife was alive and our love for each other had turned into a complex unresolvable issue, I had made peace with the situation. I did not have any right over him and I did not make any demands. I had consciously decided to overlook all those childish arguments he used to try and convince me to carry on with our relationship. We stayed together as a couple even during the time when Delhi became a state and he was nominated as its Speaker. He moved to another house, his time was divided between the Government of India, his practice and his family.[53]

He was given an official car and driver. And though he didn't have the moral courage to come to my house in this, he nonetheless managed to keep seeing me, every single day, come rain or storm, through intense downpours and heat waves. He would leave his official responsibilities and his personal duties and land up to be with me. Sometimes at midnight, sometimes during the blistering heat and sometimes as early as seven or eight in the morning. While heading off for some important official work, he would tell the driver to go wait at such-and-such place for him, then somehow or the other, take a taxi and come to my house!

It was all so childish and yet so exciting. If he didn't manage to come, there was absolutely nothing I could do about it. I knew there was tension in his house, how could I destroy the few moments of stolen peace he got at mine? The half hour, the forty minutes we got together, would simply fly by and vanish into thin air; our conversations would remain unfinished and he would be gone. We had been meeting like this for close on 22 years!

My older son Asad was with me in those days. He was married and had children. The kids were brought-up exactly as they would have been in any 'normal' household, despite Noor's presence in my life. Every single day, Nuruddin came over at lunch time laden with different varieties of seasonal fruit. My grandchildren were used to having him around.

I am indebted to both Asad and Salima for accepting the unusual circumstances of our situation in such a mature and amiable way that it appeared as though we were just another ordinary family. Of course what I went through emotionally was another matter altogether. I never went out with Nuruddin in public. Whenever he came to my house I tried to keep things pleasant and uncomplicated. But it was a Herculean task, which I

---

[53] During his four terms as a member of the Delhi Corporation, Nuruddin Ahmed served as the Mayor of Delhi for three terms, from 1960 to 1965. The Government of India awarded him the third highest civilian honour, the Padma Bhushan in 1964, for his contributions to public affairs.

faced, every single day and still managed to keep my sanity and my feelings under control.

My friends and family came and went. They also met Noor. Tongues must have wagged, fingers must have been pointed. We were successful in making sure the people whom we met regularly were those who supported us. They were respectful and cordial to Noor and never made us feel embarrassed about our relationship. The credit for this, first and foremost, goes to my children, and the maturity, love and broad-mindedness with which they handled this unusual situation. And then to divine grace. I believe God's grace and blessings have always been with me. I have gone through such severe hardships and testing times. Even the love Noor and I shared, for twenty five long years, was like a continuous trial by fire.

So much time has passed now. It is difficult to find words to express what those circumstances felt like and how they made me feel. It was similar to what Faiz sahab has written so beautifully in this couplet, '*dast-e-tah-e-sang-āmada paimān-e-vafā hai.*' (A vow of commitment to the beloved is like a hand trapped irrevocably under a heavy rock.)

In a conservative world shackled to age-old customs and restrictions for centuries I had chosen to break free and walk out, all alone, on to a painfully complicated path filled at each step with dishonour and humiliation. And I believed, quite naïvely, that I could do this without ruining my reputation; that I could appease the longing of my foolish heart and not feel the thorny prick of my conscience. But how was that going to be possible?

If you choose to walk over *pul-e-sirat*, the metaphorical bridge in hell, thinner than hair, sharper than a sword and surrounded by hot flames of fire, you must stand prepared to fall or be slashed to death. I was prepared. Sometimes I stumbled, and sometimes I stood up again. But never once did I try and get my way using unfair means. There were moments when I felt utterly lost, as though I was enveloped in total darkness, unable to see the way forward, when my courage also failed me. Then from some unforeseen direction, a ray of light would suddenly shine through and lift my defeated spirit. Once again I would hold on fearlessly to the fragile bond of love we shared and move forward confidently. Here I am only narrating what *I* went through. But honestly both Billy and Noor journeyed with me through this painful agony. Both were casualties of this love.

Billy must have definitely loved Nuruddin quite intensely. After she moved to India, she even transformed herself into a typical Indian wife – just for his sake. But after he met me Nuruddin could not walk away, he became emotionally involved with me. When you marry a woman from another culture you remain committed to the marriage, but gradually, over time, due to cultural dissimilarities, a void starts to creep into the relationship. An Indian man starts yearning to communicate in his own language with ease, to share those age-old traditions, customs and rituals with his life partner. As the marriage progresses, the lack of this communication intensifies. He starts missing the feminine grace, charm and coquetry of a typical Indian woman. Men start meandering; some seek refuge in alcohol, some start gambling while others start having small insignificant affairs.

Now after a long passage of time, once again I felt I was standing at a crossroads. My relationship with Noor, which had passed through so many phases of love, was still an unnamed undefined liaison. 'What do I call it – this that I had nurtured with my own blood and placed on a high pedestal?' I often wondered to myself. Within society nobody talks of the relationship I share with Noor. With their silence they have bestowed dignity on us. I am extremely grateful to them for this. But what was I to do now? With her death, Billy had shaken the foundation of my relationship with Noor. Now society may expect us to give a name to this relationship. Can I find a new way out of this tangled web? How do I do this? I am so tired, so very tired. If I say anything to Noor, I lose face; if he takes refuge in silence and does nothing, it shows him in poor light. Oh God, I respect him so much, I must try to understand the reason behind his silence. After all that is what I have been doing for all these years. Whatever he wants me to accept, I do dutifully. The situation we were in reminded me of this verse by Faiz Ahmad Faiz,

> *'Ahd-e-wafa ya tark-e-mohabbat,*
> *jo chaho so aap karo*

Apne bus kee baat hee kya hai
hum se kya manwaaogey.'

Be it the promise of love or breaking off of our bonds,
You do as you desire…
I have no powers.
Hence what is it that you want me to accept now?

Days turned into months and months became a full year. One day around the time of maghrib prayers Nuruddin came home and said, 'Come on, come with me.'

It was the month of March, the days had started becoming warmer.

'Come where?' I asked.

'Just come.' He replied.

I went and sat in his car. He drove straight to the mosque on Parliament Street, stopped the car and said, 'Get down.'

I couldn't understand where he was taking me. But I went inside. He walked with me towards the *hujra* where the Imam of the masjid was sitting. Nuruddin asked me to sit and turning to the Imam said, 'I have come to have my nikah done.'

My heart leapt with joy.

'I wish he had told me before.' I thought to myself, elated. But then how would that have been Nooram?[54] The Imam turned to me and asked, 'At what amount should I fix mahr?'

I promptly said, 'mahr fatmee,' the bare minimum.[55]

How much was that exactly, I had no clue! I was just so excited I could barely fathom what was going on around me. Then I realized someone was congratulating us. I looked and saw that there were two other gentlemen in the mosque. Later I found out they were witnesses to our marriage. One of them was Mohammed Tahir sahab, a Member of Parliament from Bihar's Purnia district and the other, a young man from amongst Nuruddin's followers and admirers in Delhi by the name of Mohammed Yunus.

---

[54] While Noor means light, Nooram literally translates to 'My Noor.'
[55] Traditional mahr dating back to the Prophet's time where the dower amount was notional.

After this extraordinary nikah ceremony, Nuruddin brought me back to my house at 13 Cornwallis road. He sat peacefully for a while, had dinner and then off he went, once again, to Alipore Road. What a one-sided show and how extremely romantic! How can a person who has gone through such exciting trials in her life not write her story? After our nikah Noor changed his timings. He would come in the mornings and head off to the Supreme Court straight from Cornwallis Road. After office he would come back to my place, stay till as late as he possibly could, usually till after 11pm. His older son Farid was staying with him and God alone knows what Nuruddin wanted to prove to him. Farid was at the time working in Air India and had been posted in Delhi.

I was not happy with the way things were going between us. A couple of times we had sharp arguments. I flared up. But it was only a passing phase. How could I bear to keep him unhappy for long? I knew him well enough to know the mental trauma he was in. He had an extremely strong personality; Everybody who knew Noor had tremendous respect for him. They saw him as a man of principle, a virtuous and noble human being who was bold and fearless. But he was afraid. He was afraid of himself. This was the basic contradiction in his personality.

When Nuruddin married Billy she was barely 17; he must himself have been just 22. In 1950, when he started coming to see me, my son Saeed was with me. He was extremely affectionate towards Saeed and would often tell me that Saeed reminded him of his youngest son, Feroz. He talked to me about his family, praised his daughter Ameena and told me how smart and intelligent she was, how faithful Billy was. He spoke of all the hardships Billy had suffered for his sake since she moved to India, how well she looked after him and the kids, that she had learnt how to cook a wide variety of Indian food and basically, had turned out to be a hard-working woman and a successful wife. When I heard all this the picture I formed in my head was that he was happy, he had a loving family, and I often thought, how wonderful that the husband and wife love each other so much. In the September of 1947, Nuruddin took his family and left for London only to return to Delhi two years later all by himself. He stayed at the Marina Hotel and made meeting me a regular part of his daily schedule.

Honestly it was extremely difficult for me to try and gauge the impact Billy's sudden death had on Nooram. Over time I realised that every Thursday he would visit her grave. He had food distributed there, said namaz and spent quite a bit of time there. Billy's grave is located in Dargah Sharif, Shah Kalimullah Wali which falls on the way from Alipur Road to Cornwallis Road. Not that I felt bad about this or that his actions bothered me. But one of his friends, Qazi Abdul Wadood, did have a problem and went so far as to say, 'Why are you doing this? You couldn't remain faithful to her in her lifetime and now you are trying to show what a loyal husband you are.' Abdul Wadood shared an informal friendship with Noor, he could say what he liked. I did think that visiting her grave every week was a bit odd, but for me to say anything would have been highly improper. Till Billy was alive I was constantly aware of how excruciatingly painful my presence must have been for her. I used to wish I had not existed in Noor's life.

After Billy came back to India in 1955, I made a conscious effort never to be seen in public with Nooram. Yes, he would come home to see me, sit there for a while and leave. She knew this, in fact the whole wide world did. What can I say in my defense except that all of this was written in my destiny, I had no control over it. The kind of hardships I have suffered all these years can only be expressed in Faiz sahab's words,

> *Karz-e-nigaah-e-yaar ada kar chuke hain hum*
> *Sab kuch nisaar-e-rah-e-wafa kar chuke hain hum*
> *abb ahtiyaad ki koi surat nahee rahee*
> *qatil se rasm-o-raah siva kar chuke hain hum*

I have paid my debt to the glances I exchanged with my beloved,
I have sacrificed everything along the way for this commitment
There is no possibility of being cautious now
I have strengthened my relationship with my sweetheart, my slayer.

Billy had already had a heart attack. Then one night she had a violent bout of coughing and couldn't survive it. That night Nooram lost both a friend and a confidante. Who can understand what Nuruddin must have gone through emotionally and psychologically?

How could I make an issue about how he chose to react to his loss? Nuruddin had had two heart attacks himself. I did not want to make demands on him which his heart was not willing to accept. He was asking Billy for forgiveness for making me his wife.

In the middle of 1969 I began constructing a house in Panchsheel Park in South Delhi. Some years earlier, one of my acquaintances in Lucknow by the name of Mr Sahay had asked me if I had bought any land in Delhi. When I said no, he got after me to become a member of the Panchsheel housing society. I sent off a request to the Society President, Mr Burman along with the membership fee of Rs110. Some ten or fifteen years passed. One day I was informed that Panchsheel Park Society was ready to allot a 311-square yard plot to me. I paid Rs 9000 and got the plot registered in my name. Then I went to Bhopal, sold off the two pieces of land I had there for Rs 65000. Land prices had escalated rapidly from 1955 to 1969.

14

The Worst was Yet to Come

———————— ❧ ————————

I can't recall clearly in which year Chunmun was admitted to St Mary's School in Nainital, it was probably 1969. Asad completed the admission formalities while Salima and I got busy with the tedious task of getting her uniform, home-clothes, bed sheets, towels, bedding, trunk etc., organised. Chunmun was barely nine. Chunnu Begum had recently learnt to ride a bike. While taking rounds of the house on her cycle, she rode into a pothole, fell full-force on her knees and got hurt rather badly. She entered the house limping, blood all over, miserable with pain but not a tear in her eyes. I was horrified and rushed her immediately to the doctor. They gave her an anti-tetanus injection. The wound was cleaned and dressed. I didn't scold her. How could I? My darling grandchild was going to boarding in three days.

Till 1974 when Chunmun was in St Mary's, I made all the necessary arrangements of getting her dropped and picked from Nainital. Almost every week I wrote letters to both my grandchildren. Every October, during her ten day mid-term break, I went and met her. By now I could afford the expense of travelling to Nainital. Back when my own kids were studying there, I could not do this. Chunnu was, Mashallah, doing well, getting good grades in class. Like her father, she excelled in sports. She won a prize in the 100m dash; I still have this with me. Then God knows what happened but she began complaining of recurrent pain in her ankle. The diagnosis was that the bone in her ankle had grown bigger, which is why though she could walk about easily, but if she attempted to run, it hurt. The doctor's advice was that the protruding bone spur should be surgically removed as it could grow in size and cause future complications. I wrote to Asad and Salima about this. They replied saying it would be difficult for them to come to India at that time and that I should have the surgery done.

I was extremely anxious. I had heard a few cases in which patients had passed away simply after sniffing anaesthesia! It is absolutely imperative in any surgical procedure for the anaesthetist to be technically skilled and extremely vigilant. Of course the orthopaedic surgeon has to be experienced as well. Anyway, I went and met with doctors at Lucknow Medical college, fixed a date for the procedure, booked a room and putting all my faith in the Almighty, had Chunmun operated. The reason I am writing this is because it's not easy to handle complicated issues like this all by oneself. It requires tremendous courage and effort. One has to keep one's mental and emotional state in check, take the entire responsibility and move forward with an attitude of '*que sara sara…*'

Even today when I think of that time, I get anxiety attacks! My maid Sonia, servant Abdul and daughter-in-law Naushaba, helped me immensely. Chunnu herself, proved her unconditional love for her grandmother by being extremely brave throughout this difficult time. She could have been stubborn, insisted her parents come for the operation, but she didn't. A million thanks to God, the procedure was a success and Chunnu's foot became absolutely fine. She was able to run about once again like she used to.

I had already sold off the plots I owned in Bhopal. I started asking around and found a good architect to draft a design and finally found one. Nuruddin went with me to meet him, scrutinised the blueprint closely and even suggested some changes. It took another seven or eight months to get the layout passed by the government. Luckily by the time construction started, I still had some money left. When the foundation stone was being laid, Nuruddin came with me to Panchsheel Park and had the work started. After this I took over the responsibility of supervising the construction of my own house.

Meanwhile on 28th March 1970, Naushaba and Saeed were blessed with another daughter. They named her Shahana and we started calling her Sherry. I was busy trying to figure out a way to get another contract at AIR so I could stay on at 13 Cornwallis Road till my place was ready. But this did not happen – I had to vacate the house before the end of 1971. My friend Chitra Jagtiani had a house in Nizamuddin East. She rented it out to me for Rs 500 a month. That same house has been let out for Rs 5,000 today. Amazing how the value of property has escalated. The house at 26 Nizamuddin East had three large-sized bedrooms, two bathrooms, separate drawing and dining areas and a veranda which opened out onto a huge expansive lawn. We moved there in September 1972. My sons, daughters-in-law and their kids became regular visitors. When we were moving out of Cornwallis road, Naushaba came down from Lucknow and was of great help to me. After this, Naushaba, Saeed, their two kids, even Naushaba's brothers and sisters would often come and stay with me. During winter, Pipo and Chunnu would arrive from boarding. Basically the house was always buzzing with activity. We were never short of space and could accommodate everyone comfortably.

A year later, in 1973, Nuruddin had another heart attack. Since Tirath Ram Hospital was close to his house he knew the doctors there well and he was admitted there. I stayed with him at the hospital for 12 days. Every day I would come home after 8 in the morning, take his lunch and head back to the hospital by 1.30 in the afternoon. I'd sit around for a couple of hours then drive back to Nizamuddin to get his dinner. I still had the physical stamina to make two-three rounds back and forth to and from the hospital. By God's grace his health began stabilising and on the 13th day he was discharged from hospital.

During the entire time he was admitted in hospital, I got this feeling that he did not want me to come face-to-face with his son Farid. I didn't confront him; Noor wanted to stay in denial about reality. I just prayed for his long life and I did not want to add to his mental trauma. After his second heart attack I had become even more careful about his physical and emotional wellbeing. As far as possible I tried to keep the atmosphere in the house calm and peaceful. But Farid and Ameena would constantly express their anger and disapproval of me, completely oblivious of the mental anguish this caused their 70-year-old father. Nooram loved his kids unconditionally; they refused to accept me but Noor could not break his ties with me. This struggle and its constant tension, ultimately took its toll.

In 1974 Nooram had to attend a case in Srinagar. He took me with him. We stayed there for a few days and then headed back to Delhi. It was after this that I began to notice he was starting to look quite run down. His appetite decreased and his health started taking a turn for the worse. Temperamentally he was the sort who would not let any illness get the better of him. But despite the fact he was getting weaker by the day, he continued going to the Supreme Court and driving to my place. Though as soon as he came home now, he would go and lie down. Since Farid had been transferred from Bombay to Delhi, Nuruddin wanted to be back in his own house every night and by 10-11pm he would head off from my place to drive back to Alipur Road. I would be worried sick because while his food intake had reduced considerably he was still maintaining the same hectic schedule – driving eight or ten miles to the Supreme Court, reaching my place by midday, heading back late at night to his own; and all of this without having anything substantial to eat through the day. With great difficulty he would agree to have a bit of orange juice or some soup, but nothing nutritious was really going into his body. He would refuse to listen. His own reasoning was so persuasive I became helpless against it.

Chunnu's vacations had started and she was in Delhi. On Thursday 5th January I told Noor he should stay at Alipur Road and rest all weekend as I was taking Chunnu and going to Lucknow. I felt if I was not in Delhi perhaps he would get some rest, that he wouldn't be obsessed with driving over to be with me as soon as he woke up.

I came back on Monday and by 11 in the morning, Noor was with me. He looked extremely tired and weak. That day he rested at home and didn't go to the Supreme Court. I remember we cooked fish for dinner, there was soup and some other stuff. He nibbled at his food, as though he were merely tasting everything. Around 10 at night he got up to go to Alipur road. I stared at him transfixed. He seemed so frail that as soon as he left, I made Chunnu get in my car and we drove behind him till he safely reached his gate. Then she and

I came home. He spent the whole of the next day at my place and once again when he got in his car around 10 to go home, I followed him with Chunnu. We did the exact same thing on Wednesday as well.

On Wednesday evening I gathered courage and telephoned Farid. 'Your father is quite unwell, I have spoken with Dr Mathur at Wellington hospital, please speak with him and make arrangements to admit him there for a complete check-up.' Nuruddin would never have agreed to go to hospital if I had asked him to. He was growing alarmingly weak, but he would not change his habits. He was obsessed with the idea of maintaining dual allegiance – he wanted to convince his children he loved them and had also made my worth and the love we shared, his religion. Nooram was an extremely intelligent man with a highly distinguished personality. He was competent, there was no one better at law than him, he was the life of any social gathering and at home, he was peaceful, balanced and jovial. But he could not unravel the intricate web of his own emotions. Ultimately he got entangled in this and it cost him his life.

I called and informed Farid that the necessary arrangements to get Noor admitted into Wellington had been made, he should bring his father there the next morning. He did, and on Friday morning, Nuruddin was taken from Alipur road straight to the hospital. His secretary called and told me all this. I took whatever necessary things I needed and went from Nizamuddin to the hospital. As I reached, I saw Noor getting out of his car at the entrance. He was being made to sit in a wheelchair. Farid and his Munshi were with him. I walked to his room and began setting up his things. Nuruddin's condition was not good, but nonetheless when he entered he was smiling and wanted to chat. The doctors advised against this. They emphasised that he needed absolute rest. Taking instructions on what to do from the nurse I began to take charge. On the suggestion of the doctors, we employed a private nurse for the night. Noor was displeased. He turned to the doctors and insisted, 'I am only comfortable with my wife – I would like her to look after me doctor. I don't need a nurse.' But when the doctors explained that a medically proficient person was required, he grew quiet. Though a nurse was present, I took care of most of his needs. It was only in the wee hours of the morning that he managed to fall asleep. After this I was able to get some two hours or so of rest. Around 6 he called out my name. I got up and went to his bedside.

'Did you get some sleep?' he asked.

'Yes… for about two hours.'

Someone from the hospital brought tea. Noor had a little and closed his eyes. After a while he opened them again and said, 'Have you been sitting like this all night?' I convinced him that I had rested and even managed to get some sleep. After some time we tried to get him to eat a toast, but he vehemently refused. He kept saying, 'But I am not hungry at all.'

In between he was given medicines, the staff at the hospital tried to get him to have some juice, but it proved to be quite an uphill task. As a result his body never got any wholesome nutrition.

Around two in the afternoon I asked him gently if he would agree to have a toast and somehow managed to convince him. I dipped and softened the toast in warm tea and fed him myself. He ate the entire toast meekly, without putting up a protest. I was surprised and kept wondering, 'How has he suddenly become so obedient?' I grew worried as he was uncharacteristically docile. I stared at his face, scanning it intently, watching for the slightest sign of change. The doctors were with us in the room, as was the nurse. Time passed slowly. At six in the evening, I gave instructions to the nurse and left to get some necessary things from home. When I got back by 7.30 Farid was standing in the corridor outside the room.

'How is he?' I asked, worried.

'You should go inside,' he replied seriously.

I entered and saw the doctors standing around Noor's bed. He was on oxygen. My heart sank. They reassured me that they would be removing the tubes soon. By 8.30 that's exactly what happened. Noor seemed calm and peaceful. I pulled my chair up to his bed and sat down next to him. My restive eyes were fixed on his relaxed face. Nuruddin was lying peacefully. His eyes were shut. There were no signs of any physical discomfort. Around 9 o'clock at night, all at once he took a long-drawn deep breath, opened his mouth wide and let the entire breath out in one-go. His head slumped to one side. I shouted nervously to the nurse 'What just happened?' She ran for

the doctors without answering. In the flash of an eye, a whole group
of doctors rushed into the room and began massaging his heart, they
administered one injection after the other and God knows what else
they did to him. I sat stumped, like a statue, watching this painful
scene unfold in front of my eyes. Then they stopped and started
walking out slowly. As they passed, one of them bent down and
whispered apologetically, 'We are sorry Begum sahaba, he used his
heart most injudiciously.'

I heard the sound of these words. They seemed to be coming
from some far off place. I had turned to stone. Farid did not come
inside the room. For a long, long time, I sat alone in his room, my
hand lying unknowingly on his chest trying to feel the sound of
Noor's heartbeat. I kept thinking, 'His heart is still beating ...why
are the doctors saying it has stopped?'

Fakhruddin Ali Ahmed (Fifth President of India) entered along
with some other people. I got up from Nuruddin's side and went
and sat on a chair. Fakhruddin came up to me, gently placed a hand
on my back and stood for a few minutes. Someone got a chair for
him. Mohammed Yunus, the young man who was a witness at our
nikah put his arms around me and started crying uncontrollably.
Farid turned to Fakhruddin and said, 'He died because he wanted to
earn more money.'

This was a direct attack on me. That Noor died due to the
constant stress of wanting to earn more money so he could support
me and take care of my expenses. I was shell-shocked. How could
Farid have said something like this about his own father? The father
who literally gave his life in the hope of winning favour with
his children.

Noor's secretary had already called and informed Raffat.
Fakhruddin sat for a while and left. By then Kamman, Ajju and
Raffat arrived. The decision being made was that Nooram should be
taken straight from hospital to 10 Alipur Road. In that one instant,
my presence in his life was completely obliterated. I did not want to
create a scene. This calamity was mine and mine alone. I shall remain
grateful to the people who were kind enough to stand by me during
this catastrophic time in my life.

'Let's go home, Khalla,' I heard Ajju saying.

I got up to leave. As I was walking out, I took Nooram's watch and his wallet, both of which were with me, and handed them to Munshiji.

I came home and found several well-wishers, including my dear friend and soulmate Begum Anis Kidwai, who had come over to Nizamuddin to offer their condolences to me. Oh how I wanted to cry uncontrollably, but I was a prisoner of my upbringing; I did not know how to let myself go. The strong shoulders that could have taken the burden of my sorrow had left me and gone, no one else could help me bear this grief.

Somehow that painful night passed. In the morning Kamman told me we had to go to Nurduddin's house at 10.30 for the funeral. Mechanically, like a lifeless puppet I sat in the car and reached Alipur Road. Kamman and Raffat were with me. Other relatives and friends also left for the same venue along with us in their cars. When we reached, we found a chair had been placed for me in the bathroom of the back veranda. No seating arrangements had been made for the people who accompanied me. Kamman got Munshiji to arrange some chairs. I am eternally grateful to all the well-wishers who came to my house and took the trouble of accompanying me to Alipur Road. Those who stood by me unconditionally, despite the unconventional manner in which I chose to live, were empathetic and discerning people. They were capable of understanding the grief and joy of others, the kind who would not harm anyone.

I have no idea how time passed at Alipur road. Men and women kept coming and gathering around me. I sat quietly, head bowed in prayer for the soul of the departed. Some lady came, began lamenting so loudly I was forced to look up. It was Rabban baji and with her was her daughter Sakina, Begum of Rampur. Oh my dear Lord, how could I console her? Thankfully she quietened down.

Somewhere in another part of the house, my Noor was sleeping eternally. A huge crowd had gathered there; Fakhruddin was also somewhere there. Later I learnt it was Sultan Yar Khan who said, 'Ask someone to bring Nuruddin's Begum sahaba inside to see his face for the last time.' The message was conveyed to Kamman. She held me in her arms and took me inside. The weight of my grief felt unbearable, I could hardly walk or see where I was going through the steady stream of tears. But Kamman kept holding me tight. I bent over the body of my beloved Noor and silently, in my heart said good bye to him for the last time. I could not see much but I knew the room was packed with people. It felt as though the whole town had turned up for his funeral.

The fact that our love was now being displayed publicly like this was killing me. For 25 long years we had kept our feelings for each other private. With great dignity we suppressed our sentiments and suffered quietly so that our love would not be misunderstood, so that it would not become a stigma, a source of entertainment for others. This is exactly what was happening today.

By four in the evening, Ajju, Raffat and Kamman brought me back to Nizamuddin. Many people came to pay their condolences. My sister Begum Ali Zaheer and daughter-in-law Naushaba arrived from Lucknow by the afternoon flight. Hajra Begum and Chunnu were already with me. Kamman, Raffat and Hammi took charge. Kamman's husband Ammar also arrived from Aligarh. My servant Shakur, poor guy, was doing whatever he could to take care of everyone's needs. Kamman kept a grieving Sonia far away from me.

Sakina Begum Rampur, dropped by again in the evening and stayed till two in the night. She did this for several days. Bea, Begum Bhopal also came a few times. I wanted everyone to leave me alone so I could scream, shout and weep my guts out. In front of people I would sit pretending to be in control of my emotions. Chunnu, who had more or less been brought-up by Nooram, was also with me. His death had a deep impact on her. She loved him immensely and was extremely close to me. Whenever she saw me sitting by myself, she would come quietly, hold my hand and snuggle in. I wanted to hug her, cry my heart out, but how could I do this? How could I inflict the burden of my endless grief on a young teenager?

As the days passed, the inflow of people reduced slowly. Three days after Noor's death Beevi said to me, 'Now come back to Lucknow and stay at Kashana-e-Raza.' Dear God, how could my sister say things like this? I felt extremely hurt, but I didn't say a single word. The next day she said the same thing again. 'Saeeda, you must go back to Kashana now.' This time I didn't remain quiet.

'You don't have to worry about me... I will stay right here.'

She took offence at my curt answer, 'You never listen to me and end up doing stupid things.' Tears welled up in my eyes; I got up and went into another room. Then Beevi began complaining to Hammi, 'See, I give Saeeda practical advice and she is refusing to understand.' Hammi's reply was, 'Apa, the advice you are giving means that Khalla should simply forget the hardships and sacrifices she has endured for the past 27-28 years, wipe her slate clean and change the direction of her life?' My sister did not bring this topic up again.

A week went by, then ten days, Nooram was no longer with us but I had to get my life back on track. Fewer people were visiting now. Earlier it had been my routine that every day after breakfast I did the daily expenditure account with Shakur and gave instructions for what should be cooked for lunch and dinner. When he saw me sitting all by myself for a long time, Shakur took the opportunity to get back to our routine. He came and placed the book of household expenses in front of me. Glancing cursorily through the pages I said, 'From now on, keep an eye on what you spend, we can no longer afford to live like we used to.'

Shakur sat down on his haunches in front of me, folded his hands and said pleadingly, 'Please don't speak like this Begum sahab, till I am alive Inshallah you will always continue to live like you have been doing.'

I realised we were both crying and I thought to myself, Dear God, do such things happen... Shakur whose salary is barely Rs 150 a month, an uneducated man who has worked his entire life as a cook, he is being so sympathetic towards me and my own sister wants me to give up everything I have worked towards and return to Kashana-e-Raza? God knows what happens to people. Can we really ever know them? On what scale should one judge them?

One day the Begum of Rampur, Sakina, called me and said she wanted to fight a case on my behalf. 'Sultan Yar Khan will be the lawyer, I hope you will not back off,' she said.

'I won't,' I replied. Nothing further was discussed. Sakina was known to be emotional. She often said things like this in one of her spontaneous outbursts. For ten days she had been instructing me, 'You, must fight for your rights as a wife.' I did not want to get into any argument with her. I knew quite well that I did not want to be involved in any legal battle. I had no right over Noor as a wife. Yes I had gone through a legal nikah with him but that was not for any financial security, it was purely out of emotional and psychological compulsions. During the nikah I had kept mahr as mahr fatmee – the absolute bare minimum.

After we got married, Nuruddin supported me financially for three years. Prior to that, each year he gave me Eidi, a gift for my birthday and would send my car for repair to the same garage where his used to go. He would even pay for the repair. Initially, I protested but then started accepting it gracefully. The only thing I ever gave him each year was a birthday gift. He was quite stingy about getting new clothes stitched for himself, so I would either buy him sherwaani cloth or a kurta with chikan embroidery, which I used to get made especially for him from Lucknow. The sherwaani cloth was good quality thick silk, the best of which cost six rupees a yard in those days. I used to buy this from Gandhi Ashram. He always grumbled lovingly while accepting my birthday presents as they were costly. His logic was, 'You don't earn the kind of money that you can go about buying me such expensive gifts.'

I disliked this. I thought if I am giving you something with joy and love and you should accept it gracefully.

When I was at the MP's house on Feroz Shah Road, (where the rent was Rs 150 a month) the taxi fare to office was one rupee. If I took a cab to work for the 7pm shift, I would end up spending Rs 30 every month. So for a month, I walked to office, saved this entire amount and bought Nooram five yards of the best silk available as a birthday present! Of course I didn't tell him how I managed to save this money. If I had, he would have given me another long lecture. Here I am today, sitting all by myself, the one who lectured me so lovingly has left and gone forever.

Farid and Ameena were concerned I might try and claim my rights legally as Nuruddin's wife. Munshiji came two times to meet me and was quite sympathetic towards me. He also cried about his expenses as he had lost his livelihood. At the same time he tried to gauge my thoughts, to see what my future course of action might be. I had no plans. Quite cleverly he tried to ascertain who were the witnesses of our nikah. I told him one was an elected MP from

Purnea in Bihar called Tahir and the other a young man by the name of Yunus from Delhi. As he was leaving, he once again complained about money. I cut a cheque for Rs 2,000 and gave it to him. At that time I probably had about twelve or fifteen thousand to my name in the bank.

My life was now stuck at a strange new bend. I had spent twenty five stormy years living with uncertainty, barely three of which had gone by with some semblance of stability. Once again I was caught in the middle of an emotional whirlwind. The Nizamuddin house felt empty and deserted as did my spacious large bedroom. The man who once shared it with me, had left me and gone away forever, without any forewarning. And here I was, still alive. I wanted to scream. Cry my heart out hysterically but I told myself, no, I will not cry here, this house also belongs to my children and this torturous grief, it is only mine, no one can share my sorrow. Those days, I would take my car out and drive off in any direction. I would drive and weep at the same time, loudly, I'd howl my guts out. When I got home I hid the raw emotions bleeding inside safely within the folds of my aching heart.

Quite often I would go to Noor's grave. But I never found an iota of peace there. He is buried at Dargah Sharif Shah Kalimullah Wali, a perpetually crowded place. On his tombstone it says, 'Deeply Mourned by Ameena, Farid, Feroz, Sasha.' It was absolutely essential to write this epitaph. To announce to the whole wide world that aside from these four human beings, there was absolutely no one else in Nooram's life. How meaningless and so very unnecessary. How does it matter now if I was a part of his life or not?

For a long while his children remained worried that perhaps I would stake a claim on the money he had left behind. For several years I heard rumours from here and there about what they were allegedly saying about me. I remained quiet and still am. I will perhaps never be able to explain my relationship with Noor to anyone. It was an unbreakable bond, a reality which turned into a wisp of a dream on 14th of December 1974. When I met Nuruddin in 1950 I had no idea that my life was about to take such an off-beat direction. This *sher* sums up the reality of the relationship he and I shared:

ishq kehta hai khamoshi se basar ho jaye
dard ko zidd hai ke duniya ko khabar ho jaye

Love says let's be discreet, let no one find out
But pain insists the whole world should see its agony.

Only God knows how I managed to balance these two contradictory emotions – endure the heartache of being in a socially taboo relationship and still keep it a secret. It was almost as though some unknown force was guiding me. I believe it is the deep sense of gratitude I have always had towards the Almighty that has helped me maintain stability and balance in life. Now without Nuruddin there is only emptiness in my life. But when memories of the countless moments of joy we shared together appear on the canvas of my mind, I smile. I am reminded of this beautiful couplet by Hafiz,

harr chand peer-o-khastaatan, wa-naa-tawaan shudaam
harr geh ke yaad roye tu kardum jawaan shudaam

No matter how old, frail and weak I may be
Every time I recall your face, I feel young again.

15

The Sum of All Sorrows

———— ❧ ————

I was overwhelmed with sorrow as though the sky had fallen on me and doomsday had arrived. But this doom was my personal doom; it was my calamity, it did not affect my family, nor was it a disaster that threatened my country. I felt as though I was sitting in the middle of a fierce firestorm but the intense flames consuming me could not be felt by anyone else around; not even those sitting close to me. The burning fire was only within me. This was my personal hell. Perhaps if I died in its ruthless blaze I would find salvation. But can life ever be that kind?

A woman is invincible; she is a tough creature. By making her a mother, God has placed an enormous burden of responsibility on her which she must cope with all her life. God knows how many problems were waiting to be resolved in my life. The most critical was to find a suitable house for myself. Nizamuddin felt too big and empty for me now. I had to find something smaller. I had already spent several days searching for a place and found nothing that suited my requirements. Raffat and Hammi came regularly to see me. Kamman was with me. I had sent Chunnu to Kuwait to be with her parents. I was alone in Delhi but I had the love and companionship of my nieces and nephews.

I spent the entire month of January 1975 looking for suitable accommodation. Home owners would show me their apartments, we would fix on a rent, eager to let out the place they would end the meeting and tell me 'Please come tomorrow to sort out the important details before you move in.' When I went the next day, their attitude would be different; they'd give some lame excuse or the other or say they had changed their mind. Gradually I began to understand, no one wanted to rent their house to a single woman.

One day, Raffat, who was witnessing my futile attempts at finding a place, said, 'Khalla, why don't you come stay with me? I can give you a bedroom, a dressing area, veranda, a kitchen of your own and even a servant quarter.' This was more than enough for me. I arranged some of my furniture in Raffat's drawing room – the rest in some of the other rooms of her house and ended up staying with my darling Raffat for one whole year. And I stayed most comfortably. She helped me resolve an extremely difficult issue. I can never forget Raffat's generous gesture for the rest of my life, in return for which all I have to give are my blessings. In the time when I was at Raffat's home, Naushaba, her brother Azad, Salima, Chunnu, Ali and other members of the family often landed up during the holidays. Raffat welcomed and made space for all of them in her house aside from looking after them cheerfully and hospitably. In early 1976, Chunnu (who had come to Delhi on vacation) and I went to Muscat together. Asad had left his job with Air India and had taken up another one in this Middle Eastern city which was the capital of Oman.

By the summer of that year I moved into my own house in Panchsheel Park. Another phase of my life began. A new home, a new locality, unknown neighbours and me all alone, by myself. But I had to reconcile to these circumstances, train my faithful servants to adjust to the unfamiliar surroundings and teach myself to live with strangers gracefully and cheerfully. Both my sons were abroad. Their own compulsions and commitments did not allow them to come and help me put my life in order. I was left to deal with all those pressing demands of this materialistic world, for which women have for centuries depended on a man. But then I had been walking alone, bearing my own cross for God knows how long now. Sometime in my life Nuruddin had appeared, fleetingly like a phantasm, a mirage – there one minute, then gone forever. Often I wonder, as Taskeen Qureishi did, *'kisase poochein, humnein kahan chehraa-e-roshan dekhaa ha?'.* (Who do I ask, where did I see that radiant face?)

Noor was lost forever, somewhere in the desert of endless time. I had to course through this meaningless world holding on courageously

to the reins of life for the sake of my children. I had to smile and
tend to my home and see the buds of my efforts bloom into flowers.
I am grateful to both Sonia and my cook Shakur for standing by me
and supporting me faithfully through this challenging phase of my
life. They were extremely dependable and helped me deal with and
solve, all those monotonous problems that seem insurmountable in
daily life.

In fact, it is absolutely imperative in the story of my life to
introduce readers to my trusted servants. The children called Shakur,
Shakur Baba and Sonia, Sonia Maa, Maa and baba being the
Hindustani words for mother and father.

Shakur was our cook. Initially he worked with my sister, then he
came to work with me and stayed for almost 40 years. He had a very
unique personality. Sonia never refused any job asked of her. She
was extremely hard working and did all the housework untiringly.
She was sincere, utterly frank and so honest that if you spread the
riches of a king in front of her, she would not be tempted in the
least. Sonia adored my grandkids, in fact when Pipo was just three
years old, he would say, 'I will marry Sonia Maa.' Shakur baba
was the grand old man of the entire area where we lived. He had
managed to win the hearts of the residents of E-Block Panchsheel
Park within just a few days of his arrival. If he spotted a child in front
of a neighbour's house while heading off to market (red gingham
kerchief-cum-duster thrown stylishly across his shoulder) he would
affectionately run his hand over the child's head and ask, 'Do you go
to school young one…? What class are you in…? oh I am sure you
must always come first.' Then patting the child fondly on the back,
Shakur would continue on his way. A few houses down, if he met
a housewife, he would greet her courteously with adab or namaste
and ask, 'I am off to market, would you like me to get something
for you?' And so it was that within a short span of time all our
neighbours became friends of Shakur baba. He always managed to
help them in some way or the other. This is a successful personality
trait to have in today's day and age. But poor dear Miyan Shakur
was absolutely petrified of his wife. If you saw him with her it would
be hard to imagine this was the same carefree man who struts about
confidently in the by-lanes of Panchsheel Park in his inimitable style.

Wherever Shakur worked, he became an integral part of the family. But because his wife was extremely ill-tempered, she soon realized that no one in the household really liked her. She wanted Shakur to keep changing employers in the hope that perhaps someone might find her as likeable as him. At the time I moved to Panchsheel Park I was the only Muslim woman with a house of her own in the entire colony. Shakur's wife started filling his ears, 'Oh... come on, let's go from here, why don't you try and find a job somewhere else... if you were to die here, no one will even come forward to give your dead body a shoulder.' Miyan Shakur's classic reply always was, 'But who knows where I will die?' Another imaginary notion that niggled at her was that her husband was constantly having an affair with the other women working in the house –the maid or the sweeper woman. Quite often we would hear her lamenting aloud, 'Oh my husband is cheating on me... this is the 13th woman he is having an affair with!'

Among the working class, such over-dramatic outbursts proved to be entertaining. Whenever they met, these small stray incidents were food for gossip. It filled their free time with laughter and the bitterness of the incident would simply lose its pungency. These matters hardly ever reached our ears. If they did, we dealt with them by simply looking the other way. That's how slowly and gradually our home formed a personality of its own, one that appealed to the people who visited us and we began to hear nice things being said about the residents of E-28 Panchsheel Park.

The years passed swiftly. Asad was now working in Muscat. Both his children were studying in America. Saeed had settled there as well. His first wife Naushaba had asked for a divorce and they had separated by mutual consent. Saeed stayed on in the US while Naushaba moved to Lucknow and made it her home town.

In August 1975 my brother passed away. When Bhabhi called to give us the news, Hammi and I took the next flight straight to Bhopal. I informed Ali; he was posted in Siliguri, West Bengal at the time. After four days, Hammi flew back to Delhi. I decided to stay on for another two days and had my return journey booked by train. One day prior to departure, I got fever. The doctor advised against travelling and my ticket was cancelled. By the end of the week, Ali reached Bhopal.

When Ali arrived, Bhabhi seemed immensely displeased. All at once she became withdrawn and aloof. After a few days my fever reduced. Bhabhi came and placed a piece of paper in front of Ali and me on which was written, 'Begum Mehdi Ali is the sole inheritor of Mehdi Ali's entire property.' Ali's name was not mentioned anywhere. What Bhabhi was showing us was merely a piece of paper – it was not a government registered document and it had not been notarized either. Thus it had no legal value. Aside from this, there is no concept of 'Will' under Sharia Law. According to Islamic inheritance jurisprudence the share of a wife and a son are pre-determined and the division of property has to be done in accordance with what is stipulated.

In order to gather support for herself, Bhabhi got all my brother's friends together and started lamenting that a great injustice was being done to her. Her son Farrukh and Ali began arguing, each tried to prove that he had a greater right over his father's property. I immediately asked Ali to stop quarrelling in front of his elders. Then I turned to Bhai's friends and told them that if the property was to be divided according to Sharia, Bhabhi would only get an anna of a rupee as her share. My suggestion was that out of the two houses my brother owned, one should be given to Ali and the other, put in Bhabhi's name.

Bhabhi was not at all happy with my proposal and created an extremely unpleasant scene. But Machchan bhai's friends supported my idea. A short while later we learnt that one of the houses had already been sold and some of the money from the sale had even been used up. My advice to Ali was, 'Take whatever is left from the sale, be content with what Bhabhi agrees to part with out of the household items, take these and go back. If you decide to fight a legal case sitting all the way in Siliguri, all your money will go paying the lawyer's fees – no one will get anything.' Thankfully both sides agreed.

All this happened in 1975. About a year or two later, Ali's maternal grandfather Janab Tajjamul Hussain sahab also passed away. His wife had died earlier. Ali became the sole heir of Tajjan miyan's entire property. Ali was working in a tea estate in West Bengal and it was difficult for him to get leave, come down to Lucknow and deal with matters related to his grandfather's property. He wrote to me asking

what he should do. As was my habit I replied, 'Bete, I will try and
help you resolve this matter.'

Anwar was a trusted and faithful employee of Tajjamul miyan.
When I asked him about the condition of the property in Biswan
I learnt that close friends, relatives and even businessmen, were all
trying to grab whatever they could of miyan's property, that one
wall had already collapsed, the house itself was in a rather pathetic
condition and that it would be best to sell it all off. But selling a
house or even a piece of land is an extremely complicated matter.
God knows how many people are sitting greedily in the hope of
an opportunity to wrangle a piece of land for themselves or simply
appropriate it at a ridiculously low price.

I was a complete novice in these matters and didn't understand
the degree of complication involved in buying and selling land.
I would speak naively to people, they seemed upfront, they gave
reassurances and then would simply move off without helping. God
knows how many trips I had to make to Biswan and the strange
characters I met there. But Anwar was with me constantly, guiding
me through this irksome process.

Matters pertaining to real estate are filled with deceit and quite
often one has to face unpleasant, distasteful situations while dealing
with them. It took me four tedious months of travelling to and from
Biswan, to sort through the thick web of fraud that the buyers had
created. Then with great difficulty Tajjamul miyan's entire property
was sold for Rs 90,000. If I had been able to match the cunningness
of the buyers with shrewdness, I may have managed to get a bit
more. I was unable to do this.

Meanwhile in Lucknow there was no one staying in Kashana-e-
Raza after Abbas Raza died in 1968. Asad was of the opinion that
the house should be sold off. I advised against this. After all Kashana
was their ancestral property, it had, quite literally, been constructed
under my watchful eye and it was the birthplace of my kids. My
emotional attachment to it did not permit me to even consider the
option of severing all ties with Lucknow.

But as the years passed, God knows what problem cropped up
that prompted us to rent Kashana to the Uttar Pradesh government.
Slowly and gradually we began hearing rumours that if you lease out

a place to the Government of India, chances are they will never vacate the house and that eventually they would usurp the entire property; that too for free. Asad and Saeed were both living permanently abroad. They could only come down to India for a week or ten days in a year. But matters relating to maintaining or selling property can definitely not be handled within such a short span of time. Both my sons once again decided the house should be sold off. They came to me and said, 'Can you stay for a few months in Lucknow and get Kashana-e-Raza sold?' In the interim, Asad managed, through help and mediation from his father-in-law Dr ZA Ahmed to get the UP government to vacate Kashana. The boys were clear they did not want to rent the house again. I agreed to go to Lucknow and take on the mammoth task of selling Kashana.

My sister's house was next door; I stayed at her place. Ali Zaheer sahab's secretary, Raza sahab, was appointed to assist me. The two of us began tackling the nightmarish task of finding a suitable buyer. Selling property is an extremely difficult job for which, first and foremost, one has to be extremely unscrupulous and should be able to lie and cheat as though it were part of your innate nature. Badmouth this one, praise that one, make false promises and all this without adhering to punctuality. I had to face this every single day. Raza sahab was an expert. He guided me through this painful process expertly.

Kashana-e-Raza was strategically located on Clyde Road (now Rana Pratap Marg) bang opposite the National Botanical Research Institute of Lucknow. Due to this special proximity it had, residents of the city often called it Garden House. Spread across 60 acres of prime land, the Botanical Gardens stretched from Rana Pratap Marg, all the way across to the southern banks of the Gomti River. Kashana's location was by itself a unique selling feature of the property. When people heard that the massive house was up for sale, well-known jewellers of Lucknow came to meet me and hinted that they would be willing to pay more than the market price for the house. But the condition they put forward was, they pay more than half the money, in 'black,' under the table. Basically on paper, show the government that you are selling the place for less and do not disclose the exact amount to the tax authorities. I did not want to sell the house in this manner. I did not have it in me to work in an underhanded deceitful fashion. I told Asad what I was feeling and he also agreed that our conscience would not be able to bear the burden of hoarding 'black' money. But every offer we got came with the same messy stipulation.

Finally, after getting completely frustrated with the entire process, I sold Kashana to the UP government for a paltry sum of money. Now the Sugar Syndicate office stands in its place and I often wish I hadn't sold the house whose very design I had helped create; each and every stone of which had been laid under my supervision, whose façade was drafted expertly by Mr Griffin, one of America's foremost architects and whose impressive structure and innovative modern layout had created an uproar in Lucknow society at that time. When Griffin visited Lucknow he fell deeply in love with this alluring city and decided to live here forever. Unfortunately life betrayed him. He died shortly after shifting to Lucknow and is buried there.

In every Shia household, one room is always assigned to observe the mourning ritual or azadaari. This room, or azakhana, is decorated in the same manner as an imambara; in one large wooden cupboard a silver taziya, (a replica of Imam Hussain's tomb), is kept with silver *alams* (emblems of the army) decorated with beautiful gold embroidered banners. Every Thursday during majlis when the cupboard is opened, one can see the beauty of the imambara. When the majlis is over, everything is folded, wrapped and put back and the cupboard closed once again.

When Kashana was being sold, I wondered what I should do with the imambara. Initially I wanted to have it kept in the azakhana at Mehmoodabad Estate but that did not work out. After getting thoroughly frustrated I finally had the cupboard, along with the taziya and alams kept at the imambara at Shahnajaf on Rana Pratap Marg with faith that God would take care of things from here onwards. I had them write in their records that 'the azakhana which once belonged to Begum Mohammed Raza has now been given for safe keeping to the Shahnajaf Imambara.'

In 1978 Ali came from Jalpaiguri to spend his holidays in Delhi with me. Ali's maternal grandfather was a good looking man with a pleasing well-rounded personality. His nani was tall and extremely beautiful. My brother was of medium height. Ali has taken after his mother's side of the family, he is tall and handsome. One day I met my friend Lajwanti Yunus who introduced me to her friend, Shameem. Ali was with me at the time. A couple of days later Lajwanti called and said Shameem would like Ali to meet her sister Shaista, if they both like each other, it would be a perfect match, as Shameem's sister is not only tall, but also extremely beautiful.

The two met with each other a few times and then the marriage was fixed and we headed to Hyderabad with Ali's *baarat*. In the wedding procession from the groom's side, there was Kamman, Ammar, Sabiha, Shanti, Pipo, Sherry, Shizzie and of course me. We were given a grand welcome and after about a week's stay headed back to Delhi with Ali's wife. The bride and groom stayed a few days with us and then went off to their own home in Jalpaiguri. The marriage is successful, the couple are well settled and have two adorable girls.

In December, Chunnu and I left for Muscat via Bombay. We were both going there for the first time. Our flight took off around 9am. Soon after departure, the air hostess made an announcement. 'We will shortly be serving breakfast to our passengers.'After about half an hour there was another announcement. This time it was the pilot. 'Due to some technical issues, we will be heading back to Bombay.' Well that was the end of breakfast. As passengers we were suddenly both anxious and petrified. I turned to my 14-year-old granddaughter and promptly started narrating all sorts of stories to her. I told her about her father's childhood, all the mischievous things he used to do and some interesting tales about her 12-year-old brother when he was a child, basically I kept on talking to keep her from getting worried. Forty minutes passed quickly and the plane landed safely at Bombay International Airport. We were asked to remain in the plane, and were told that the mechanical failure would be fixed in half an hour. They kept us seated for a full hour and a half and even turned off the air conditioning. We had to tolerate the oppressive heat and humidity that Bombay is so famous for. To add to this, we were famished.

Finally, around 11am, the aircraft took off and straight away we were served breakfast. We had barely finished our meal when the pilot made another announcement in a rather sheepish voice, 'We are sorry to inform our passengers that the same technical problem has cropped up again. We will be heading back to Bombay. We would like to request you all to remain calm.' Immediately, Chunnu turned to me and began prattling off some long-winded story about what she does in school and told me that some of her teachers are quite strange. She then started mimicking their accents and imitating their manner of speaking and talked to me non-stop for a full thirty minutes. Instinctively I understood what she was trying to do. I felt a deep sense of joy that the two of us understood each other so well and were that close that we could comfort one another. Then by God's grace, we landed safely at Bombay airport. But this time I protested that we would not sit in the aircraft. We were taken off the plane and made to sit in a special lounge on condition that none of us leave the room.

Fixing the aircraft took the entire day. Chunnu began feeling unwell; she used to get air sick. When the situation was tense Chunnu contained her sickness with great courage and never made it obvious to me that in reality she was feeling ill. However when we were literally imprisoned in the airport lounge and several hours had gone by, she could not control herself any longer. I gave her the nausea medicine, got her to lie down on a sofa and gently placed her head on my lap. She was better after lunch. We finally reached Muscat at 10 at night! Both Asad and Salima were at the airport to receive us. They had also spent the entire day worried sick. But we reached safely and were very happy to be with each other. I stayed in Muscat for four months.

Muscat is a largish 'hamlet,' sparsely populated yet well-planned with all the creature comforts of a modern city. The local people were extremely pleasant and the place had an easygoing happy feel to it. Two or perhaps three days after I arrived Asad threw an office party at his house. Everyone was invited, from the company's owner, the President, Manager, General Manager, to the rest of the administrative staff. The influence of British rule on this port city was glaringly evident as the Managing Directors of almost all Omani companies were Englishmen. Quite a few British people were at the party. During the course of the evening, an Omani in his traditional Arab dress happened to be seated next to me on the sofa. Sitting beside him was an Englishman. After a few awkward moments of silence, I decided to make conversation with the Arab gentleman in English. He replied in broken Hindustani that he did not speak English. I grew quiet and kept wondering for how long I would be able to just sit about like a statue. At the same time I knew socially it would be highly inappropriate to ignore the Omani gentleman and start conversing with the Englishman sitting next to him. While I was still figuring out what to do, the Omani gentleman said abruptly, 'I… driver.'

'Aah… okay, okay, very well… you are the driver.'

'I driver company Asad Raza.'

My first thought on hearing him was 'He is the driver and he is taking his boss's name? He is calling him Asad Raza not Asad sahab?' While I was still processing this in my mind, another Arab gentleman came up to meet me. He spoke fluent English, we were introduced and I was told he was the actual owner of the company Asad was working for. After greeting me he turned and addressed the driver, 'How are you Mohammed Ali?'

'Very well, Mohammed Zubair,' the driver replied.

They began speaking with one another in Arabic and throughout their conversation there was absolutely no use of any terms of respect such as 'huzoor,' 'ale janab,' 'your excellency.' The driver, the peon, Managing Director, General Manager and even the owner of the company, all ate together on the same table and ended the evening saying good bye to one another as social equals. I was most impressed by this egalitarian attitude.

In February Asad said, 'There is a direct fight to America from Bahrain. I am getting a free ticket. Should I send you? The ticket is valid for 15 days?' Saeed was already in America; I happily agreed and along with Salima and her six month old baby girl Ayesha, we left for Bahrain. We stayed there for a few days with Asad's good friend Dr Syed Ahmed. Then we left for America and after a tedious non-stop 17-hour flight finally reached New York. Saeed was at John F. Kennedy airport to receive me. The entire city was covered in snow. Naushaba's sisters, Ghazala and Yasmin, welcomed me to their house and after staying for two weeks in the US, I came back to Muscat, via Bahrain.

New York felt like a whole new world. There were large expansive marketplaces full of all sorts of unique items sourced from across the globe. The huge stores were devoid of people and full of goods – one needed a whole day to roam about in them. Aside from the United Nations, there is really no other historical place worth a visit. Basically New York is a big modern city – let the Americans enjoy it!

By April of 1978 I was back in Delhi and got busy settling back and fixing things in Panchsheel Park. I had retired from radio and was no longer employed, so there was no change in the rhythm of my day-to-day routine. But no one escapes the ups and downs of what life has in store for them. The years kept passing by. Saeed was busy tackling the difficulties he was facing trying to settle alone in a place like America. Asad used to make frequent trips to the US in connection with work. He realised that Saeed was rather lonely and given the kind of situations he was dealing with, needed someone to share his life with. In December 1980 Ali's sister-in-law Shahla Khaleeli visited Delhi. Saeed was here on vacation at the time. The two of them met several times and then Saeed and Shahla expressed a mutual desire to be with each other and were married in January 1981.

In the Summer of 1982, Asad, Salima and I went to America together. Their kids Pipo and Chunnu were already studying there. We all stayed with Saeed and had a fantastic time together as a family. The three of us left the US with the satisfaction that Saeed and Shahla were Mashallah happy with each other and would be able to handle whatever challenges life threw at them. In February 1986, Asad, Salima and Chunnu stayed a week to ten days with me in Delhi and went back to Muscat. As was my habit, I tied an imamzamin on each of them when we said goodbye.

Then March started. That year the festival of Holi (Hindu Spring festival also called the 'Festival of Colours') was on the 26th of the month. I didn't plan on stepping out of the house, people become very rowdy during Holi and more often than not, their behaviour crosses the bounds of propriety. Around 1.30 in the afternoon the phone rang. I picked up the receiver. Ruqayya was at the other end. Till today, that one sentence she uttered echoes in my memory. 'Khalla, Bunny fell from the ninth floor and is no more....' Bunny, my nephew Kazim Zaheer's 26 year old young son! I have no idea what I said to Ruqayya or what else I heard – all I know is that the next minute I was in my car driving at top speed to Hailey Road. It's difficult to describe the scene there; it felt like the end of the world. Zakia, Bunny's mother, was beside herself with grief and kept fainting. The broken remains of the boy's body had been sent to Okhla to Sayyadain Manzil. By evening, Kamman and Ammar came down from Aligarh. All the relatives from either side continued to arrive. Everyone was deeply affected. The young man had vanished just like that from this world, within seconds, leaving his parents to face eternal grief. Oh God what is this divine game of Yours?

I believe when news of Bunny's sudden death reached Muscat, Chunnu, who was the same age, cried bitterly. She was badly shaken-up with the incident. Almost every day I would go to Zakia's place and try to spend as much time with her as was possible and then drive back home to Panchsheel. Two weeks passed. One day I had barely reached Panchsheel after returning from Zakia's, when what do I see – Ajju-Raffat and Akku-Zakia entering my house.

'Arrey how is it you are all here?'

They looked at one another.

Then in a very controlled quiet tone, Ajju said, 'Chunnu has had a car accident.'

'Is she alive?' I shouted, alarmed.

The four of them were quiet.

'Why don't you say she is no more... say it. SAY IT!' I kept screaming.

Everyone was quiet.

What could they have said? Within just 15 short days, we had to prepare for the funeral of another young soul. What happened, how did it happen and how did we find the courage to bear it – how can I find the words to express all this?

Asad and Salima brought my beloved Chunnu's body to Delhi. Dead from inside, stone-cold emotionally, I went about doing whatever was asked of me. Twelve years after Noor's death, my darling child, Huma Fatima Raza, had abruptly been taken away from me – for ever. That child who called me 'my very special grandmother,' who was extremely close to me, who was not only like a daughter to me but had over the years also become a close friend, who was constantly trying to fathom the depths of my complicated emotions and nature, who had developed great qualities in her personality at such a young age. Why did this terrible misfortune fall on us – it is beyond us humans to try and fathom. In the prime of her youth, my beautiful 26-year-old child had been snatched away from us.

Today, though a thousand layers have covered the scar of that unbearable loss, whenever I think of her, the wound oozes fresh blood, I grow restless and besides myself with grief. The truth of what I feel for you my dear girl, can only be expressed through these words by Iftikar Arif:

> *Tum se bichad kar zinda hain*
> *Jaan bahut sharmindah hain.*

> You are gone and I am still alive
> O my darling it shames me so.

~&~

'The moving finger writes and having writ, moves on'
                                             – Omar Khayyam